The St‹

Mary Hill Dobbs © 2014

ISBN-13:978-1493592470

DEDICATION

Dedicated to my Mom and Dad, Judge William J. & Mrs. Mary (Sparks) Hill, & older Sisters; Carolyn Hill Glasson and Pat Hill Lindsay who forever shaped my life: with their love and intellectual guidance.

CONTENTS

ACKNOWLEDGMENTS

I want to acknowledge the excellent help I have received from my grand daughter Erica Jordan, a computer whiz, in preparing my columns for publication. Also, I extend my heart-felt thanks to my high school classmate and ongoing friend, Dorothy Cutright who was an English major in college and has made my this book "more readable" via her red proofing pen!

Plus, all of my innumerable friends and readers who have provided information and positive feedback through the passing years. Among those are; Marilyn Barkley who sent me my first fan letter, plus providing me ongoing encouragement, throughout the years!

Also special thanks to my friend, Dixie Lee Kuhn Howard, who recently took a first place in LLC's Foundation 2014 Photography Show. She applied some of her same talents in taking the picture of our Cumberland County Courthouse (3/14) and using it to design my book's cover.

All of my columns have previously been published in both or one of the following weekly papers: "The Toledo Democrat", "The Golden Gate Gazette"(no longer published), and "The Collier Citizen" owned by Naples News in Naples, Florida. I had resided in Naples, as a Snowbird, during my first 20 years of retirement.

Through the years, some of my columns have been published in others' books with my consent, with me retaining ownership rights. Billie Chambers, the editor and owner of "The Toledo Democrat' shared with me today that she certainly has no objections to my columns, that she has published through the years under my by- line, "The Steeple Scroll," being published in book form, as she knew I had maintained ownership rights. I also want to acknowledge my appreciation for the encouragement and help she has given to me as my Editor.

Special thanks to my long term Naples friend; Kaydee Tuff who had first edited and published my columns in Naples using my by-line; "Under the Sun," in the: "The Golden Gate Gazette." She later edited my columns using my same by-line for the "Naples News" when they were first published in "The Collier Citizen"

I thank, Nancy Evans; Editorial Office Manager for the "Naples News" for giving me their permission to use my columns, for my book, which had been published in the "Collier Citizen."

Also, thanks to Carl Walworth who gave me permission to include my Mother's column, "Down Cumberland Way" that they had owned and published in the "Journal Gazette" in October of 1954. Finally, love and thanks to my immediate and extended family for their; inspiration, encouragement, patience and help!

CHAPTER 1
LEARNING IN AND OUT OF SCHOOL

Toledo High School Reunion--*June 1, 2001*

Toledo High School (THS) graduated 748 students, between 1890 and 1949, whose influences have been far reaching. During some of those years there were no graduates. There is some evidence that THS began as early as 1861. Available records indicated there were at least sixteen graduates in the 19th century.

As I write today, I am aware there is only a small percent of us who have actually experienced what I am writing about. Yet, THS impacted many lives and continues to do so today. It has been more than 50 years since the last diploma was awarded. I think it is important to acknowledge and record this history for which we are indebted and owe thanks to our forefathers' and foremothers' ingenuity and labor. All of us need to be reminded, that we have built on the shoulders of all the generations that have gone before.

Today, the Ben Tire Ltd. and The Neal Tire Company occupy the final site and part of the former THS building. If you look closely, you can see the School's original front door: which was a door of opportunity for all that passed through it.

For the past 21 years during the Toledo Festival, graduates and attendees of THS have met to celebrate, renew friendships, and share memories. Bill Mock, from the Class of '37, has served continuously on the THS reunion committee. Other current members are: Margaret Furry Venatta (a 3rd generation graduate), Evelyn Elliott Livingston, and Vera Jackson Scales, all from the class of '46 and Oma Oakley Layton, Chairman and Merna Smith Childers, both from the class of '49. They exemplify the THS spirit.

This year during the Spring Festival one hundred plus people, including my spouse (class of 45) and I (a dropout from the Class of 48) gathered at the Toledo Town Hall to continue this tradition. This is a diverse group with no description fitting all. The youngest graduates, the Class of '49 (also the largest class with 28 students) graduated more than 50 years ago. The oldest graduate in attendance this year was Miss Geraldine Croy from the Class of '26. The oldest living graduate is Grace Parks Tinsman from the Class of 23. She resides in the Cumberland Nursing Home. Her son Max was in attendance and shared this information.

A count was not taken to establish which family had the most graduates in attendance, but I would guess it was one of these three: Grissom, Lichtenwalter or the Roberts Family.

The above information can be categorized as statistics. However, of much more importance are the lives which have been shaped and molded by THS during all or parts of three centuries: 19th, 20th and 21st. Although no graduates emerged during the last half of the 20th century, today the influence of former graduates and students continue, to be a vital part of our society.

The Toledo High School Reunion Part II--*June 1, 2001*

Students received a solid educational foundation at THS. Some became farmers, doctors, lawyers, mechanics, broom makers, secretaries, educators, merchants, and musicians. I am highlighting the contributions of only two graduates, although each graduate or attendee has contributed to our culture in some way.

Mrs. Bertha Hanker Sparks, a piano teacher, was a member of the first graduating class in 1890. She was a petite lady who wore a hat and white gloves about town when I was a THS student in the 40's. I suspect if a poll was taken, there are people in our community now who were her piano students. (Oma Layton, when previewing this column, confirmed she had been her piano student).

Another THS graduate, Pearl Cougill Connell, Class of '22 was known by many of you because she had taught in our schools for close to 50 years! She taught hundreds of students. Three generations of my family called her teacher. My husband, in the one room school at Hickory Corner for eight years, my three children during their first year of school at the Toledo Grade School, and also my granddaughter Stephanie. Mrs. Connell taught my husband more than "readin', writin', and rithmatic." She took Harold and his classmates to see their first movie, "GONE WITH THE WIND". She brought her clippers to class and regularly cut their hair (all boys). While she was instilling manners and teaching the fundamentals of group behavior, she occasionally used her paddle to reinforce the forgetful. No doubt many of you could relate stories about Mrs. Connell and/or other teachers who were THS graduates that both challenged and inspired students to learn and reach for goals they had not thought possible.

The lives of these two graduates tell only a fraction of the influences that THS has shed on our community. I cannot bring closure to this historical tale without acknowledging the innumerable unnamed people who contributed to the success of THS. Think of the many school boards who served trying to stretch the limited dollars, teachers who taught on subsistence salaries, often boarding with students' families, janitors who cleaned, repaired and made do, parents who paid taxes and sacrificed. This was all done with the goal of providing quality education.

Another key difference between students attending high school then and now needs to be recorded. Many students living in the rural areas but were unable to graduate due to lack of transportation. Some had no choice but to terminate their education upon completion of their area's one-room schools, eight grades. Public transportation was not provided until the late 40's. Then, many roads were not usable during the winter months. My husband, who lived north of Toledo, often found the Burma Road impassible. His older sibs, Louise and Lewis, from the class of '29, frequently had ridden their horses to THS. My Mother (Mary Sparks Hill) from the Class of '25 graduated as her parents were then retired and had moved to Toledo. My sister (Class of '47) and I attended THS because caring aunts provided housing. If you take public transportation for granted, remember that THS' students did not have that right until school consolidation in 1948.

Attending Toledo High School was a privilege which has made a positive difference in my life as well as for untold others. There is no way to truly measure the impact THS had on individuals and/or our total society.

We Need a Swinging Door--*February 4, 2007*

Does shutting a psychological door seem like pie in the sky or something you'd talk to a shrink about? Psychological means relating to the mind or mental processes, so envision a door to your mind with hinges.

The following quote is on a poster that sits above my computer. It explains why we need to mentally block out some conversations:

"Great people talk about ideas
Average people talk about things

Small people talk about other people. " Anon.

I fell in love with the plastic poster when I purchased it at a resale shop. Even the graphic design of the poster defines its message. The top row is written in larger print with the size of each line declining in size.

When you find yourself in the midst of small people talking about or trashing other people and you can't leave nor have the facts to defend them, your immediate defense may rest in your ability to shut out or ignore their hurtful words.

As children, our parents legitimately tried to provide guidance in a variety of areas. I now think they were trying to help us avoid some of their own pitfalls as I attempted to do the same for my children. However, as an adult, I always question others' motives when they give me advice that I did not seek.

You probably know how to create or shut a psychological door although you may not be familiar with the terminology. Think back to the times that you had to meet a deadline; maybe it was writing a report for school or at work. Then, you simply put other things out of your mind and totally concentrated on the necessary task at hand.

Can you see the value of doing the same thing when you want and need some private time to make some decisions, meditate or simply be free of others' agendas?

To learn how to shut your mind's door to outside distractions, begin with some quiet time; if you are a busy mother choose the time when your children are napping or at work; use your lunch hour. The bottom line is finding some time to give full attention to meditate on the issues that are important to you. Once you've learned how to consciously shut your mind's door to outside distractions, you can find time to do so in the midst of busy activities.

When I was involved in counseling I taught others how to do mental imaging. You select and store pleasant mental images such as a walk in the rain or scenes of moving water,(two of my favorites) that can be immediately recalled to create a door to block distracting and stressful issues when they occur.

Try it! Brief respites throughout a busy day can maintain mental clarity that helps you deal with tough decisions or implement new ideas that you want to test. Periods of relaxation can raise our energy levels and creativity. After all, it is our mind that is our body's "control tower" and it needs private time to sort out the many choices that we routinely encounter.

MY DESK

My desk has many unique characteristics. It is wood, old, untidy, familiar and a friend. You may wonder how an inanimate object has these qualities. Most of these traits have developed over a period of years.

The poet, Joyce Kilmer tells us... "Only God can make a tree".

Some skilled craftsman of old made my beautiful desk from God's tree. My husband acquired it at an auction many years ago, thinking when he painstakingly refinished the beautiful oak grain that he would sell it for a few dollars profit. I fell in love with the desk and it was moved from his workshop into our family room.

The previous owners had given my desk loving care. There are a few ink stains and a number of worn places on the inside. Overall it has aged better than I have. Being old is admired in furniture although the same is not always true for humans.

The untidy part belongs wholeheartedly to me. Maybe, I could argue that items stored in my desk have an unorthodox filing system. I kind of know which cubbyhole contains what. My desk has a fold-down writing surface which hides the clutter when closed.

Untold is the time I have spent at my desk. I am familiar with its squeaks and groans, which reverberate when it is overloaded with books. I have memorized the uneven places on its writing surface.

My desk is a true friend. It remains silent about my battles to balance my checkbook, the letters I must write to say I'm sorry, and the many times I have had to check the spelling of the same word. You get the drift; it never talks back or criticizes (unlike my computer).Consequently, the grain of the wood, age and untidiness are qualities that an inspection could verify. The fact that I can reach into my desk in the dark and retrieve a pen shows I am familiar with its contents. Merely reminding you that my desk has never tattled fully validates the strength of its friendship.

My Computer is Misbehaving, Again--*July 13, 2003*

Having an "acting out" computer seems worse than an "acting out kid," well almost. Of course, it has been awhile since I've had a kid around. Just the same, my non-functioning computer upsets my household. I was going to say my entire household, but when there are only two bodies in your household saying entire sounds like a little much, although my stress is at the orange level.

My normal routine is to check my online mail early in the morning, usually while I still have a cup of hot coffee in my hand. Therefore, when I tried to get online and got a series of error messages, it was frustrating. One of my less favorite error messages reads, "The computer ou are dialing is not responding." That information seemed to be a bit obvious. Harold can always tell when I'm having computer problems, by the sounds coming out of my computer room, which adjoins our kitchen. On those mornings, he's learned it's better to just keep his face hid behind the morning paper when I come in to refill my coffee cup.

Our rain gauge showed almost four inches of rain, so after checking (asking Harold to crawl under my desk to do so) and trying all the things that I knew to do i.e. check for loose connections etc., I concluded my Internet provider might be having problems caused by the storm.

My Internet provider said they did not have problems from the storm, but, apparently I had because of the loud hum on my phone line. He suggested that I call my phone company.

Getting through to a real person on the 800 phone repair number was quite an accomplishment as a recording kept giving me a series of four or five choices to select from while interspersing the message with " We are receiving a high volume of calls and you might want to call back later." By then I had waited five minutes and could not think of any good reason why I would want to hang up and go through all the selection process again, particularly when I had no reason to believe that calling back later would make the hum on my phone go away. As I waited, I did surmise that if they hired a few more people if might help to lower our nation's rising unemployment rate as well as my rising frustration level.

Finally, the truth of the saying "Good things comes to him that wait" materialized and a live human voice asked, "How can I be of assistance"?

I explained my line-noise problem, which he could hear. He replied, "Give me three minutes to do some checking and I will call you back," and causally added, "If the problem is inside your house, there will be a $91 charge." That was food for thought.

He was prompt in replying with the news that the problem was in the house lines. I inquired, "Is there   any thing I could do to correct the problem?" He suggested that there might be low batteries in another phone and advised that I unplug all the other household phones and then see if the hum remained on the computer phone connection.

I began to feel encouraged when Harold discovered one of our phones had corroded batteries and changed them. The line noises disappeared!

However, my computer flashed the same old error messages; correcting the low battery problem did not solve my computer's problem. I was back to square one.

When Harold had checked the phone wire coming into our house, he had noticed some cracks in the line. He thought it was worth a try and ran new wire from the outside box into the computer line. After he plugged the new wire into my computer tower, I got online my first try, and have had no more error messages. I also noticed the sun was shining and heard birds singing. Computer problems are a bit like life: you must keep plugging away.

Dollars --*June 1. 2003*

"Teach your dollars to have more cents (sense)."

What a truism: life would be simpler if we could master this skill! My visiting cousin from Missouri, Frances, recently shared the above saying with me and it continues to replay in my thoughts. She said it was not original with her.

Our use of money, whether we handle a little or a lot, impacts our daily life. To the extremes, murders, divorces and many lesser conflicts have been centered on money. However, many of us think if we had a little more money, life might be better.

It is hard for me to discuss money in a neutral manner. How does a person know if they have sufficient resources to adequately meet their needs, particularly for retirement? There are financial consultants who help people address these issues. However, at best, their plans are projections based on past conditions and performances. I think most of us would agree that our markets in the past twenty-four to thirty-six months have not exactly matched other periods in history. Untold companies have gone "belly-up", also wiping out the employee's pension plans. Many people who had planned to retire in the near future now must continue working to pay their bills with little hope of ever retiring. Younger people have cause to wonder, and rightfully so, if Social Security and/or Medicare will even exist when they reach retirement age, not that anyone should think they could live in the future on Social Security benefits alone.

Our country is now more in debt than it has ever been at any time during our nation's history. It is hard for me to comprehend the logic in our President signing a bill to raise the national debt in order to secure the money to pay for a tax cut. However, I freely admit there are many things that I do not understand regarding financial transactions. I do seriously doubt if I had borrowed a very large sum of money from my local bank that they would be in the notion of giving out bonus checks to me instead of me making my loan payments to them. Neither individual nor governmental debts vanish into thin air, history teaches us; all of them must be repaid.

Through trial and error experiences, most of us have learned a few ways to stretch our limited dollars in order to survive. Early on as a newlywed, I learned if I wasted or spent money unwisely, one thing for sure, we ate more peanut butter before the next payday arrived. Probably you also, can recall how you had dealt with some early financial binds and needs which had occurred in your household. Some we can smile about today, which were no laughing matter when they first happened, while we were trying to learn how to make sense (cents) out of dollars.

Actions Speak Louder than Words--*June 21, 2003*

'Thank you' means that you have done something special that I'll never forget." Chris Gallatin

Actions speak louder than words, may have been my mother's favorite saying. I heard those words, most often, when I had been trying to convince her that I was old enough to participate in some activity or when I was being disciplined.

Thus, I shouldn't be surprised that this truism is a key factor for me or at least just under the surface when I must decide if someone is credible. Remember when we were growing up and muttered under our breath, "When I'm in charge, I'm not going to do and say things like my parents?" Now I know that's not so. Once in awhile I hear myself sounding just like my mom and consider it hard earned wisdom.

One thing that's true, if I had known how difficult the role of parenting really can be in the best of times, I might have had second thoughts about launching into that role before I was twenty.

Having had the attitude that I knew it all as a teenager positioned me for some rude awakenings. As a new parent, it didn't take me long to learn that my parents were a lot smarter than I had thought they were during my teen years; at home, although it took me a bit longer and some maturity on my part before I could admit that truth to them. Today, I have extra love and thanks in my heart for my parents because they didn't give up on me, when struggling to parent and discipline me, as it must have been a tempting choice, for them many, many times. Thoughts of my adolescent years were recently triggered by the comments of Dr. John Besore III, given at a memorial service which I attended for the daughter of a friend. He said, "Love and the gift of life are the greatest gifts we receive."

Wow, I quickly searched for a pen and jotted down his words. I didn't hear much else that he said that day; because I was so busy analyzing and rethinking his statement about gifts. Now with the passage of a few days, I think he is correct in his ranking of gifts.

In addition, as I meditate, another profound truth surfaces: my mother is the one human being who had the most to do with me receiving both, the gifts of life and love. Mother's actions, indeed, spoke louder than her words.

Blue Moons Have Changed with Time

Most families have symbolic codes which they use to represent wishes and pipe dreams. Early in my marriage, my husband and I selected Blue Moons to represent all those desirable yet non-essential or unaffordable items. At that time, a typical Blue Moon would have been a vacation to an exotic place, an expensive car, or even household help, of which could not then find a niche in our budget.

The time did arrive when college tuition and the other long list of essential expenses that accompanied raising a family began to lessen. At that time, we began to have some resources to potentially divert to some items which we had dreamed of earlier in our marriage.

But guess what? Living life and the passage of time had changed most of our wants and desires! No doubt, life has or will impact you in a similar fashion.

I should have learned about this changing phenomenon from observing my parents. From my earliest childhood memories, my parents talked and dreamed of taking a trip around the world. They pointed out the places on the map that they hoped to visit someday. They had sacrificed to pay their life insurance premiums in case they did not survive to fulfill their parental duties. Their policies had clauses which permitted them to be cashed in at maturity, thus providing the funding for their dream trip. A revised version of their trip did materialize with a few flaws. During the 1960s, they took a train trip to Mexico. However, Mother experienced an acute attack of arthritis and had to use a wheel chair and their insurance cash did not stretch at the same rate as it might have done in the 1930s. Later, using other resources they added a happier chapter to their dream and took an extended tour of Australia and New Zealand and a tour of Canada.

Harold and I no longer want to visit exotic places as our mobility is limited. When I began working full time, some occasional household help became a necessity instead of a Blue Moon because I had wanted to be able to relax and walk through my house when I returned home from work.

Now we are more conscious of our fragile environment and certainly do not want a larger car to add any additional pollution. Every time we fill our car with gas, we are very pleased that it averages 35 miles per gallon. Our Blue Moons for today have taken on new definitions. Primarily, they are the unhealthy items with excess sugars and fats which continue to be temptations that occasionally somehow end up in my grocery cart. Such is life!

Back to Routine--*January 15, 2013*

Are you ready for your routine to be restored? A short definition for routine taken from my Scrabble Dictionary is "a regular course of procedure." Doing what, we are used to doing or habit may be another way of defining routine.

Do you have the gifts exchanged that didn't fit and the ones you didn't like returned with the "Thank You" written for all? And by the way, have you memorized what all the buttons on you new phone or computer do? Will it be a secret feeling of relief to send all the kids back to school, which should be underway by the time you read this?

I'm asking some of the above questions from memory as it's been a very long while since I've had any children in my home to feel good about getting them back into school and, at my age I don't want to be learning to punch new buttons on my phone or computer, I am pleased when my older ones continue to work! These are some of the differences that come to mind as I now live in a different stage of life. In fact, I like routine and habit. I could paraphrase it as being: orderliness.

I have been thrilled to have part of my great-grand children in my home at various times during the Christmas holidays. All of them have been here with the exception of the two boys that belong to my USAF grandson.

As we all journey into 2013 with different goals, plans, desires and hopes we all could encounter some failures, bumps and delays co-mingled with joy, achievements and successes along with some unexpected and unplanned happenings. There was a time in my life that I wanted to know what my tomorrows held and to even borrow some of them for today's use. However one lesson "my maturity" has taught me is to fully live in the now or present, as each new day is a gift: don't waste any of it longing for something else that you may not even like when it does occur!

Washing Machines & Haircuts--January 16, 2006

Thoughts are energy; you can make your world or break your world by your thinking. Susan L. Taylor

Some days are like a puzzle, which has missing parts. Earlier in the week; after my washing machine repairman had made his third visit, I loaded my washing machine from the overflowing laundry basket. I was feeling relief that my washer problems were finally over.

While making my bed in the next room, I heard a suspicious sound of running water... When I approached the laundry area the water was running all over the floor and quickly soaked up my socks.

After turning the washer off and saturating several towels, I composed myself so I could call the repair service once more as we have extended service on our appliances.

I suspect the office girl recognized my stress-filled voice prior to her asking for my contract number. She was sympathetic and said everyone was very busy but the technician would try to work me in on Thursday......and then added sometime between 8 a. m. and 5 p. m.

Thursday began as a fairly normal day. Husband Harold agreed to wait for the repair person, while I left to get my hair cut. Psychologically that was an upper. I didn't have to wait at the beauty shop and I loved my haircut. Inwardly, I was wondering if I had sufficient cash in my purse to pay, plus cover a nice tip. When I inquired as to what I owed, Mona replied, *Nothing, this is your tenth haircut and it is free.* I completely dismissed the washer doldrums and went by the store to purchase sea scallops for lunch.

Shortly after lunch, the repair man arrived and said he could return in a week with the major parts needed for the repairs. I headed to the pool thinking twenty laps might lessen my stress before a trip to the Laundromat, which is my least favorite place.

When I returned from the pool feeling a bit relaxed, I found a message had been left on my phone saying that the parts for the washer were no longer available. Harold concluded, "That means we need to shop for a new washer"

After rethinking the past week, I have concluded:

I need to *stop sweating the small stuff.*

We do not have a blue tarp on our roof like those whom are still waiting for hurricane repairs.

My thirteen year old washing machine has had a normal life span.

Washing machine type crises will continue to occur.

An occasional haircut kind of surprise may moderate future crises.

LESSEN LIFE'S OBSTACLES--*July 27, 2001*
"Nothing is so good as it seems beforehand" George Eliot

How do we cope with frustrations which we have been unable to resolve? We know all the ways of trying to deal with them which have not worked, such as simply worrying. If new solutions fail, we can learn to take another look at past choices, which may have been the culprit.

A psychologist advised me to think about something pleasant when I am worried. He said it is impossible to think about two things at the same time. This is a bit like distracting our children or changing the subject when they are focusing on something that might be harmful for them. I have tried his suggestion and found I continued to feel a sense a floating anxiety. And besides, that is a temporary solution.

Try putting the problem on a shelf for twenty-four hours. Most things we worry about don't ever come to pass and the passage of time might resolve the issue or at least lessen its importance.

There is the possibility that if you can rethink the whole issue with a clear mind and find a solution, if not a perfect resolution, at least a plausible one.

If you are a person of faith, Proverbs tells us to ask for wisdom. This may be the place to begin.

Two heads are usually better than one. Consider discussing the issue with a friend or with a trained professional.

Then if that does not bring relief, finding a way to prevent the same problem from recurring is worth pursuing.

Many of our problems arise in direct response to earlier choices we have made without considering the consequences. A bit late we discover our choices are not as good as they "seemed beforehand". We can change future choices.

If we do this we might prove the truth of the old adage; "Something good can come out of everything."

Life's Zigzags--*October 5, 2003*
I don't remember too much from my high school geometry class. It

seems as though I was more interested in learning about the opposite sex than learning how to compute the circumference of a circle.

However there is one theorem that stayed with me: a straight line is the shortest distance between two points.

Maybe I recalled that one because it was easy to visualize. I did not need mathematical tools, i.e., compasses, protractors or formulas to prove its truth. When I had cut through an ally or across someone's empty lot on the way home from school, the proof was obvious.

I have found that it is one thing to mentally know a truth and quite another to apply that truth to daily living. It merely takes a brief glance backwards to count the zigs and zags present in any one day.

Take as an example, a recent day that I tried to make a quick trip to the grocery store in a town near my home. First, the phone rang when I was ready to go out the door. A friend wanted me to drop off some papers pertaining to a joint program that we were doing. That took some time because the night before I had wanted to watch a special program on T V and thought I could get up early and finish the paperwork the next morning. Didn't happen, also my husband had asked me at breakfast to deposit a check at the bank. When I attempted to make out the deposit slip; I discovered his check was not endorsed and he was already outside on his morning walk.

My original purpose for going to the grocery store had been to purchase some ingredients for a new recipe. I then needed to recheck the ingredients I had in the kitchen cabinet to determine which items I needed to purchase at the store.

Eventually, I got out the door and into the car only to discover my gas gauge was in the red zone. That meant going straight to the gas station was my number one priority as soon as I had discovered which way Harold was walking to get his John Henry on his check. Then, I could drop off the promised papers, which I had hastily taken the time to complete. Finally, I could achieve my original goal of going to the grocery store.

I have shared these examples of trivial zigzags in an ordinary day. Because I would be embarrassed to have shared some of the major zigzags in my life which took much longer periods of time to correct. For example: dropping out of high school during my senior year to marry the love of my life and not getting into college until my youngest son started to school. That involved a lapse of twenty years!

I cannot deny there often had been many happenstances of beauty joy and wonder occurring when I was experiencing some of the zigs and zags in my life. During my delayed trip into town, I had looked up and seen the beauty of a gray heron in flight, which returns each summer to a nearby pond and the white tail of a deer bobbing through the bean field. In addition, at the bank and the gas station there were pleasant encounters with friends and a time to chat.

The twenty years which lapsed before I completed my education were not wasted either. The joy of raising my children had included many days of playing and reading with them under the shelter of my Cottonwood Tree, which I have written about in earlier columns.

I also had spent many happy years working closely with my husband on our small farm. Although I must admit after I had completed college I had made a better teacher than I had earlier working as a farmhand. At least I think I did.

A straight line is indeed the shortest distance between two points and may be the most efficient route for a robot. However, for the rest of us I think it's all right to zig and zag a bit and encounter your friends and have some unexpected fun and happiness along life's journey.

Is it Time, Money or Choices?

"We are free to the point of choice, then the choice controls the chooser." Mary Crowley

One day, when I was waiting in line to check out, I overheard the young checkout girl say to her helper, "I have everything in place for college, except the time and money." I smiled and said "They are the same two issues, which I have often found wanting in my life and continue to deal with today." I could have added that past choices are the prevailing factors.

Throughout my life time and money have seldom flowed proportionately. I think back to my childhood when it seemed as though time would last forever. I doubt that never ending time was my exclusive property. Can you remember the number of years that appeared to stretch between each Christmas and/or your birthdays; as a child? Or how long it took for a few days to lapse when a fun trip had been planned? Even the length of a single summer day when you could lie on your back and count the trees, flowers and animals formed by the fluffy clouds overhead?

Many times in my life, money has been a scarce commodity relevant to time. I can recall when I had been in the first grade how long it took me to spend my penny in the school store which was opened, during my lunch hour.

My treasured coin was always tied in the corner of my hankie. Earlier in the day I touched it and anticipate what I might exchange it for. I considered a BB-Bat, Mary Jane or a Babe Ruth candy bar, or even a pencil if I really wanted to please my grandmother who had let me earn the coin doing chores.

In maturity, I gradually began to have more money flowing through my hands. It seemed that when there was time to do some fun things, the money was already earmarked for essentials and/or supplies for our farm. As our family grew: such items as fertilizer, taxes, the children's teeth, insurance premiums, college funds, or a new set of tires all had legitimate first claims.

There were times for modest vacations; often visiting family who lived in other states, Sunday drives with a stop at the Dairy Queen and treats for after school events.

Finally, in our family we began to have money, without prior commitments. There actually was some money available for vacations without the fear of overdrafts or robbing our savings. Clothing could be purchased other places than the year end clearance sale or rummage sales and even the possibility of replacing worn furniture became an option. But guess what? You already know! There was no time and little energy. Our jobs were demanding and our children were involved in many activities with school and/or friends. Then there is now: retirement. It is a wonderfully different period of life; relevant to time however our income is a set amount.

As I look back, I see more clearly that my husband and I made choices; marriage, having children, living on a farm, seeking a warmer climate in the winter, which have controlled our time and resources.

By now, I think you get the drift that throughout one's life, time and money will always be key factors, which are controlled by past choices.

An Extraordinary: Role Reversal--*August 20, 2011*

Recently, I awakened early feeling very uncomfortable and was fortunately able to schedule an appointment to be seen later that day, by the doctor.

I had anxiously walked over to the Clinic a bit early, as I was wondering if my body is simply wore out and about ready to call it quits.

Ahead of me, I saw a lady and a little girl getting out of their car. The lady walked in ahead of me and the little girl step behind me to hold the door open for me to enter. I thanked her, and then added, "I bet your mom taught you; your good manners." She nodded her head affirming my statement.

Her mom proceeded to the desk, and I stepped down by the wall, to give her some privacy at the registration window, as I waited for my turn. I noticed the little girl walked over to the section; where the toys and books were stored, as I thought of how attractive and well mannered she was.

Then my thoughts, returned to my discomfort and anxiety and I began wondering; what my pending appointment might reveal.

All of a sudden, the lovely little girl reappeared smiling, with a book and sat in the empty chair next to me saying, "I'm going to read to you about our body." Being surprised, I said, "O k and mumbled, "thanks."

She sat close and opened a large book in my lap to what appeared to be a picture of the skeleton of a human body and began to share with me the amazing information that she knew about how our body works as she pulled out the tabs and spent several minutes explaining in some detail the interior functions of a person's body.

I need to fill in a bit of information here, as before I began to write today, I returned to the Clinic to get some basic information about the book she had used to teach me as I also, wanted to order a copy. The title of the book is: See Inside Your Body by Katie Davnes and Colin King. An explanation states: "This is an Usborne Flap Book, with over 50 flaps to lift."

A brief explanation printed on the back of the book reads:

"Follow your food as it travels through your body. Take a deep breath and explore your lungs. Let your mind boggle at what your brain can do. This exciting book packed with lively illustrations and fascinating flaps, is bursting to reveal your body's amazing secrets."

This little girl astounded me as she pulled the flaps down, one by one to show me how food entered the mouth and moves down the esophagus en route to the stomach and on through one's digestive system. But to my amazement she added other details saying, "If you do not chew your food good; you could choke."

In my efforts to get some information as how she could look so young and yet be so well informed, I asked, "How old are you"? She informed me she was six and would be in the first grade. I then inquired if she knew my great-grandson Jackson, who will be in the first grade at Cumberland. Her mother, overhearing my question responded that she did not go to school at Cumberland.

The girl continued to turn the pages and pull the tabs while explaining to me the functions of the heart, lungs and other systems of our body. She explained with some detail how all parts of our body work together. I was amazed by her knowledge and shared with her that I was an ex-teacher who currently is seventy-four years older than her. I also told her, that I couldn't believe how much she knew and was teaching me about the anatomy and other functions of my body.

About this time, the nurse called for me to go with her to an examining room and I did not see my beautiful young teacher again, nor even know her name.

However, in a short period of time; this young girl, had profoundly impacted my attitude, behavior and actions! Her teaching, along with my learning from my doctor knowledge that could (and now has) eliminated my discomfort I left the Clinic that day a changed person feeling emotionally upbeat, with a song of thanksgiving to God in my heart.

I have no idea, why this attractive young girl; decided to explain and share the book with me. She unknowingly, had reminded me that my body although; with its "ageing, wear and tear," is a remarkable creation, that probably can continue to function reasonably well into the future.

Paving the Way With: WHAT IF"S--*February 2, 2013*

"We're still not where we are going but we're still not where we were."
Olga Korbut

Does anyone seriously say, "Who cares what the future holds?"
Or do they just reach the age that they are indifferent to future happenings?

Will people continue to plant trees that they will not likely harvest their fruits nor enjoy their shade, while continuing to enjoy the shade of their forefathers' plantings? I have a friend who is planting trees that the unborn can enjoy.

Politicians must think there will be some future government and /or society. But instead of sitting down and communicating across their aisle until they could agree on the best way to finance our government, they chose to continue kicking any resolutions and bill- paying plans down the road. What role does habit play in our personal actions or those of our government? Does it take a crisis to bring about change?

Let's checkout our forefathers who shaped our current environment. Suppose there had been no Revolutionary War? Would we be more like

Canada to our North or Mexico to our South? Because I'm writing as our President's Day approaches, think if there had been no Abraham Lincoln: would it still be legal for Americans to own other human beings? Of course, some have more or less continued to do that by engulfing others, with credit and debts they cannot afford.

Also from the past we need to thank all of the scholars that have made our world a better place through their teaching and research that, for example: produced vaccinations, plus other knowledge that keeps us from reinventing the wheel. Shouldn't our current generation continue their examples?

Back to answering one of my earlier questions; 'Do people reach the age that they are indifferent to future happenings? I'm answering for myself with a definite no: I haven't reached that age and don't think I ever will as long as my mind continues to function. Here is why: I have two children, five grandchildren and six great-grandchildren, (sounds like I'm writing my own obituary) who are part of our future. Thus, because of them and many others, that include a host of friends and extended family, I care very much as to what the future holds!

Ms. Korbut's quote above implies that we may not have met all of our societies' most desirable goals; but nevertheless, we have made progress. For instance, my descendants have forefathers who fought on different sides during the Great War of Emancipation and had a grandfather who enlisted during WWII, when he was past forty years of age and had a house full of kids. Plus, I have a Grandson who is currently serving in the USAF. No doubt, all of these did, or continues to do what they thought was important for our Nation. Thus, I care about doing whatever I can to make our future a better place for others, even though it may now be limited at this stage in my life to: trying to write, tutor and encourage children, as well as voting on all election days and assisting in teaching my Sunday School Class, plus giving thanks to God for friends, family and each new day.

So never mind the: "What If's," let's stay on the job!

Persistence--*July 23, 2006*

"If we are facing in the right direction,
All we have to do is keep on walking." An Ancient Buddhist Expression
How do we acquire persistence?
Is it genetic? Does it come from knowledge and/or trial and error?

A couple of well-known examples of persistence come to mind, along with experiences from my own life.

My first example of persistence relates to the inventor, Thomas A. Edison who was considered by many to be a genius. He invented the electric light bulb in 1879. Prior to inventing the light bulb, he had numerous failures. He and his associates worked on at least 3000 different theories. Many of us would have given up. Edison said, "I tested no fewer than 6,000 vegetable growths, and ransacked the world for the most suitable filament material."

My second illustration is a quotation from the New American Edition of the Bible found in chapter eleven of Luke:

> "Suppose one of you has a friend to whom he goes at midnight and says, 'Friend, lend me three loaves of bread, for a friend of mine has arrived at my house from a journey and I have nothing to offer him; and he says in reply from within, 'Do not bother me; the door already has been locked and my children and I are already in bed. I cannot get up to give you anything.'
>
> I tell you if he does not get up to give him the loaves because of their friendship, he will get up to give him whatever he needs because of his persistence."

From my own experiences I have found support from others has helped me to persevere and achieve goals.

My parents had the goal of sending all seven of their children to college. I married early and began my family, which put college on the back burner. I finally entered college when my older children were in high school and my youngest son entered kindergarten. However, through the passing years I had never lost the desire to secure my college degree. The fact that my parents had inspired my goal was reinforcing throughout my years of waiting.

Success from persevering has also given me courage to pursue other difficult goals.

While I was earning my degree (1969) in Education at Eastern Illinois University (EIU), I had taken some beginning classes at Lake Land Community College (LLC). Then LLC was a new concept in public higher education, as Illinois had passed the Community College Act only a few years earlier, in 1965.

While taking classes at LLC; I discovered first-hand how its new and exciting student-oriented concepts had made higher education more accessible. After teaching a few years and loving my career in education; I decided it would be inspiring to play an active role in the governance and policy making of LLC. The college was growing by leaps and bounds and impacting so many lives in a positive ways.

To make a long story short no woman or elementary teacher had ever been elected to LLC's College Board.

Persistence, along with the help and encouragement of many others, made my goal possible. I spent less than one hundred dollars on gas and postcards to communicate my ideas to the voters in LLC's 15 county district. Much to my own surprise; I received the highest vote count of all the Trustees who were elected.

Returning to my original question, Edison answers for himself. He said, "Genius is one percent inspiration and ninety-nine percent perspiration." Thus sometimes persistence is perspiration.

The Good Book tells us that sometimes persistence is more effective than friendship in achieving a goal.

I think my own desire plus inspiration and support from others, has fueled my ability to persevere, even when my goals were not visible. Perhaps some of these ideas will help you to persist in order to achieve your goals.

The Excitement of Mail--*July 5, 2002*

" The only way to have a friend, is to be one." Ralph Waldo Emerson
One of the joys of writing is receiving feedback from readers. It is reinforcing to know that someone, somewhere, at some time reads my column and finds it worthwhile and/or has had like experiences and takes the time to give me their reactions.

Since I can first remember, there has been something exciting about getting mail, not that I ever received much mail as a child. As children, my sisters and I would race to the mail box when we saw our rural carrier's car approaching, hoping he would hand the mail to us so we could be the first to see what had arrived. I had hoped my current issue of the *WEEKLY READER*, would be in that day's mail delivery or if I had sent in some cereal box-tops for free exotic gifts, I would wait in wonder and excitement hoping my prizes would arrive that day.

Once, I recall sending in for the Lone Ranger's official badge. Too bad I did not save it. I see on the *ROAD SHOW* that trinkets from the past now have considerable value.

On rare occasions, when I had my chores finished before mail-time, I would climb up into the Chainy Ball Tree which shaded our mailbox like an umbrella. This gave me the advantage of spotting the mailman as soon as he came around the bend in the road. Also, I then thought, I might be hidden from being assigned additional chores or called back to correct my sloppy performance on my earlier tasks.

In retrospect, I now know Mother knew my whereabouts all the time. Perhaps she also knew the joy I derived from my secret rendezvous.

This week an unfamiliar address appeared in my e-mail letter box. Upon opening it, I found it was from Jack Bowles, a friend from my school years. In high school, all the girls had crushes on Jack, as he was tall and extremely handsome.

Jack, in his e-mail was responding to my column from a couple of weeks ago, in which I had written about my Dad. Not only was I excited to hear from him but also appreciated the poem and feedback he had included.

I had seen Jack a few weeks ago at the Toledo High School Reunion, which had been held during the Toledo Spring Festival. At that time, he told me that he was a regular reader. He had given me *THE LITTLE BOOK OF FAMOUS QUOTATIONS*. I knew he really had been reading The Steeple Scroll, to give me such a thoughtful book, as a quote is often the source of my inspiration when I write. What I find meaningful about quotes is someone else's ability to express a thought so concise. It is as though they used a brush to paint a Van Gogh example of truth.

I have enjoyed browsing through his book the above quote, along with several others, had caught my eye. However I could not conceptualize how to use it.

Thus, I am now using the quote to say "Thank you, Jack for taking the time to give me the feedback and I am enjoying using your thoughtful gift." Also thanks to many of you who have given me feedback and encouragement at various times.

Hellos and Goodbyes--*January 1, 2007*

I usually like hellos better than goodbyes. This preference is probably connected to an abnormal fear of separation I had experienced during my early childhood. However, the changing of the years may be an exception to that feeling.

When I was a child, I became upset any time I was separated from my parents and threw what my Grandmother Hill, who was my substitute caregiver called "mad fits". I then believed if I couldn't see my parents they no longer existed and somehow had vanished.

In time, I learned from example that they always returned. The good news for my Grandmother was that it was a rare occasion that involved both of my parents being away from home at the same time.

Because I have continued to feel some discomfort when separating from love ones, I have tried to avoid goodbyes whenever possible.

Even when visiting love ones as an adult, there have been times that I have quietly dressed, written a thank-you note and slipped out of the house on my departure day; before anyone was up. I simply chose to believe if I didn't say goodbye it meant that it wouldn't be so long before I would see them again.

Last evening, Harold and I took our usual walk to watch the sun set over a near-by lake. Watching the changing colors reflect on the water with a few seabirds flying westward served up a large dose of serenity.

For once it had seemed peaceful and o k to say goodbye to 06'. None of us can know what the New Year holds as Iraq continues to cast an unknown shadow.

Later, I had gone to bed early thinking of welcoming the New Year with happy dreams. I had to scrap that plan when others were celebrating with loud fireworks. I wondered if they were celebrating the old year or welcoming the new one: probably a mixture of both.

All of us can look backwards and know we have been able to cope thus far: giving us confidence that we can do the same during 07'. Being an optimist; I can even guess that there might be some pleasant surprises surfacing along the way as 07's calendar sheds its pages.

Responsibility in decision making--*July 3, 2007*

"Our physical freedom stops when we encounter someone else's elbow."
Anonymous

Since my return to central Illinois a few days ago, I have been looking backwards. As I approached the small town that surrounds my county's Courthouse, my heart flooded with memories.

I was reminded of the first time I saw it more than 60 years ago. I was a teenager at the time and my family had moved to rural Illinois from Norfolk, Virginia, where my Dad had been stationed at the close of World War II. The courthouse also triggered fond memories of my Dad, Judge William J. "Bill" Hill, who had served as County Judge for many years. He taught my sibs and me about the responsibilities linked to the freedom of making individual choices in our lives.

While sorting through a VIP file, I ran across an essay written by my sister Pat Hill Lindsay, who had been an important part of my life. Her essay reflects some of the values we learned from our Dad. I share it below:

"Strangely, and perhaps not so strangely, my thoughts center around an old, old dichotomy. It makes me restless to contemplate the seeming paradox. I am not sure that the problem is unique; rather, I'm sure that it is not. The sense of aloneness that comes when I realize that this has happened before is difficult because I prefer problems that can be resolved and forgotten.

What would I do with only myself to consider? What would I not deny myself? These have to be pertinent questions to consider even if the answers are clouded by conformity. I considered them for an instant or so. The feeling of aliveness and awareness was almost shocking with intensity. Freedom is the word that best describes the free reign of thought and emotion that was given a few moments play. It didn't last long because with it, as always, was the descent into reality and its counterpart -- responsibility.

Civilization and society are the result of the dichotomy between freedom and responsibility in the larger world that we live and move in, but the aloneness comes when we must confront it in our personal lives. The agony of decisions is that they have to be made over and over again. Reaffirmed may be the correct word.

Somewhere along the way from childhood to adulthood, the groundwork is laid, the rules are learned or perhaps formulated and we are set or conditioned. If we vary too far from the norm, we pay a price for our variance. We learn this and though we might yearn or fantasize, we transgress at our own risk.

Though this realization is far from unique, nevertheless, it is an alien soil that we tread upon when the awareness of the freedom that exists bursts upon our realization with such unexpected force.

This then is the aloneness. This knowledge that we are alone, that we have more choices than we know, and paradoxically, knowing that we have very few because the same intuitiveness that floods our being with freedom makes us also aware of the consequences.

Thus the freedom/responsibility dilemma remains a lifelong balancing act for me since first transmitted from my parents. However, my values, faith and ongoing life experiences continue to play an important role in shaping my decisions."

This is the end of Pat's essay and explains why she always about went off the charts on most of her I Q Tests!

Taking Photographs--*March 28, 2005*

" We don't see things as they are, we see them as we are." Anais Nim
Having a photo taken sounds easy but it isn't for me. How can a reasonably simple task become so complicated? Recently I was asked to submit a current photograph. I immediately went into a dither because having pictures made is my least favorite thing to do as I usually freeze at the sight of a camera's lens. I rank its impact in the same category as feeling claustrophobic in a crowded elevator. I've tried to analyze and determine why this is the case, which immediately added to my frustrations as none of us like to look inward. Somehow it is always easier to diagnose others' problems or shortcomings rather than our own. I think part of my hang-up relating to pictures is the fact that I have always been larger and taller than others around me-- my classmates and even my older sisters, as I passed both of them in height, while in grade school. I must have inherited their share of family height genes; along with my own. At birth, I had a head start, as I weighed thirteen pounds. When my first born was delivered weighing a few pounds less, I really had empathy for my Mother whenever I thought of her giving birth to me.

When in the 6th grade I had already obtained my adult height of 5 foot 10 inches. Thus in all classroom pictures I was always the tallest even taller than all the boys for a few years. Sometimes I was mistaken for the classroom teacher. No matter how many times my mother told me, I would be happy being tall someday and had me practice walking tall with a book on my head. In private, I continued to slump and try to blend in a crowd, whenever possible.

With this recent request for a photograph, I decided to go to Wal-Mart and have it taken quickly and not get worked-up about it. I thought I had learned to choose my battles and not sweat the small stuff. Didn't happen. The photographer said it would take three weeks (which I didn't have) to get the proofs back.

A friend who has a digital camera agreed to come to my home and take a picture and e-mail it to the party who needed it. I felt relieved when my friend sent me a copy in fact I rather liked the picture and printed off a copy to keep. My friend sent me an e-mail the next day stating the person wanted a picture of me smiling.

Back to square one and yes my Mother (as always) was right. I have stopped slumping and learned it is good to be a tall adult, even advantageous when I want to see in a crowded room and on most other occasions. Now if I could just learn how to smile in front of a camera. Mother could probably teach me-----

"No one can make you feel inferior without your consent." Eleanor Roosevelt

Technology Has Changed our Modes of Cleaning
--April 24, 2006

Is spring house cleaning a formal procedure in most homes today or was it a job that went with earlier generations? Maybe it was necessary because most homes had depended on coal or wood stoves for heat and washboards to clean their clothes and bedding.

Fifty years ago, when I began housekeeping, we did not have all of the automated appliances, or furnaces, which eliminate the physical labor from many of today's household tasks.

Today, self-help advice is available everywhere telling us how to improve the quality of our lives. Simplify is often at the top of the list. Simplify is one of those incongruent tasks, which is easy to talk about while it is very difficult to achieve whether we are carrying in a bucket of coal or setting the thermostat.

Thoreau has said: Simplify, Simplify, and Simplify. He did it in part by physically removing himself from civilization. However that was not an option for my mother's generation or me in the beginning years of my household chores.

Women have always had innovative ways of coping with the work at hand. My mother came to marriage, eighty years ago: fresh out of Toledo

High School where she had graduated at the top of her class in 1925. However she had no experience in scrubbing clothing in a wash tub and cleaning house. She was a younger pampered daughter and had escaped those tasks by studying and doing homework.

Reality without technology set in when she had moved to my Dad's home in eastern North Carolina. She was far from her Illinois family, when she proceed to birth to three daughter in five years. I was daughter number three.

None of our current technology of the day was available when she became bogged down with all the cleaning chores.

However, Mother was an excellent seamstress and her loving parents had sent her a new treadle Singer Sewing Machine.

There was a wonderful black woman named Caroline that had several daughters living down the road from us. She made her living washing, ironing and cleaning for others. In the depths of the Great Depression, Mother certainly didn't have the fifty cents to spare, which Caroline earned from doing the weekly washing for others.

Caroline did not know how to sew nor own a sewing machine. You guessed it! Mother bartered a deal to make dresses for Caroline's daughters and Caroline in return scrubbed the clothes until they were sparkling white and hung up in the bright sunlight. What a wonderful tradeoff for both women. As I became old enough I helped early in the morning to fill the big black pot in the yard with buckets of water to have hot water steaming for Caroline on wash days.

Even though this was a dark time in our nation's history when segregation was in full force my parents taught us to treat all people alike. I have many happy memories of summer days, when Caroline's daughters came along and we played in between helping with the washing chores.

The word of Mother's dress making skills spread about and Mother sewed for others as she found time, thus earning extra "pocket money". Sometimes the change was used to order bright prints form the Sears Catalogue,

After our marriage, Harold and I visited my relatives who continued to live near my childhood home in North Carolina. During one visit I purchased a painting, which I now treasure from a local artist. It is of Caroline standing by the front door of her modest home with her twin wash tubs setting on her front porch. She was known and loved by many, as she had raised her family by doing the laundry for a whole generation in that community.

The oil painting hangs only a few feet from the louvered doors that hides my washer & dryer. It is a constant reminder of the changing technology which has freed most all   American women from back breaking drudgery. It also triggers many happy memories from my childhood.

The Roles of Waiting &Wasting: When Pursuing Wants--*January 7, 2006*

"Want is a growing giant whom the coats of Have was never large enough to cover." Ralph Waldo Emerson

Waiting can be the most frustrating drain and waste of our time. Waiting is out of our control when we want something to happen. We have the option of removing ourselves and walking away in anger. That means if we are waiting for some essential service, we would need to risk the same waiting cycle at a future time. If we are waiting in a checkout line to purchase food for an evening meal, there may not be a viable alternative. The same may be true when we are waiting in rush hour traffic or have the need to consult with a busy doctor when you are sick.

Wasting is closely related to waiting as it saps time and energy that could have been utilized in a constructive even pleasurable manner.   Bernard Berenson, a man who must have devised a plan to prevent wasted hours said. "I wish I could stand on a busy street corner, hat in hand, and beg people to throw me all their wasted hours." If we only knew his secret. Our wants can fall anywhere between essential needs and requirements to wishes and desires with elaborate visions of grandeur. Benjamin Franklin said "Our necessities never equal our wants." Pursuit of wants consumes much of our time and energy. Others at specific times in our lives; primarily our family and/or friends have tried to select and dole out wants, which were available or things that they thought we wanted.

Many factors in our lives from desires to abilities and resources continue to impact the fulfillment of our wants.

When we make poor choices waste is a factor unless we label those undesirable wants as learning experiences.

As we eternally pursue our wants; waiting and wasting will always be present because Emerson's words remain true.

Who Are We?--*May 29, 2005*

"To live is to change." Anon.

When you encounter someone that you have not seen for twenty years can you call them by name? Do you ever give thought to who you are and how others' perceive the changing you and equally if not more important, how do you cope with the ongoing changes in your life? That is a horse of a different color and can be kind of frightening.

My first thought is that others who live in our area probably know me as I have lived in the area for sixty years. That is not necessarily true. I could describe myself as being a retired social worker, a wife, mother, grandmother and great-grandmother. Someone could reply that description fits another person. I cite these examples to demonstrate there are a variety of ways in, which all of us recognize casual acquaintances.

A common method is associating people; with their workplace. When we see a person in a location other than their work site we realize that we should know them but may not. When I encounter a young adult who greets me saying, "Hello, Mrs. Dobbs" I immediately suspect that he/she was a former student from my 6th grade homeroom class. My former students have a distinct advantage in recognizing me because of my voice and the fact that I had already reached physical maturity before, I had taught them. Today you can probably mentally hear your former teachers' voice. I can certainly hear some of mine. For me to call my former students by their name is a different story as they have undergone considerable changes since their early adolescence.

Another way we identify people is through family associations. People older than me, often knew me as Bill Hill's daughter. My Dad had been active in Cumberland County's government and many people knew him in that role. Strangers to me, sometimes share humorous stories, which had originated with my Dad, as he was a great storyteller.

People younger than me may have known me as my children's mother and/or in my role as a grandmother.

Recognizing and measuring the changes, which have taken place in our own lives, is a very difficult task. We learn new things through everyday life experiences. There is no reason to think that ongoing changes would cease at some pre-determined age nor would we want them to. Changes usually are slow and gradual, nevertheless changes do occur. Their origins can be physical, emotional or in the intellectual realms of our lives. Some changes can have positive results while others may impact our lives negatively.

During crises and as well as, in ordinary times we must learn new skills to cope with the results of changes. It is never easy.

Sometimes we realize we no longer enjoy doing things that we once did. It doesn't mean that a former activity was bad; it simply means there are other things we would rather be doing in those same scarce time slots in our transitory lives.

Thus keep in mind as we try to recognize the changes in others we need to remind ourselves that it is even more important to understand and adjust to the ongoing changes in our own lives.

Caregivers Need Care--*October 5, 2008*

If I ask, "Have you ever been a caregiver"? I suspect most everyone would answer yes, as six year olds who have held a bottle for their baby brother or sister, could be included along with those who had given constant care to loved ones, who could not care for themselves.

In the past, I would have answered yes, because I had raised a family and provided intensive care for family members and others, during shorter periods of time. I use to wonder why there were support groups for caregivers. Now, I fully understand why, as I have provided extensive care for my husband; Harold who had to deal with the effects of post surgical pain.

Firsthand experience is a good teacher, although it may not be the most efficient or the less painful way to learn! I now realize the importance and wished I had reached out, more in the past, to lend a helping hand to others caregivers. However, when I was younger, I might have thought it being too intrusive.

I'm aware that many of you have already experienced the trauma of being the primary caregiver for a loved one in pain and that some of you who are experienced caregivers are going to wonder how I lived so long without fully knowing what's involved in being a primary caregiver. I can't answer, other than to guess; it was luck.

I am sharing my experiences as a caregiver not to complain, because it was a labor of love that ended in restored health for my husband. Rather, because, I hope some of the things I learned might prove beneficial to some of you, who someday may have a similar experience and/or occasions to provide help and support for family, friends or others. My husband's post surgical pain called for medicines that would impacted his thinking, for a period of time. Thus, I needed to remain with him around the clock. When exhausted, I made an important decision that all caregivers need to do: I asked for help. I call our daughter; who is a nurse and she caught the next flight to come and help with her Dad's care, which was an "upper" for both her Dad and me. She was able to stay a few days until Harold was home and we had other help.

Life goes on even when you are a caregiver and during Harold's recovery was the time; my eye needed a corneal transplant. Our son Roger came to help with his Dad and took charge for a few days. My neighbor; Cathy was able to take me for the outpatient surgery where I received the corneal tissue, that was a wonderful gift from a donor that has improved my sight. My son and I had a role reversal for a few days, which was a new experience for all of us! Soon, Roger needed to get back to his work and in a few days; I was again the chief caregiver for Harold.

Many of you may know from first hand experiences that providing ongoing care for someone you love is a stressful experience. We are use to thinking that if we try hard enough we can quickly make "things all better". I was forced to realize that our ageing bodies are a bit like Rome, in that they cannot be rebuilt in a day.

I usually overeat and gain weight when I'm experiencing stress but being a caregiver made me lose weight because eating didn't seem as important as resting when there was some free time. This made me recall when my children were young and I sometimes took a nap when they did, to catch up on lost sleep.

I discovered that even little acts of kindness made a big difference during my exhausting days and nights as a caregiver. I can't thank enough our friends and neighbors who: stopped in to provide respite care when I needed to run errands, prepared meals and or did my grocery shopping , called and/or sent e-mails of encouragement and remembered us in prayers. It all made a positive difference!

Thus in conclusion: I want to repeat the importance of anyone giving assistance, as they can, to their family and/or friends who are in the midst of being primary caregivers. Most important, I hope my "learning on the job experiences" will be helpful when you find yourself in a similar role.

Always remember: it is not just O. K. but ESSENTIAL for a caregiver to ASK for and to ACCEPT help.

Making Decisions--*February 13, 2011*

"Man like every other animal is by nature indolent. If nothing spurs him on, then he will hardly think and will behave from habit like an automaton. (or robot)." Albert Einstein, Out of My Later Years (1954).

Do people have a system that they used consistently to make decisions? Habit is a major factor; as many decisions are made over and over again; without thought and yet there are some life shaping or critical decisions, which must be made on the spot, with little time to analyze. Thankfully these situations, don't surface very often, as whatever decisions are made under pressure can sometimes resurface in the form of regrets if one is out of practice, in exercising one's mind; even as they sometimes have slacked up on exercising their body.

Relying on habit is not all bad as our thought patterns would be in turmoil if we had to rethink and test every decision. Habit was defined correctly by George Santayana as being "stronger than reason" in his *Interpretations of Poetry and Religion* written in 1900.

Webster states that habit "is an action that is acquired and has become so automatic that it is difficult to break." I'm reminded of the multiplication tables and/or addition facts as an example: as the solutions simply pop-up when needed.

My neighbor, Bev was visiting when I was thinking about this column, so I grabbed my pencil and yellow pad and asked her, "How do you make a difficult or critical decision when you have ample time, to make up your mind?

She replied, "I think, pray and ask for guidance." She continued, "Sometimes, my answer comes through something I've read or something that a none-involved person has said." Then she added, "A dream may be the source of my answer or perhaps the solution was in my sub-conscious mind all of the time. I think we need to trust our own experience and instincts."

I couldn't agree with her more! In fact, her answer was very similar to what mine would be. Our life's experiences both past and present contains valuable information and like shifting gears; we can quickly revert to reasoning. We are constantly learning as we read; books, magazines, our newspapers and/or when we are observing others, participating in conversations, attending worship, meditating and etc. The beauty of all these learning experiences is that our mental computer sorts and stores worthwhile facts in order, so they can be recalled; whenever the need arises.

Thus, even though; we let habit rule in most daily decisions, we do have the potential to switch-on the grey matter: to analyze and think in order to decide upon the best solutions; whenever necessary. Napoleon was aware of this more than two centuries ago when he wrote; "Nothing is more difficult, and therefore more precious, than to be able to decide." *Maxims 1804*

But, remember our brain like our body: benefits from regular exercise.

Is New Always Better?--*September 16, 2006*

Some things you keep. .They're good for you, reliable and practical. . So you hang on, because, something old is sometimes better than something new. Anon.

How do we choose between the new and old? Or is this one of those "it depends" decisions?

When I was a child, a book mobile made regular stops at a crossroads near my rural farm home. I always looked forward to its visits and checked out as many books as possible as reading was my favorite pastime.

I found it exciting whenever there were new books on the shelf. A new book always had a special feel, scent and look; all its own besides the anticipation of discovering the excitement, which any book's pages might reveal. Without doubt there would be no handprints or tears on the new book's cover nor folded corners that had marked some previous reader's place.

Opening the cover of a new book continues to arouse my curiosity. However, with the passing of time; I have learned to love and equally value old books. I'm reminded that ideas written about mankind by Plato, Aristotle and other Roman and Greek philosophers; before the time of Christ are applicable today.

When I read a book that was first published a hundred years ago, I think of the authors and the time that they had lived and written. I try to imagine how different their world was from mine.

I wonder about the people who had owned and/or read some of the old books before me. Did they enjoy reading the book? Maybe the book had merely collected dust in someone's bookcase.

Growing up, I was the third daughter in a large family. So guess what: I wore a lot of "hand-me-downs" until I grew taller than my sisters. My Mother was a talented seamstress. She made my hand-me-downs fit and often she had been able to disguise their earlier appearance.

I always loved wearing a brand new dress even if it had been made from printed sacks that had once contained flour or chicken feed.

For special occasions such as my birthday and Easter, I was permitted to select my fabric and buttons from the Sears & Roebuck catalogue for my Mother to sew. The catalogue contained real sample pieces of material in several different colors, thus adding to the decision making and excitement of choosing the yard goods. I fully understand the meaning of "wish book" as I spent many hours looking at the new fall catalogue when it had arrived in the mail.

In time, I learned that clothing tailored to fit was more attractive than ready made clothing. Now in maturity, I continue to wear some of my old favorites; both because they feel comfortable and I have developed emotional attachments to some pieces hanging in my closet.

Today, I asked my husband if he liked new things better than the old. He replied; "I like you best and you are old." After I got over the resentment; I decide it was a back handed compliment and truthful. At the very least he must think like the above quote that I am "reliable and practical."

I think deciding whether the new or old is best: surely needs to be left, in the "it depends" category.

Slow Down, It's Worth It--*September 5, 2004*

Earlier in the week, my granddaughter called me during her lunch hour. I was surprised to hear her voice as she continued in a sober voice, "I have a suggestion for your column."

I encouraged her to share it as my curiosity was aroused; wondering what she had in mind.

She asked me to please write something to encourage drivers to slow down in road construction zones. She added there had been an accident at her job site earlier in the day.

I needed no further encouragement because my family has been involved in road construction for more than 50 years. My husband helped to build some of the Interstate Highways in our country as well as other roads. My son and granddaughter are currently involved in construction work. We recognize the fact that on every construction site someone's father, mother or child is working to improve or construct the roads, which we all need.

My granddaughter provided the following statistics, which pertain to people killed in Illinois during 2003 (where she works) by careless drivers in work-zone related accidents.

The total killed was 44 people, averaging almost one person per week. Thirty-nine were passengers or drivers in the work zones and five were construction workers showing that it is also a risk for the drivers when they speed in work zones.

I do not have the current statistics for the state of Florida and/or Collier County. Regardless, the need for caution and full cooperation of the driving public is universal in all construction sites, more so amid summer's last holiday and a busy hurricane season.

There are speed laws posted in most construction zones to slow the traffic, plus flagmen or women to stop and direct traffic as necessary. Drivers who are frustrated or running late are more likely not to slow down and end up injuring and/or killing themselves or workers. Most of these accidents can be prevented by obeying the law and showing consideration for the workers.

Fines are doubled for failure to slow down in work zones as some drivers will only respond to fines. Apparently they fail to realize that drivers are also killed in construction work sites.

The next time you enter a work zone remember the workers are there to improve our roads. Mentally substitute the faces of some of your loved ones for the workers.

Take this grandmother's word, "It will be easier to slow down and be patient.

Concentration--*March 24, 2002*

"It is order in all things that rests the mind." May Sarton
What does it mean to concentrate?
Centering, compacting, focusing, consolidation, converging are all

related words to concentration.

The meaning, I like best is "A point where rays come together." How seldom this happens. However, occasionally it does occur, seemingly without rhyme or reason. We need these times of affirmation in all realms of our lives.

Our minds thrive on order. Not order which someone else has dictated, as we all rebel when someone attempts to preempt our own agenda. Rather, I mean order that is the absence of stress. Disorder hinders clear thinking. Near the close of the day I decided to go for a swim hoping to work off the day's outpouring of stressful events. First I thought that would consume the energy that I needed to prepare the oysters I had planned to serve for the evening meal, but I threw caution to the wind and grabbed my towel.

As I approached the pool, its solitude and the beauty of the palm fronds barely moving plus the noise of a deciduous tree's large brown leaves falling on the pool's deck caught my attention. The sight of the tree, full of spring green leaves, while discarding its old brown ones reminded me that all living things are ever recycling. Upon entering the sun drenched pool, without another person in sight, I immediately felt rewarded for my efforts. The sun was close to setting. Each time I swam towards the west my view of the setting sun through the trees was more brilliant with color than it had been during my previous lap. The water softly lapping against my body literally drained the stress from my mind and body.

As I floated on my back to rest, I was rewarded with another of nature's gifts. I saw flock of gulls that were flying into the sunset and reflecting the colors of the setting sun. At first there seemed to be no order in their flight, then several gulls made a perfect "V" formation. I've read that the lead bird breaks the air currents thus making the path easier for the ones following to glide. In a few seconds a lone straggler, which I could readily identify with, came along bringing closure to the scenes of beauty.

From nowhere, a feeling of security and well being engulfed my surroundings: the same "centering presence of love" that I had felt when I had met my parents' approval, as a child. I can only guess what caused the aura of my parents love, approval and presence to surface.

Maybe swimming had been the catalyst, which had always been a happy time with my parents, during my childhood. My family had not swam in a pool, rather bathed in a nearby stream, often during the sunset, following a busy workday on our labor intensive farm.

Or could it have been my thoughts of preparing oyster stew for dinner? On special occasions, during my childhood, Dad would bring home a quart of shucked oysters. Mother, then fried the large ones and used the smaller ones to make a large pot of stew with freshly churned butter floating on the top. Occasionally we had a peck or two, to roast in the yard, over a fire covered with tin. A wet burlap bag was placed over the oysters, to create steam. Each member of the family took turns being served the delicious seafood, as rapidly as Dad could open the cracked shells. Thus, anytime I cook oysters, I am reminded of my parents.

My swim today was a perfect image where the "rays of my life came together" for a few moments of love and serenity.

The Crayon Box--*April 5, 2003*

"We could learn a lot from a box of crayons: some are sharp, some are pretty, and some are dull with weird names and all are different colors. ... but all exist in the same box." Shared by Barb Titus from her: Thought for the Day.

My friend Barb adds; *A Thought For the Day,* to most of her e-mails. Thus, I always open her e-mails with eager anticipation because she attaches such though provoking ideas.

I found the *Crayon Box,* as quoted above intriguing. When I contacted her and asked permission to quote she told me it was not original with her and that her source had not credited anyone.

It contains so much wisdom and could describe many communities beginning with our world, North America and particularly our own United States (U S). It makes me think of the melting pot theory , which has been used to describe groups from around the world that have settled in our large cities during the Twentieth Century; the box representing the U S and the crayons our diverse population.

It is extremely troubling that at our entry into the Twenty First Century, we still have not outgrown our prejudicial attitudes against others because of some of the differences listed in the above Crayon Box quotation; traits over which some individuals have, no control. The University of Michigan's case currently before the Supreme Court, that is attracting so much attention, indirectly speaks to this issue.

I recall a minor prejudicial incident that had been painful for me, as an adult student entering a Midwestern college. My freshman Speech professor singled me out in class telling me I needed to go to speech therapy before he would allow me to be in his class. The therapist interviewed me and sent me back to class with permission to re-enter my speech class with the message: I did not have speech impairment; rather I spoke with a Southern dialect, which was normal, as I had grown up in the South.

If we were drowning would we resist a lifeline thrown to us by a person who possessed characteristics of the Crayon Box; different from ours? Would we refuse an organ donated, that would save our child's life? Would we reject a firefighter that would carry our love one from a burning building? There are untold scientists who have discovered medicines and developed procedures which daily improve our quality of life, whose descriptions are very different from ours.

Of course, we would not reject help from any of the above and daily appreciate the contributions of others. We all possess some of the Crayon Box qualities.

Think about the symbolic Crayon Box the next time you are tempted to make a snap judgment or prejudicial remark about another person who is different from you in some way. I will.

'If we cannot now end our differences, at least we can help to make the world safe for diversity." John Fitzgerald Kennedy~~ 1963

CHAPTER 2
NATURE'S BEAUTY AND FURY

Cleansing Rain: Without & Within--*July 12, 2006*

"I shut the door on yesterday and threw away the key.
Tomorrow has no fears for me since I have found today." Unknown
Last night after the rain Harold went out to check our rain gauge.
Returning with a big smile, he reported that we had received one inch of
rain. We chatted awhile about how helpful the rain was for everyone's
crops, plus the tomatoes in his garden.

Later in bed, I enjoyed the clean moist air that flowed through my open
window. I went to sleep with pleasant thoughts in anticipation of my
early morning walk on our newly washed earth.

This morning I decided my paper and a second cup of coffee could wait
until later as I was eager to get started on my walk.

At first, I was disappointed by the fog and my limited vision. I had
anticipated seeing the sun glistening on each droplet of rain clinging to
the dark green corn leaves.

I soon discovered my sense of smell was working overtime to
compensate. The rain had left a lovely clean fragrance in the air and I
decided to look inward and contemplate my objectives for the day as I
walked.

Today's experience reminded me how easy it is to spoil your day, when it
does not unfold as you had planned. To my regrets, I have been guilty of
that in the past; prior to learning that time is a transient gift to be
treasured.

The quote above was found in some notes which had been left in my
husband's book, which had been purchased used on E-Bay. It revealed
that the book's preceding owner had learned the profound lesson of living
in the present. At least, they had taken the time to record notes about it.
We need to be reminded that the present moment is the only time we
have for sure. It's up to us to use it wisely.

The Roof Cats--*May 9, 2005*

We had a stray tabby cat show up in our back yard when we returned to our farm home for the summer. It has created a dilemma, which I hope some of you can tell us how to resolve.

At first, Harold and I thought "The Cat" might belong to some of our neighbors. Not so, at least it didn't leave. The Cat soon discovered our compost pile, where we put our table and other vegetation scraps. Although The Cat kept its distance, it checked for food whenever we open the door.

At first, I thought of asking my friend Judy, who places dogs to find "The Cat" a home. Then we got the idea she might have babies.

We first thought it strange when we saw The Cat climbing up our rose trellis and then jumping onto our roof several times in one day. My first thought was that maybe she was seeking a tasty lunch from a bird's nest in the roof's soffit or the baby squirrels, which sometimes jump from the branches of nearby trees onto our roof. Not so.

My first suspicions were confirmed. When it warmed up enough for us to sit on our screened porch, we could look up and see three furry balls running on our roof. The Cat had delivered babies on our roof; in a sheltered spot where an overhang provided protection from the rain and a piece of the soffit had been torn loose, by the winter storms.

Even if we had found a cat lover, immediate placement became a moot issue. We began to buy cat food so The Cat could nourish her babies. I had no idea how much it cost. The Cat preferred the table scraps; thus we make a greater effort to share.

The Cat immediately makes friends of any children who come around. I am in a panic and asked them not to touch the cat because I would guess The Cat has not had shots.

The bottom line is: we can't keep The Cat or her off springs. We are not able to get on the roof nor could anyone else get close to the kittens as they run inside the soffit.

At first, The Cat seemed to rein in her babies when they strayed too close to the edge. However, there is one which didn't obey. It fell off the roof when we were watching. The Cat immediately jumped on the rose trellis and leaped to the ground and began licking her fallen baby. Shortly, the baby followed The Cat to her food pan and eagerly began to eat with no apparent after effects from her fall.

The Cat made several trips between the roof and the ground trying to care for her separated kittens. She seemed to look towards us for help. I sensed her frustration and had empathy, as I have had various occasions when my kids didn't mind leaving me feeling at my wit's end.

Harold came to the rescue. He got the ladder, gently scooped the kitty up into an empty flower pot, and dumped the cat back onto the roof. All was well for a few days. That is until the venturesome cat jumped off the roof again. I've come to the conclusion that mama cats have as much trouble controlling their offspring as some humans do, maybe more. Of course, I can't understand cat language and sometimes I used to think my kids did not understand me. Now I know it was simply a case of selective hearing.

We decided The Cat had to resolve her own problems. When Harold was working in his shop a few days later, he saw The Cat was in the corner nursing her ground baby.

The kitten keeps its distance from us. In the meantime, The Cat is apparently still feeding her roof babies. They sound as though they are full of energy, when I hear them running in the night.

Maybe it's possible; The Cat will teach the remaining roof babies to jump off the roof. Harold has "put together" a wooden path of sorts, which they could walk down from the roof.

In the meantime, maybe some of you, who are wise cat lovers, will share ideas as how we can reunite this "active bi-level" family on "terra firma" so we can proceed with a placement plan.

Assignment Resulted in Tattletale Tales

"There's a magical tie to the land of our home, which the heart cannot break, though the footsteps may roam." Eliza Cook

My sister and I both enrolled in Eastern Illinois University as adult freshmen when our youngest sons entered kindergarten. That was prior to the time when the university had an adult re-entry center, which now assists and guides mature adults wanting to pursue a new career.

On that long ago day, I had struggled to get through the registration and book lines. Close to tears by the end of the day, my sister and I finally found a moment to compare our schedules. We had been elated to learn by some stroke of luck, we were both placed in the same English composition class.

Prior to our first class, we had decided not to reveal the fact that we were sisters. We felt our "maturity" would already set us apart from the younger students. Later we learned that was not true, as the recent high school graduates were very accepting. We had wanted to blend in the class and not attract any attention. The anxiety of earning and bringing home grades for our own high school children to see was sufficient stress for us to manage.

Incorrectly, we thought it would be easy for us to keep our identities a secret as we had different last names and no one had ever thought we looked alike.

Our first classroom assignment disclosed our secret. Our scholarly instructor, Mrs. Robertson, requested that each student write a short in-class essay about a familiar body of water. I felt like I was home-free as I am a swimmer and was always attracted to moving water as I find it soothing. A few weeks earlier, I had panicked when my assigned writing subject on my college entrance exam had been, "The Sex Life of a Newt."

I chose to write my first essay about Cowhorn, a favorite childhood swimming hole located near my childhood home in eastern North Carolina. I relayed how Cowhorn felt and looked like iced tea, as it flowed out of a thick swamp into the sunlight along the side of the road where the trees had been cleared and the water flowed under a bridge. Cowhorn had made a perfect swimming hole, as it had a white sandy bottom and you could always see your feet in the bright sunlight. One hazard was that copperheads and water moccasins also enjoyed sunbathing in the shallow water.

On that first day of class, we had walked out of the class discussing how good we felt about our first assignment. All of a sudden, without sharing we instinctively knew that we had both written about Cowhorn.

Thus, it came as no surprise at the conclusion of the next class, when Mrs. Robertson asked both of us to remain after class…

We had unexpectedly learned an important lesson on that first day of class: one's heritage reveals more about you; than your name or looks.

Animals = Creative Home Entertainment--*July 18, 2004*

Birds and rabbits perform daily matinees in our yard, which my husband and I observe from the comfort of our screened porch. The curtain rises many times on any given day and both the price and serenity of our choice seats is right. Our conservation filter strips have lessened the erosion caused by water runoff and have increased our animal population.

Young rabbits play Ring Around the Roses and Follow the Leader, as many as five rabbits playfully circle our olive bush and other shrubs. When one breaks rank, usually another one will follow. The only time I don't enjoy their performances is when they stray into our garden.

We rarely see the pheasants but often hear their familiar sound coming from the filter strip.

I sometimes think our bird populations have been "people watchers" as they have acquired some bad traits, which humans regularly display. We have a dominant bully, which regularly visits our finch feeder. The finch bully is so busy knocking off other birds that it forgets about eating. There is one exception. The bully Finch does not get after the small Bluebirds who come to the feeder. I suspect that, one of the bluebirds has put the bully bird in its place during some previous visit.

The small but mighty humming birds empty their feeder as often as the finches. We have red ribbons attached to their feeder, which flutter in the draft of the birds' powerful wings. The cardinals serenade us and the papa bird's color is always magnificent.

Young robins are also frequent visitors to our lawn. They play the hop-hop game and sometimes two robins get hold of the same worm. Bob whites are regular residents and answers our calls. We have an ample supply of jays who quarrel with each other and are fussy with us if we get too close to their nest.

One of our favorite summer visitors, which returns each summer, is a large blue-gray heron, which we occasionally see flying overhead. We also see it around the Johnstown and Bradbury bridges making us think it must nest somewhere along Muddy Creek. From time to time, we see deer, which also have their habitat along Muddy. We are most likely to view the deer crossing the road, in the woods, which borders the Bradbury hill.

During the night, I hear the hoot owls and some other unknown bird which likes to chirp during the pre-dawn hours.

In total, I enjoy seeing and hearing the gifts of nature's bounty, with the possible exception of the two a.m. chirpers.

Uninvited Guests--*July 5, 2003*

Holidays create welcome guests for many families, as many of those millions of people, who had been on the road this Fourth of July weekend, were headed for happy reunions with their families.

My daughter and her husband were among the travelers. They traveled west for a long awaited reunion with their son, who has recently returned from the war zone. I shared her happiness, while feeling pain for all those families whose children were killed in the conflict and for those who continue, almost daily, to meet death and injury in Iraq and/or Afghanistan.

All week long, I have had destructive nightly visits from both an uninvited and unwelcome guest, who has been busy uprooting plants in my flowerbed. I would have welcomed our intruder if he/she had uprooted and had eaten some of the weeds.

After three mornings of attempting to restore my ravaged and uprooted flowerbeds, I declared all-out war on the intruder. Harold dug out a trap that had been in storage, as several years have lapsed since our last four-legged invasion.

Harold baited his trap with apples and his favorite snack: peanut butter. Peanut butter is a staple on our kitchen shelf as it has played important roles in our life. I shared a few weeks ago, that earlier in our marriage when the grocery fund would run short, we kept a backup jar of peanut butter and a box of crackers on hand. Back to our intruder, the first morning after setting the trap, we discovered the food was gone but the trap was empty. The trap was upside down, a few feet from my uprooted flowerbed. As we again baited the trap, we concluded that our intruder was some kind of a smart four-legged animal that liked peanut butter, as he had known how to retrieve the food without being trapped inside.

Yesterday, I had slept in a bit and Harold called to me saying, "It's time you were getting up. We have a visitor." I reached for my robe wondering who I would see, when he added "Our visitor has rings on his tail." I hurried to my flowerbed, where a coon was actively showing his displeasure at being caged. We relocated the coon, away from any houses in a wooded area, near a creek.

Last night, Harold again baited the trap with his favorite food in case our intruder had extended family that was planning a nocturnal visit.

You guessed correctly, another irritated coon was in our trap this morning. I've given up on saving my flowers, but if the peanut butter holds out, in time, we may get rid of all of our unwelcome guests. Never underestimate the power of peanut butter and persistence.

My Dad's Enduring Instructions--*September 25, 2005*

My Dad was a native North Carolinian. My birth family lived on the east coast until I was in high school. I recall an "unnamed" hurricane which made landfall in the 1940's, which caught me at my grade school that was located on Chesapeake Bay in Ocean View, Virginia. My Dad who was then in the Navy assigned to the Norfolk Naval Training Station; walked through the fury of the storm to rescue my brother and me at school. Today's advanced technology allows students to be evacuated long before a pending hurricane makes landfall.

When my Dad was discharged from the Navy, my family relocated in the Midwest because my mother had roots in Illinois. Thus, I have always retained both my love of the beach and a healthy respect for hurricanes as I now spend increasingly longer portions of each year in Naples. When my Dad had some serious instructions or something he deemed important to say, he would use the preferential remark, "We need to prepare as if for a hurricane." Of course, we all knew that we could not experience a hurricane in Illinois but out of our love and respect, gave him our undivided attention and tried to obey.

Since my Dad's death, our government's technological advances in tracking hurricanes have greatly improved. Today's students are evacuated long before a pending hurricane makes landfall. However, Hurricane Katrina gave painful evidence that our government has not developed adequate plans in how to quickly rescue victims during and after major disasters; whether they are natural or manmade.

I, like you and untold other Americans, felt anger and shame at the number of our elderly and incapacitated citizens who drown or died pleading for help during the first two to three days after Hurricane Katrina had made landfall. Homeland Security & FEMA simply did not respond in time.

National Guard Units are often the first responders in local crises. Perhaps the fact that part of New Orleans' Guard Unit and their equipment was in Iraq added to the slow response.

My daughter who has served as the administrator of a nursing home facility said, "… that having in place and practicing a facility's evacuation plan is a prime duty of every administrator." Because the facilities where the deaths occurred were below sea level, they no doubt had appropriate evacuation plans in place.

If you now have disabled friends and/or loved ones in an institutional setting, ask the staff about their facility's current emergency evacuation plans as there are many potential emergencies other than flooding that could occur such as: tornadoes, fires and terrorist attacks.

We all need to thank the brave and heroic actions of the hundreds of people who did work until they collapsed rescuing thousands of other victims from Katrina's fury and rising water. In many cases it involved neighbors helping neighbors early on, along with the outstanding performance of our U. S. Coast Guard during the days when FEMA could not get its act together.

Something good can come out of failure. All evidence points to the fact that those agencies who miserably failed the old and incapacitated during Katrina have responded quicker to the threats and fury of Hurricane Rita. I hope each of you will follow my Dad's instructions "in preparing as if for a hurricane" and contact your senators & congressional reps who appropriate the funding and have some oversight for our federal emergency response agencies. Please tell them: our national emergency responses were inadequate during Hurricane Katrina and we want changes; I did.

A Silent Guest in Worship

Vision is the art of seeing things invisible. Jonathan Swift (1711)

I entered the East Naples United Methodist Church early on Sunday morning to worship after scurrying about to dress, get a bite to eat and arrive in time for the 8 a.m. service. It was exhilarating to drive down Airport Road with hardly a car in sight! Arriving at church a few minutes early I had welcomed some quiet time to meditate and collect my thoughts. That was not to be, even though there were fewer people in attendance as the migration of Snowbirds north has lessened the size of the 8 a.m. congregation. One small uninvited blackbird quickly became the main attraction, gaining and keeping everyone's attention.

As I was taking my regular seat in the back, Pastor Craig called to the ushers "Turn the lights off, open the out-side doors so the bird will see the light." The thought passed through my mind that Pastor had come with a prepared message that he hoped would provide new light and understanding for his congregation rather than for a bird. His morning message would later prove that to be true, but no success with the bird.

The bird had an agenda of its own. It remained occupied; flying about and finding perches to pause and examine the lovely banners which decorate the walls of the sanctuary as well as checking out the lofty chandeliers.

I reached in my purse for my ever present note pad & pen as I toyed with the idea that this might be creative column material. I overheard these comments as staff and entering worshipers became aware of our unexpected visitor's presence. Quoting in random order:

> "The bird will sing."
> "We may wish we wore a hat (as she held her program over her head)."
> "It's a different color than our church's symbol (a white dove)."
> "It will keep us awake."
> "It's better than having 'Bats in the Belfry'."
> "If it gets hungry it can participate in Holy Communion."
> "Someone needs to cover up the bird during service."
> "Maybe it has plans to build its nest."
> "During my 15 years of being a pastor, I've never had a bird in the sanctuary."
> "The bird feels safe."
> "A special guest."
> "One of the flock, recognizes the Good Shepherd."

Our uninvited guest did indeed make the congregation more alert, with no one napping that I could see. Most worshipers believe that God is an unseen guest at every service. Perhaps today's bird was a bearer of good news telling us that rain is on the way to alleviate the drought, even as a bird had been for Noah in his ark, revealing that the rains had stopped.

Hurricane Wilma: Viewed at a Distance
--October 27, 2005

The passage of time sometimes has a tendency to dim and/or remove one's power to choose. Hurricane Wilma's slow journey provided time to refresh my memory with some basic values that my parents first modeled and taught me. I am also unexpectedly writing about, as well as experiencing, the topic of stress again in a big way!

When Harold and I perceived that we might physically be in Wilma's projected path, we pondered what action we should take. I was reminded of Rule #1: Protecting and nurturing life is always more important than things.

This lesson was modeled by my parents in many ways. One that comes to mind is that nutritious food and proper medical attention are always of prime family importance. When money was scarce, those essentials took precedent over new clothes or toys.

Rule #2: Always be mindful of and check on others. During Wilma's sojourn, we have experienced, first hand, being the recipients of this rule. It was comforting to have our children, grandchildren, extended family and friends call and check on our plans, while extending their love, and offers of housing and transportation. One of my North Carolinian cousins, who now own a house on Topsail Beach and have dealt with many damaging hurricanes, called and encouraged us to escape Wilma's wrath.

Rule #3: In the midst of stress, remember to relax and don't lose your sense of humor. While exhausted and waiting in the airport for a flight north, we noticed a family arrive with two laughing teen age daughters. One girl was holding a blue ice cream cone. The other girl put her arm around her and hugged her, apparently comforting her. I thought, "Isn't that nice" as it appeared that their vacation had been interrupted. However, when her head was close enough, she took a big lick off the other girl's blue ice cream cone. All the weary travelers smiled. Curiosity got the best of me.

"What flavor is your ice cream?" I asked.

She smiled and replied, "Cotton candy." The mother shrugged and said, "I thought cotton candy would be pink."

I laughed and replied, "So did I," and decided it must be another of those generational issues.

Rule #4: Don't lose your imagination in the midst of stress. We looked out the airport window at some dark and ominous clouds. Harold nudged me in a little bit and said. "What do you see in that cloud to the right? "A pig's snout," I replied; Harold agreed, reminding me of those carefree childhood days, spent staring into the clouds and seeing all kinds of fluffy images. For a few minutes, all our stress evaporated.

P. S. I'm writing this on my son's office computer. He picked us up after our late-night flight into Indianapolis and we are now experiencing a pleasant role reversal! Son takes in parents! We are tracking Wilma's journey on his TV with much less stress.

Nature's Scenic Road: To EIU & Work
--September 15, 2011

Today I traveled a scenic road that I have treasured during much of my life since I had moved to Illinois, with my parents, in 1945.

However, because of its beauty I never learned to take it for granted or to think it will look or be exactly the same, the next time I traveled on it. I'm referring to the blacktop road to Charleston, which goes through EIU's Campus and is also known as Fourth Street and/or Lincoln Log Cabin Road, when going toward Toledo. I have lovingly named it my: "Hilly Road."

I first traveled this road as a special treat when a teenager in the late 40's when my oldest sister; Carolyn was a student at EIU. After Carolyn had graduated from high school in North Carolina, she had worked in an office on the Norfolk Naval Training Station during WWII. Instead of flying the coop, she chose to continue living with our family, in order to save most of her salary to help pay her future college expenses. At EIU, Carolyn boarded in a private home on 6th Street in Charleston, sharing sleeping rooms with other girls, who also had cooking privileges in the basement and access to the living room for dates(if the need arose) and other social events. This was an economic way to be near the campus without the costs of living in the dorm.

Carolyn and her room mates would all take canned or fresh baked and/or garden produce from home in season to share and help reduce their mutual food cost. Carolyn had six younger sibs at home, including me, and on the weekends that she came home, some of us would get the privilege of going along on Sunday afternoon for the ride, up and down the beautiful hills while sitting on the back seat and sniffing the good aromas escaping from Carolyn's food box(that shared the back seat) and often contained Mother's angel food cake, pies , fresh baked cookies, a platter of chicken plus a dozen or so, baked sweet and Irish potatoes. Later, on Sunday, Dad would return my sister; Pat and me to our Toledo apartment in order for us to attend THS. We also got a food box as this was in pre-school bus days when we didn't have the rural roads to support buses. I am now keenly aware and thankful for the many sacrifices my parents made to keep their kids in school as I, like my parents, am a strong believer in the importance of education.

Years later, when my youngest son David first entered grade school, in the 1960's, I began commuting to EIU to take classes that coincided with his time in school. The thrill of viewing nature's beauty on the "Hilly Road" never left me from the time I was first exposed as a treat, riding along when Carolyn returned to EIU, until going there today for a reunion dinner with my former co-workers at DCFS in Charleston where I had been employed for several years.

Driving north on my "Hilly Road" today was a bit like a trip down memory lane with all kinds of remembrances flashing in my heart, as if on a mental T V screen. Nature's Fall paintbrush has already been working overtime in coloring a few of the magnificent trees in the wooded areas, while tinting the soybean fields from shades of golden yellow to a pale brown in the fields which have been harvested. The well-kept lawns surrounding the lovely homes sitting on the side of hills, landscaped with rows of evergreens and/or brightly colored fall flowers, made me wonder if some of my college acquaintances and former professors; from long ago, were still in residence.

Today as I drove over the hills and valleys, engulfed with beautiful views, whenever I looked upward with the sun gleaming on the trees giving me a moment to recall the many times I had ventured over these same roads; glazed with ice and snow during the twenty-five years that I had been en route to school and/or work, murmuring prayers and hoping that I didn't slide off the blacktop or crash into another car. This also brought to mind loving memories of my DCFS office mate, Marge Ramsey who resided in Charleston and insisted that I "sleep over " in her lovely restored Victorian home, whenever she thought I might be at risk driving home on my iced "Hilly Road." At that time her husband, was a practicing caring obstetrician who spent many nights at the hospital; whenever his patients were in labor, she somehow graciously made me feel it would be good for her to have me to keep her company.

En route home and each time I travel my "Hilly Road" and go by the cemetery where Lincoln's father is buried, I am reminded of the now; historic people who had trod this same beautiful journey on horseback or afoot so long ago. I have read that the Lincoln shrines in Illinois are the number one choice that tourists from abroad want to visit.

Shortly after a couple more curves in the road, I observed the Janesville Cemetery and saw the progress of dedicated citizens who are now working towards restoring it without tax support. Sometimes I stop to visit the graves of so many of my forefathers, along with Harold's, whose contributions during their lives had made life easier for Harold and me. Also, this is where I plan for my ashes, along with Harold's, to be interred ,and, thank goodness, the chore of selecting our memorial marker was behind us prior to Harold's passing.

When you next want to plan an inspirational trip to see some of nature's beauty, don't overlook a drive to Charleston via my "Hilly Road."

LOOK BEYOND--*August 11, 2008*

Do you ever get caught up in "tunnel vision"? I do. When I consciously analyze a situation I can move beyond it, because in a tunnel is the last place I want to be. Recently, I have been writing about the advantages of living in a rural community, namely Cumberland County. I do not want to retract anything I've written about its many pluses, merely to add another dimension: ALWAYS remember to look up.

During the recent past, I, like millions of other people from around the world had been listening to news blurbs about how the Chinese government was preparing to conduct the current Olympic Games.

I knew cost was not an issue because their wealth is no secret. The United States imports much more from China than it exports. Anyone only has to check the source of the merchandise in any Wal-Mart store to verify this. Also, China owns many of the US bonds that have been issued to fund the billions of dollars of debt that our country has incurred during the last few years.

Thus, it soon became apparent that the quality of the air was China's number one problem as they prepared to conduct the Olympic Games. They took many temporary actions in an effort to improve the quality of the air such as shutting down factories in the area and limiting the number of vehicles on the streets.

As I was listening to the news reporting the levels of smog and air pollution in China, I began to look up to check our own environment. Immediately, I began to look beyond and view the clear blue of our sky laden with white fluffy clouds that look like air boats. I was then reminded that the clarity of our air is another bonus that goes with living in rural America!

However we are not off the hook, China cannot be given exclusive ownership of all the world's smog. Some of our cities continue to deal with it although we do have some federal laws which seek to control a number of the harmful exhaust fumes which come from autos, as well as our industrial areas.

My husband, Harold, is an artist at heart. When he was able to pursue his hobby of woodworking, he created many beautiful designs, and he continues to see art designs in the clouds whenever we are walking. Do you recall as a child lying on your back and seeing both imaginary and interesting designs in the sky?

We all know that walking is an exercise that helps to maintain our physical bodies, but it's also good for our mental and psychological outlook. Being surrounded by natures' bounty, whether it's the clean air, beautiful skies or animal and plant life, can help to clear our minds and reduce stress.

The next time you are outside, take the time to deliberately look up. It will help you to look beyond whatever stresses or daily cares that are on your mind. I find looking up is a bit like using an eraser on a blackboard as it cleans the slate, at least for awhile.

While you are looking up, whisper a prayer of thanksgiving that you are living where you can clearly view our beautiful sunrises and sunsets and all that is displayed between nature's morning and evening shows.

Tree Cutting & Changes--*September 18, 2006*

"Poems are made by fools like me, But only God can make a tree." Joyce Kilmer

A few weeks ago a lineman from our electric power co-op stopped at our house on a routine check. My husband talked to him about having a tree remove from our front yard. Our birch tree was leaning towards the power line.

Originally, the tree had twin trunks but one had died a few years ago. We were afraid that a wind storm would bring the remaining part down into the power line.

The lineman agreed to remove the tree but said that he was not sure if they could cut the tree this year. Before he left; he marked the tree with a big red X so the cutting crew would know which tree to remove.

At first, every time I turned into my driveway the big red X caught my attention. I didn't like the looks of it. I guess I have read too many novels about marked people and things. I finally got used to seeing the mark. Yesterday when we returned home, Harold exclaimed, "The tree is down!" Harold is always more observant of details than I am. When deer or other animals are in the fields, he always spots them first.

The red X and all the rest of the tree was scattered across our driveway in pieces and piles. On the ground it seemed as though there was more bulk to the tree than when it had been standing. I was reminded of a scene from a few weeks earlier, when its leaves had gracefully fluttered, creating scenes of beauty in the bright moonlight that I had enjoyed watching.

As I thought about how long it has taken the tree to reach maturity, with ample portions of sunshine and rain, I felt a sense of loss. I was reminded that man can remove a tree but indeed, "Only God can make a tree." Adjusting is an everyday occurrence with nature. Humans have the same potential to change and direct their attention to other issues. Somehow, it seems as though we instinctively have an extra need to cling to the familiar for awhile longer.

The tree had overshadowed some pine shrubbery and a smaller ornamental tree. Also, there is a dark red peony bush which seldom had bloomed because of the shade.

Next year, I suspect the direct sunlight will produce changes in all of them, possibly very pleasant ones.

Kept After School--*September 20, 2003*

Hurricane Isabel gave me cause to remember a day from long ago when I had been kept after school by a "No-named" hurricane. I smile when I tell this story because my children have inquired, jokingly I hope, if I'm referring to the times when people traveled in covered wagons, when I discuss hurricanes, without names. Admittedly, the science of predicting the path of a hurricane was unknown sixty years ago, along with many of our other newer technological advances, but I'm getting ahead of my story.

I grew up on the east coast where storms were a normal part of my childhood. The "No-named" storm that I remember best stands out in my memory because it made landfall unannounced when I had been at school.

Let me take you back to the early 1940's, I'm aware that many of you were unborn at that time. In the 40's, there was no TV with cable stations giving hourly reports on the track of hurricanes and certainly no sophisticated storm monitoring equipment , with early warning systems. My "No-named" storm arrived in the midst of WWII when I had been accustomed to air-raid sirens sounding for nightly blackouts, not sirens warning of intruding storms, as I lived next to the Naval Base in Norfolk, Virginia, where my father was stationed.

I had attended school in nearby Ocean View, which was located on Chesapeake Bay. There had been no school buses and my siblings and I rode public transportation to school. My sister was in high school and upon getting off the bus; she received a transfer to ride a streetcar to her school, which was located closer to downtown Norfolk.

On the day the "No-named' hurricane struck my school, prior to our normal dismissal time, the skies had turned gray and ominous. The high winds and heavy rains had pelted the windows and caused the landscaping bushes and uprooted trees to fly like missiles gone astray. The broken power lines had left the school in the dark.

Earlier in the day, some parents had come to school to pick up their children. My mother had young children at home and my dad was teaching on the naval base.

As the storm strengthened, some students began to cry as the teachers tried to distract their attention from the angry storm. Later in the day, all remaining students were moved into the inner hallways.

I do not know how long the storm had been raging when I saw my dad enter the hallway. His naval uniform had been soaked and plastered to his skin and his pant legs were rolled up; never had he looked so good, as I ran crying towards him.

My dad being worried about the safety of his kids, had walked to the school in the midst of the falling trees, ripped up street car tracks, downed power lines, and other debris that had blocked the roads.

In time, the roads were open and the police took us home.

Sixty years have lapsed since the "No-named" hurricane created havoc in my life, on the Virginia coast. Time has brought great technological advances to our nation as evidenced by Isabel's approach; which allowed a half million people to be safely evacuated from areas which were threatened.

However, some things do not change: the fury of hurricanes has not been conquered and fathers still want to protect their children from harm's way.

Too Wet/Too Dry: Just Right (Soon)?

Goldilocks said, "Papa Bear's bed is TOO hard, Mama Bear's bed is TOO soft, Baby Bear's bed is just right." THE THREE BEARS

What a change to return to Cumberland County with a surplus of water from Southwestern Florida's drought conditions. I think that too much water may be better in the long run than too little moisture. At least the plants, trees and lawns are not dying. Also, people are not being arrested for violating the water restriction ordinances, nor living under the constant threat of fire. Plus here, there must be an ample supply of water for human and animal consumption, as I have not seen anyone hauling water.

Of course, I know some of my farmer friends will reply that you can't grow anything if the seeds are not planted. I am keenly aware of that as I look out and see the water standing in our fields.

Before returning home to Illinois, when I went out the front door to get the morning paper, I would often smell smoke. Frequently I was unable to walk outside because the smoke had created breathing problems. At least I can now walk and breathe in Cumberland County, although I might get a bit wet and/or chilled.

On our way home, we turned off the Burma Road and saw where Muddy Creek had washed sand over the road and fields and had cut a big hole by the Bradbury Bridge near Charlie and Marilyn Scott's farm home. That reminded me of a flood in the fifties, which had caused the old bridge to float down the creek several feet. I cannot recall the exact year; maybe it was 1957. Anyway, when the water receded, the bridge was pulled back into place and used to cross Muddy Creek until the present bridge was built.

On Mother's Day, we were invited, along with others, to the home of our special friends Barb and Terry Titus for dinner. While there, I took an unofficial poll asking, "Between the two extremes; too much rain or too little, which would you prefer if you had a choice?" The results were exactly even. So my poll didn't resolve anything. Not that it mattered as no one can control the choices.

Nevertheless, the rain has probably been good for the lawn mower business. Our thoughtful and helpful neighbors Rex and Becky Evans had mowed our lawn two times before we returned home. Unlike the damage TOO MUCH rain brings, Cumberland County has a wonderful supply of good neighbors and friends who are just right as they reach out and help each other without regards to the weather.

The Aura of Summer--*June 2001*

"And what is so rare as a day in June? Then if ever, come perfect days... ." James Russell Lowell (1819-1891)

June 2001 is passing by! It is hard to fathom that one-half of this year is history. Nevertheless, prior to us departing Naples, June had already managed to launch SUMMER.

What does summer hold for you? For me? While summering In Illinois, I envision ripe tomatoes and peaches, picnics and cookouts, family reunions, vacations and a more relaxed schedule.

You may notice activities involving food inappropriately dominates my summer dream list. Husband Harold and I have started a diet and my fat cells are waging war.

I have listed pleasant events, which I hope will come to past this summer. When planning or doing work, I now and then use the sandwich method. That is listing or doing the more pleasant things first, then the least desirable in the middle as the filling, and then concluding with additional enjoyable activities. Which implies, I expect to have twice as many pleasant activities this summer, which may not be the case. If not, I will have thinner slices of bread and thicker filling in my "model sandwich".

Now to the filling list or my least liked distractions of summer: weeds, moles, biting insects plus those which invade the garden, payment of taxes and insurance premiums, thunder storms and unfinished chores piling up.

Harold thinks summer is the perfect time to get all his chores completed. That is contrary to my longing for leisurely days. Fortunately for me, he is both a workaholic and a realist. He finishes his own work early. Then he has time to complete the jobs, which I had started and set aside because I could not be separated; from my computer or books.

Numerous fun ideas surface to become the top of my summer "sandwich" plan. Such as watching the changing colors in the flowerbeds and the vibrant Finches at their feeder, swimming, visiting with friends, and consuming the fresh veggies from Harold's garden. Plus, simply sitting and staring, while meditating on the wonders and beauty of summer: is perfection for me.

Some things do not change. I concur with Lowell's words written more than 100 years ago: *"And what is so rare as a day in June? Then if ever: comes a perfect day... "* and sets the tone for my kind of summer.

Toledo's Flower Lady--*August 30, 2003*

An old axiom tells us, *"Beauty is in the eye of the beholder."* If that is the case, everyone who has driven around the Toledo Square this summer has surely observed the beauty of all the colorful flowering plants.

When I go to Toledo on errands, I need to make a list, otherwise when I begin to admire the flowers on the Square I almost forget what I came to do. Natures' beauty always has therapeutic qualities: seeing brightly colored flowers growing is soothing to me; like the sound of moving water.

William Wordsworth's description of daffodils in, I *WANDERED ON A LONELY HILL* paints a perfect scene of beauty being portrayed by flowers:

A host of golden daffodils, ...Fluttering and dancing in the breeze... .

During this summer, I have enjoyed some of Anne Frank's writings. This young writer wrote these profound words about beauty and contentment: *Think of all the beauty still left around you and be happy*. Miss Frank wrote these words when she and her family were, in hiding during World War II.

Adolph Hitler, then, the ruling dictator in Germany, killed millions of

Jews during his rule, including Miss Frank in 1945 because he did not like their ethnicity.

If a teenage girl; hiding in a warehouse desperately trying to avoid death had the wisdom to write the above words about beauty and happiness: think how fortunate we are to live in a land, where the local government; in a small town places a priority on providing beauty for all to freely enjoy.

Whenever I see beautiful plants growing and flowering, I know, from my experiences, of observing Harold at work in his garden that a lot of tender loving care and hard work goes into the end results.

Thus, I began to wonder who had planted and cared for all the beautiful flowers which produces such bright colors and beauty, throughout the summer, on the Toledo Square.

One day, when I was coming out of the IGA, my question was answered. I saw a small tractor rolling down the middle of the sidewalk equipped with a water tank and garden tools. To my surprise, I discovered Joyce Ingram; my special friend from years ago when our husbands had worked together: is Toledo's Flower Lady!!

Thus, I extend special thanks and appreciation to the Toledo Town Board, Joyce and anyone else, that might be responsible for the beautiful flowers which, creates happiness for me and no doubt, many others, who choose to "behold their beauty."

Natural Beauty is a Restorative Gift--*July 20, 2006*

"To look up and not down, to look forward and not back, to look out and not, in ... ".Edward Everett Hale ;Ten Times One is Ten

Natural beauty often surrounds us, although at times; we fail to perceive and appreciate it.

Last night I fell exhausted into my bed and squirmed around to find a position that lessened my aches and pains. A longstanding habit of mine is to mentally review a day's activity prior to bringing closure, as I find it serves as a learning process. Hopefully, some of the negative or non-productive events of that day can be examined and possibly prevented from reoccurring. I gave myself a C- for a difficult day and trusted that sleep would erase some of its impact.

Nevertheless, I'm an eternal optimist because I had experienced a new day bringing a clean slate. Perhaps, tomorrow there will be an opportunity to make a positive difference in someone's day, if not in my own. I have been the recipient of many kindnesses from others of late with few opportunities to repay them. When these situations arise, I try to put into practice the "Pass it On" system.

As I turned in my bed and was facing towards the window; its outer frame suddenly outlined a beautiful picture. The moonlight was glistening through the branches of the tree outside of my window, as its leaves moved ever so slight; in a faint breeze. The lightening bugs were creating spontaneous bright spots. As if an artist had added a finishing touch, near the very top of the window, there was a bright star twinkling eons of miles away, with a message of wonder.

I reached over to the window to get a clearer view by pulling the lace panel to one side, as I was shown, once again that beauty is therapeutic for me. My aches and pains, along with my thoughts about some of the day's troubling issues all vanished, as serenity engulfed me.

I didn't have to wait, for tomorrow to bring a clean slate!

I have experienced similar occurrences; in the past, but I do not possess the key to unlock their healing serenity at will. Thus, for now, I will simply enjoy and absorb the moments of God's peace and beauty; whenever and wherever they occur.

Experiencing Earth's Beauty--*September 2, 2013*

"Lord you have done so many things! You made them all so wisely"! Psalms 104:24

The theme of the Adult Sunday School lesson that I taught yesterday was: To appreciate how God creates and sustains all of creation and emphasized the beauty of His creation. Thus, this morning when I drove out to my old farm home site that my children have beautifully converted into a family park, I was more aware of God's beautiful surroundings than usual. Lily and Bob are camping there for the long weekend and had invited me to come out to share an early cup of morning coffee, with them and to hear about their camping vacation spent with their son and his family on the Minnesota/Canadian border last week.

The Burma Road is very familiar, because I have driven it thousands of times through the years, often in haste: failing to pay much attention to the beauty of the fields, trees and sky that surround it.

Traffic was sparse on the Burma, so I opened my windows while slowing down to view the crops. There was a space in the road, that I could clearly see the bean fields on both sides: their tops seemed to look like an ongoing dark green velvet carpet; how magnificent in the bright sun! As I looked north, I could see more beauty in the rise and fall of the Burma Road; edged by the Bradbury woods and scattered trees.

Turning west, off the Burma down the Bradbury Hill and through the woods to the bridge that crosses Muddy Creek, is one section that nearly always had attracted my attention because of the changing scenes created by the trees during the various seasons of the passing years. As I descend the hill, trees on both sides of the road sometimes meet creating various sized holes above, for me to look through and late in the afternoon, I sometimes had seen: the setting sun displaying many rays of color engraving the scene, in my memory.

During the winter when the leaves have fallen the dark branches also have created attractive designs in the sky. When crossing the bridge at the bottom of the hill, I usually take a quick glance at the creek bed to see if there is any moving water.

On west, there is an old barn that sometimes contains young animals, but none today. As soon as I turned north, I have a view of Rex and Becky Evans' Farm Home that always looks like a beautiful picture one might hang on their LR wall. It looked as beautiful as usual today, but I knew it was too early to stop and say hello to Becky.

When I arrived at the Dobbs' Park, Lily and Bob had overslept a bit and the coffee wasn't quite through perking. Saturday night's wind had blown down several limbs and they had been busy gathering them into piles to burn. I think they got more wind than rain but everything looked green and had a "fresh washed aroma" to it. They placed a comfortable folding chair for me in the sun where I could continue to view God's handicraft among the trees and also could hear the coffee perking. With the buildings removed, it was a bit difficult for me to decide what part of the grounds(where Harold and I has lived for 60 + years) that I was sitting in, but with Lily's help, we decided we were close to where Harold's rhubarb bed had been in the garden.

They have all the grounds planted into a lovely grassy carpet and Bob keeps it mowed evenly. But, it still gives me a strange feeling, when I drive my car through the area, where my bedroom had been located. Nevertheless, it was a thrill to sit and visit about their recent lakeside vacation with their grandsons and their son and wife; while enjoying my early morning coffee: in the beauty of God's creation.

CHAPTER 3
FLOWERS OF LIFE

Childhood Friends--*May 24, 2005*

"I remember, I remember The house where I was born," Thomas Hood 1827

Sometimes memories flood our minds when we least expect them. It would be a great loss if we could not recall and reminisce about our past. A few days ago, my lifelong friend, Edna Carmack Huffman, called to tell me her three sisters; Sarah Rhodes, Mavis Jarman, and Marjorie Harris were on their way to Toledo from North Carolina for a visit. Many of you know Edna as a long-termed employee and volunteer at the Life Center. My relationship with Edna and her family goes back to the time we both were born and lived in a rural farm community in Eastern North Carolina..

Edna, who lived on a near-by tobacco farm, had met her husband Maynard Huffman, when he was visiting my parents in N. C. Maynard was my mother's cousin and had traveled from Illinois with his parents Wren and Vera Huffman.

To make a long story short, Edna and Maynard fell in love, married and lived west of Toledo until Maynard's death.

My parents purchased property that had belonged to my maternal grandparents and relocated in Cumberland County after WWII, as my mother (Mary Sparks Hill) had been born and grew up in Toledo, graduating in the THS Class of 1925.

During grade school, Edna's sister Mavis had been my closest friend. We were in the same grade at school and attended the same church. Often we would visit in each other's home for Sunday dinner. As Southern farming at that time was very labor intensive, we often had worked together.

Thus, I was excited to receive Edna's call and immediately began to anticipate seeing my childhood friends and Edna.

I purchased Sweet Potato Pies to serve, as both our families had grown sweet potatoes commercially on our N. C. farms. I call my sister to join us, as I knew she would be equally happy to see the Carmack sisters. I could only imagine how thrilled Edna would be with all three of her

66

sisters, a special gift of time.

The weather co-operated and last Sunday, we were able to sit on my screened porch and view the irises, roses and other spring flowers that provided a rainbow of colors, with the cardinals and other birds providing the background music in the nearby trees. We really did not need any outside stimulus; merely being together brought forth many of our happy shared childhood memories which had been in storage for fifty years.

I wished afterwards that I had taped our conversations so our children could share some of what had filled our youthful days.

Marjorie gave me permission to share one of her memories pertaining to Edna and Maynard trying to have some privacy while dating. At that time, much of the courting was done in the family parlor. Marjorie, like younger sisters, wanted to know what was going on and sat down on the sofa by Edna. Maynard gave Marjorie a nickel if she would go outside and play for a while. Marjorie said she earned a matchbox full of nickels during Edna and Maynard's parlor dates.

Edna shared another "suitor story". A neighborhood boy who had wanted to date Edna came to her house at night under the pretense of visiting her brother. Edna wasn't interested and simply went to bed, leaving him talking to her father. He finally got the message.

Our visit, like all happy occasions, went all to quickly. We exchanged addresses in hopes of keeping in contact.

What's in a Name? --*July 6, 2001*

Recently while scanning birth announcements, I discovered my birth name Mary Hill. Mental pictures blur as I try to imagine what her life might be like seventy years from now. Will she experience as many changes in her life span as I have thus far?

No doubt, similar thoughts went through my parents' mind when they tried to project what life would hold for me at the time of my birth.

I doubt that my birth notice was even printed, as the village I was born near did not have a newspaper. My Dad said it might have been several days before my doctor had business in the county seat and took the time to record my birth.

When he recorded my birth, he mistakenly used a different middle name than my parents had selected. I didn't know about the mistaken name until I was grown and needed a copy of my birth certificate. As a child I had wished many times that my name could have been Elizabeth instead of Eliza. You guessed it. Elizabeth was the name the doctor had mistakenly recorded for me at the courthouse. However, by then I was married and had taken my maiden name of Hill as my legal middle name. I never used my dream name: Elizabeth.

My Father was in the service when my oldest sister was born. Mother named her Carolyn. Dad was disappointed because he had wanted her to be named Caroline after his birth state.

My father gave the name of a beautiful historical queen, Cleopatra, who sailed the Nile, to his second born child. She did not like it and shortened it to Pat; when she went to school.

However, at home it didn't matter much what our given names were. We all had nick names. Our Grandfather was not very tactful in disguising his disappointment that we were not of his sex. He named my oldest sister Sam and me Pete. Pete was derived from the word repeat because I was his third granddaughter (a little much from his point of view).

My mother later bore three sons, but Grandfather Hill did not live to see them.

I have a strong suspicion that most girls, at least, go through a period of time as my sister and I did when they wished for another name.

My Mother in her wisdom said it was much more important how we lived and what credit we brought to the name we had been given instead of fretting about not liking it. Now I understand and appreciate her words more than I did when I first heard them.

I have also learned in time that being born a different sex from my grandfather was not an insurmountable handicap. Sorry, Grandfather, that is another one of the privileges of being born in the 20th century rather than the 19th; when women could not vote.

Also a passing thought to every Mary born in the 21st century: you may live in the White House and be our nation's first CEO from the fairer sex. Who knows? Your spouse could live in the White House and volunteer for a good cause.

Childhood Memories of Work &Play--*July 8, 2006*
"Poverty consists of feeling poor." Ralph Waldo Emerson; Domestic Life

I grew up in a time that poverty was pervasive in our nation. Historians label that era as the Great Depression. Yet as a child, I never felt poor. I fully understood that we had been, many years later, when I was a history major in college. Probably, it was because my classmates had similar lifestyles with the exception of the few students who lived in the village.

Then, most of the children in neighboring families also worked to help maintain their livelihood. As a child, I worked in the fields and in the garden, which produced most of our food. I helped to feed and care for the chickens and other livestock, which were also source of food, with some being sold or bartered for other necessities.

On Saturday afternoons, Mom would take a case filled with eggs into the village store to exchange for groceries. She sometimes sold extra pounds of butter that she had beautifully imprinted and shaped with her butter mold.

Now, I sometimes see butter molds for sale in antiques shops for outrageous prices. It causes my mind to flood with pleasant memories, which includes the dime my Mom had given me that came from selling the butter, to see the latest episode of "Cowboys & Indians" at the Saturday movie matinee.

Children throughout the ages have had the creativity to make play out of work tools. My sisters and I were no exception.

On our Carolina farm, tobacco was grown and processed as a cash crop. Producing bright leaf tobacco was labor intensive, which involved all of the family plus swapping work days with our neighbors.

The cured and sorted tobacco was tied into bundles and placed on slick, round wood sticks for transport to the market. The prepared tobacco was hauled several miles to market by local truckers. There it was slid onto wood pallets and placed on the warehouse floor; then the sticks were removed for reuse.

I suspect some of you will recall pictures and/or hearing the auctioneers in radio ads saying, "Sold to Lucky Strike" or to whatever company that had purchased it.

On market day, the tobacco was sold for cash. Then Dad went to the A&P Store to stock up on non-perishable supplies such as flour, sugar, plus large cellophane bags of puffed wheat (a treat for the kids) and soaps, although my Mother made the lye soap used for cleaning. The icing on the cake was Dad stopping at Pulley's Bar-B-Q Restaurant and bringing home paper dish-trays filled with barbequed pork. I'm sure many of you know that nothing tastes as good as southern pit barbeque. As an adult, when visiting my relatives in North Carolina, I have revisited Kinston to eat barbequed pork, but it no longer held the excitement, as it once had; during my childhood.

My sisters, Carolyn, Pat, and I used scraps from my Mother's sewing basket to decorate the smooth tobacco sticks and pretended they were characters from the funnies. Lula Belle, Captain Easy, Ella Cinders, Lil Abner & Daisy Mae were some of our favorites. We drew make--believe houses for them on the ground; much like a hopscotch diagram. Then, we would ad-lib conversations as our characters visited each other.

Another summer diversion from our work chores was to hide-out in our favorite tree or in our bedroom closet to read our newest library book. We selected books from the traveling Bookmobile that made regular stops at a crossroads near our farm home.

All of my family also read and discussed the serial stories in the Saturday Evening Post. We liked to meet the mail man so we could be the first to read about the story's latest happenings.

Thus, in the midst of work, my parents always allowed some time for fun. Emerson's quote was true for me, as I never felt poor.

Clothing with Attachments

Do you ever wonder why you have a problem cleaning out your clothes closet? Why tossing out some older items of clothing is so hard to do? And yet some newer outfits get pushed back in your closet without being worn? Maybe it has more to do with the mindset than the fit. Did you ever stop to realize our clothing collects emotional baggage just like our psyches?

I envision some male readers thinking I must have grown up in Outer Mongolia or someplace different from them, and that might be the case. I grew up in a female body and am aware that both sexes do not experience or feel the same way about many issues. Keep in mind I have lived with and loved a man for umpteen years, which gives me a few clues as to how the stronger sex might respond.

A wedding dress is a perfect example. Women who remain happy in their marriages keep their wedding dresses. You may have kept your wedding dress. Mine was street length, aqua with shimmering threads and I enjoyed wearing it on other dressy occasions. Like for many newlyweds, funds for clothing were not plentiful, and, besides, I loved the dress and the man I married!

I see ads occasionally saying, "Wedding dress for sale cheap." To me this indicates how the seller felt about the total involvement.

If you are old enough, you probably recall the pink suit which had been stained with President Kennedy's blood that Jackie Kennedy wore back to our nation's capital on the fateful night after the President had been assassinated. I'm sure other clothing was available on Air Force One. Parting with the suit meant she was parting with part of her husband. Think about your favorite clothing. Articles you like best may have been purchased when you were happy or had been worn, on special occasions. Your favorite jewelry in the past may have been gifts from someone special. Of course, you may no longer wear it if you currently feel different about the giver. Similarly, your clothing that remains on the hanger in your closet may have negative connections although you had enjoyed wearing it in the past.

The next time you are trying to clean out your closet, consider the emotional attachments. Some of those items that take up space, although they still fit perfectly, may need to go.

4-H Memories--*August 22, 2004*

Recently Harold and I went into Pank's Pizza and saw a large group of children, sprinkled with adults. Our first guess was it might be a Bible School group enjoying pizzas. I soon learned it was a pre-fair meeting of the Liberty Hill Rangers 4-H Club as they were discussing their Fair projects.

I wonder how many of you have memories associated with 4-H projects at the Cumberland County Fair. I suspect this shoe fits many of you. Either as 4-H members or as parents or both, as it does for me. We enjoyed listening in on their meeting as we consumed Pank's wonderful Taco Salad.

The Rangers leaders are Vivian Hallett & Janet Cox, and they have close to twenty 4-H members. Their lesson was on Farm Safety, with emphasis's on young people.

As their young president conducted the club's other business, I recalled the wonderful leadership skills I had learned in 4-H.

The president introduced Mrs. Pankey to the club, as she was the guest speaker. The club members listen attentively and asked good questions as she shared what it had been like to open Pank's Pizza two years ago without prior business experience.

Then her husband, Larry Pankey, was without work. He lost his job due to downsizing after working in a Charleston factory for more than 20 years. Downsizing and movement overseas has had affected so many families in both our area and country.

She reported Larry now makes from scratch from 4-7 batches of pizza dough each day as well as the pizza sauces. Each batch of dough makes around 20 pizzas depending on their individual sizes.

Daily, prior to opening, the vegetables must be prepared and the pizza oven must be pre-heated. Mrs. Pankey shared that cleaning is ongoing throughout the day and evening. That is evident when you are at the counter ordering and get a peek, at their sparkling kitchen floors.

After their meeting, when the club members were enjoying their pizzas, I talked to Vivian. She reminded me she had been a 4-H member the same time as my son Roger. She also reported that as soon as they finished eating, the Club planned to tour the Depot and other historical sites in Greenup.

I suspect some of the members who have livestock projects are camping at the fair this week, which reminds me of my first 4-H camping experience at White Lake, N. C. It was also my first experience of being away from my parents. Vegetables which had I had tended in my 4-H garden project paid my camping fees. My 4-H Club had ridden to the summer camp in a truck bed, which had a tarp covering it. Nevertheless, it was both a fun-filled adventure and learning experience. I both enjoyed and learned more than I have on later trips which cost many times over.

I cannot write about 4-H without paying tribute to my one-time neighbor and lifelong friend Mary Ruth Cooter McKinney. She for more than 50 years has positively influenced the lives of Cumberland County's youth as a 4-H leader. I send thanks wrapped in love to Mary Ruth from all of us.

Get the Box--*June 14, 2003*

Sometimes inanimate objects become an integral part of our lives, such is the case for an ordinary box in my household. The status and usefulness, of the box gradually evolved. A stonemason, Mr. Zibe Tinsman, who had built the fireplace in my living room, left the box at my home more than forty-five years ago. I can't really recall how he had used the box. Possibly, he had used the box's surface to hold the pieces of Indiana limestone, while he cut them to fit, or maybe he used the box to stand on while mortaring the upper pieces of stone on the fireplace in place.

The box has no outstanding features, style nor wood texture. Today I measured and found that it is a 12x12x18 inch hollow cube. Sometime, during the passing years, I painted it a plain brown color. After the completion of the addition to my home, the box escaped the bonfire, when the workmen piled up the scraps during their final cleanup. Although, Harold is not a "saver of valuable stuff", like me, he had rescued the box from the scrap pile and stored it in his workshop, perhaps thinking it might have some future use. I'm sure he never dreamed it would become an indispensable part of our household.

Like many objects or people, for that matter, it takes time to fully discover their talents and/or possible hidden abilities. When referring to people, we often use the term "late bloomers". I do not know what terms could be applied to a box. At first, the box's utilitarianism was discovered when Harold needed to reach some item stored on a higher shelf in his shop. The box's full versatility only surfaced during later projects.

In time came a day when the box was brought into the house to provide a secure footing for Harold when he was doing some of my many "honey-do" projects. It would be returned to Harold's shop because I did not want a plain box sitting around in my house. These work tasks involving the use of the box were repeated for a few times over a period of years. Then came the day when I fully realized the value of the box. Then it became a permanent resident of my household with no more return trips to the workshop.

The box was the perfect perch for untold chores, such as cleaning the baseboards, heat registers, sorting junk from under the kitchen and bathroom sink, weeding the flowers planted at the edge of the patio and on and on------. Using the box, I discovered, prevented both untold backaches and leg cramps.

However, this was only the beginning. The box was the perfect fix, when we needed to convert a kitchen chair into a high chair. Later the same kids and grandkids used it for a neat racing site for their miniature cars. Oh yes, now, great grandson Logan has discovered the box, proving history indeed repeats itself.

The teenagers used it to hold their game boards and/or cards while sitting on the floor. When the dining guests are greater in numbers than the chairs, the box upended, creates another place at the overflowing dining room table.

Now the box is on display, with respect, in my home, as I never know what pending crisis will be resolved when someone yells, "Get the box." Thus, with boxes and people, unexpected talents and unique solutions can emerge when you least expect them. That is, if you don't get in a hurry and throw out the baby with the bath water.

It's impossible to Save Time--*August 3, 2004*

"You put corn in the barn (or freezer) but there is no (storage) place to put time." Bob Beall

What a profound thought, and to my amazement it is absolutely correct. Then the obvious next question is how much time will be allotted and how can we best use it? The first answer is, we do not know, and the second answer is up to us.

Time is one of those seemingly simple words and consumes half a page in Webster's Dictionary. It's all inclusive and vague first definition doesn't do much to achieve clarity. Webster states "time" is, "The period between two events or during which something exists, happenings or acts; measured or measurable intervals."

No place does it state you can store an ounce or a bushel of it for future use. Thus, I have chosen to share how one of my neighbors is using his treasured gift of time.

I have named this story:

HAPPENINGS in TIME

Every time I go to town, I drive past the lovely farm residence of Rex and Becky Evans. I have known Rex and his sibs since they were a young family at home when their mother had died in an auto accident. This summer, I noticed early on that the outside cornrows in the field south of their home looked different. I soon decided that was the location of his annual sweet corn patch, which he always plants to share with his family and neighbors. I began keeping an eye on the progress of his sweet corn as

Harold and I have gone to town during the past two weeks to work on preparing a rental house for sale. One day last week, we came home exhausted wondering what we could prepare for supper with the least effort, and PRESTO, there were several ears of fresh corn on our porch! Yum, yum! We knew its source.

Saturday when we were returning home, we saw Rex and his brother Kenny harvesting more of the sweet corn. It wasn't long before Rex, Kenny, and Rex's two young granddaughters Emily and Abigail pulled their pickup truck into our driveway loaded with several bushels of sweet corn and invited me to take as much as I wanted. This is a happening in time which reoccurs every year.

Years ago, when Rex's mother had been killed in the tragic accident, she had been taking corn to town to store in a locker plant (pre- home freezer days) for her family's winter use. At the time of her death, his maternal grandparents were our closest neighbors and lovingly assisted in the care of their daughter's seven children for many years.

In appreciation, during the past several years Rex has grown and shared his delicious sweet corn with all his family and neighbors. I think there is a saying that applies, "What goes around; comes around."

A story for another day is how my friend Bob Beall (quoted above), who is a retired business man, along with other caring people(including my sister, Pat) have used their time to open and operate a homeless shelter in a nearby town which now houses and feeds several homeless men and women each night (PADS).

As Bob stated, no matter what happens, the clock keeps ticking and we have no way to store our time, only the opportunity to wisely use and share some of this gift, which is allotted to each of us: one day at a time.

The Gardner Family. Neighbors, Teachers and Friends--*August 28, 2001*

Neighbors are treasures we encounter along life's journey. Emotion colors my thinking when I pause to remember my wonderful neighbors: Mr. and Mrs. Allen(whom we nicknamed Grampy) and his wife Bernice Gardner and their daughter Eva lived across the road. Eva's brother Raymond and his wife Hazel and son Donovan(who was soon off to college) also resided nearby.

For fifty years they extended love, kindness and a helping hand to my family. Sharing the bounty of their garden, kitchen, "know how" and hearts, without fanfare, which was their everyday way of life. They exemplified the poet's words, "Let me live by the side of the road and be a friend to man."

Usually, on Sunday morning, Raymond stopped for Harold on his way to Toledo where they picked up the paper and had coffee while hearing the local news. Those visits filled a special need for Harold who had lost his parents earlier in life.

Raymond enjoyed refinishing, caning and repairing broken furniture in his farm shop. Woodworking was a relaxation as he was a hard working farmer. He taught woodworking skills to Harold, which has proven to be a satisfying hobby for him. This summer, Harold is refinishing an antique loom for our daughter Lily.

Many years ago, I had wanted a round oak table. However, my limited budget dictated that all I could do was think about it. Raymond knew this as I always had admired the tables in his shop that he had refinished for others. In time, he found at an auction (that he loved to attend) two damaged tables from which he made my table at a minimal price. Now, when my family and guests gather at my dining room table, I'm reminded of Raymond's woodworking skills as well as his thoughtfulness.

Creating a usable and beautiful finished piece of furniture for his friends and neighbors gave him more satisfaction than the money he earned for his labor. If all of Raymond's time in his shop had been considered, I am sure he earned very little in hourly wages.

The Gardner family lived up to their name. They produced bountiful vegetable gardens. Eva and Hazel both had beautiful flower gardens. Whenever my plants burst with color, I thank them, as many of my flowering shrubs and plants were starts, from their gardens.

I often found Eva and Mrs. Gardner quilting and sewing when their daily chores were completed. They made quilts for each member of their family as well as other exquisite handmade linens, which they gave to family and friends on birthdays and other special occasions. I cherished the ones given to me.

Grampy Gardner was more reserved and the least verbal in the family, although he was kind and considerate. I remember one winter that I turned too fast and ended up in the ditch. In a little while, Grampy appeared with his tractor, to pull me out.

I smile now as I recall Eva's later years when she did permit me to drive and take her places on occasions. Many times during the prior years, I had ridden with her and Mrs. Gardner to church as well as to other places. However, when Eva could no longer drive, she fiercely maintained her independence. No matter how I would protest, she insisted on giving me money for gas. This was hard for me to handle from a person who had become a second mother to me.

However, I finally realized when you have been a strong and independent individual all your life; you could not change at eighty-five. I stopped protesting, took her gas money and dropped it into the offering plate Sunday morning.

The Gardner families truly "lived by the side of the road" and were friends to many. They taught me by example "the pass it on" way of saying thanks.

Rocking Chair Insights--*October 15, 2007*

What you think of yourself is much more important than what others think of you. ~~~ *Seneca 4 B C- 65 A D*

Yesterday while cleaning, I rearranged some furniture and moved a small old wooden table in front of an east window; close to my caned-bottom sewing rocker that has an old wooden bread bowl hanging above it which had belonged to Sister Love, more than 100 years ago. The incoming morning sunlight highlighted the blemishes on the tabletop. I concluded that the beauty of the grain and design of the table overrides its flaws.

This scenario immediately triggered many pleasant memories from my past. After I had meditated for awhile, I quizzed Harold as to what the table brought to mind for him. He replied, "My grandmother's kitchen table."

Harold's Mother died when he was ten. Then, when he walked the mile home from his one-room grade school at Hickory Corner, he passed his maternal Grandmother's home. She often had fresh warm rolls and a glass of milk that had been kept cooled in the well waiting on her table for him. He said, "Grandma's table had a wide drop-leaf top that was supported by a wobbly pullout leg. Grandma had told me that her table had been brought to Illinois in a covered wagon when her parents had moved from Kentucky. The tabletop had lighter streaks caused by her frequent scrubbings with her homemade lye soap." Harold added, "It took me awhile to realize that it was no accident that her hot rolls happened to be coming out of the oven just as I passed by."

Harold's comments, made me recall the large wooden table from my childhood that I had helped to clear and scrub after family meals when it was my turn to do dishes. On Sundays or whenever we had company we used a tablecloth that made the job easier as we went to the back door and shook the cloth. During the school year, if we had homework, that was an automatic pass from cleanup chores. My older sisters and I usually managed to hit the books immediately after mealtime.

My Grandmother sitting in a nearby rocker would often point her cane at us and tell us to go and help our Mother. In time, we realized on our own that we were unnecessarily passing work on to our Mother, who often had prepared the meal for our large family, which included baking hot bread, after she had worked in the fields all day on our labor-intensive bright leaf tobacco farm.

Occasionally when I sit in my rocker I reminisce and cherish the happy times my family of nine shared during mealtimes and rarely recall my chores. I do regret that I did not help my Mom as much as I could have during my childhood.

I do not point my cane at my grandchildren but I know in my heart; when they pitch-in and help with family chores, they will like themselves better when they are my age.

Viewing Life Through a Peephole--*September 14, 2008*

Every time I drive over the Bradbury woods road, en route to our farm home, I see a limited view of the sky. This is caused by the branches of the trees overlapping in the center of the road. The road is on a hill that leads down to the Muddy Creek Bridge. It doesn't matter whether I'm headed east or west I always look up to enjoy the beauty of the views because they are always different.

Probably the most magnificent view is when I'm headed down the hill going west at sunset. The taller trees, commingled with the shorter ones, with their branches meeting at various levels over the road, form a picture frame. Sometimes they create a two-tier peephole, which I name the upstairs and downstairs paintings. The peepholes' scenes of beauty are fleeting and I must be paying attention to quickly view them while also keeping my eyes on the road.

I find these scenes to be a microcosm of life as there are many times when we see a partial look into others' real life situations that are very different from our own way of life. Yesterday we had an opportunity to view outward glimpses of the life styles of the Amish people.

Our neighbors, Rex and Becky Evans called to invite us to go with them to Yoder's Kitchen in Arthur, Illinois for lunch. We were doing household chores and quickly answered yes.

When we got into their car Rex asked if we were in a hurry to eat. We responded "no." He said, "We would drive north on the country roads and do some sightseeing along the way." It turned out to be a perfect day for looking around, because the recent rains had changed the sun-burnt brown grass into various shades of vibrant green.

Soon we were sufficiently north to enter the edge of the Amish country, verified by the horse-drawn buggies along the road. At first there was only an occasional Amish farm home. Although there had been a lapse of several years since I had worked and sometimes driven in this rural community, it remained easy for me to identify the Amish farm homes. All of the Amish houses have large gardens near their houses, and almost always have beautiful flowers gardens blooming in their yards. Another identifying factor was the horses in the barn lots, and frequently there were two homes on the same farm site which housed different generations of the family.

We noticed a great variety of specialty shops that sell anything from quilts and tools to various kinds of food. Through the passing years. making a living on limited acres had caused the Amish families to diversify in order to provide income to support their expanding families. They draw customers from people like us, from surrounding communities, as well as tourists who plan their vacations around a visit to their community.

In our high-tech competitive world, it is interesting to observe their unique and plain life style, which has remained mostly unchanged through the passing years. As they have continued to worship and reach out to help their neighbors and others in surrounding communities, as their forefathers did before them.

After we ate, I should be more honest and say "over-ate", Rex drove through downtown Arthur and out to the edge of town into the back storage lot of large farm equipment company in order for Harold to view some of the latest farm equipment.

Rex gave me a "peephole" look into what young farm boys liked to do when he shared that looking at farm equipment was something he had enjoyed doing with other guys since he was a teenager.

Having lived on a farm most of my life, I thought I knew the purpose of most farm equipment. Not so, as there was so much equipment stored in various stages of being assembled that I saw pieces that I didn't have a clue as to what their intended use might be.

For instance, there was one bright red object that was about the size and shape of a farm grain wagon, but its framework was open like a steel gate. Rex smiled and explained that the piece of equipment would be attached to a hay baler in the field to catch the bales and haul them to storage. So now, with my new knowledge, I'll be looking in the fields to see one in use.

Also, I must admit that the tour of the farm equipment store's back lot was interesting, but it wouldn't have excited me as a teen-age farm girl. Then, I was more interested in checking out the farm boys. Proof of that is the fact that I married one as a teenage, almost sixty-one years ago with only a peephole view of what marriage might hold. It has turned out a bit like a view through the Bradbury Woods filled with beauty and with lifelong love thrown in as an added bonus, as we have had the gift of living and raising our children in our farm community.

Acceptance or Change with Serenity--*July 10, 2005*

The Serenity Prayer
God grant me the serenity
To accept the things I cannot change;
Courage to change the things I can;
And wisdom to know the difference. ~~~Reinhold Niebuhr.

More than 25 years ago my daughter gave me a copy of the *Serenity Prayer* printed on a plastic card to carry in my billfold. If it had not been sealed in plastic, it would have been shattered into pieces from use through the years.

Learning how to make difficult changes and/or acceptance of the unchangeable is what the *Serenity Prayer* is all about. This little prayer tells us to ask for courage to work on changing the things we can. Obtaining the wisdom to know the difference is the hard part, as we have no need to struggle over the easy decisions.

We cannot change our height, but we can change our weight, that is with time and considerable effort. This is an easy example of knowing the difference.

The Serenity Prayer is attributed to Reinhold Niebuhr; as he used it in a sermon in 1943, although some people think this prayer may had existed in some form dating back to the time of the early Greeks. If the words were not exactly the same, the need for such a prayer has always existed for mankind.

Through the centuries, human kind has struggled both with acceptance and change. When you look back over a century, it is easier to detect changes in our society than it is when examining lesser periods of time. I have been monitoring the movement of this season's hurricanes in the Gulf and I am reminded that we most often see rapid changes in weather related issues even though they may not always be easy to accept.

Accepting things which we cannot change can also be difficult. Always remember, there are changes which we can make in our daily lives, which will impact ourselves as well as others in a positive way. Change must first occur in our attitude or thought processes. That is the hard part. Once we accept the fact, that change is possible, we can proceed with action.

Serenity and peace of mind can come from either acceptance or making difficult changes, whichever wisdom dictates is the better choice for our lives at any given time.

A Listing of Memories: Gifts, Which Money Can't But *April 24, 2005*

"Life can only be understood backwards but it must be lived forward."
Susan Kierbegaard

Do you make lists? I think my first list might have been made during my childhood at Christmas time. Being a child born in the era of the Great Depression, most of my lists were usually so called *wish lists.* I enjoyed looking at SEARS & ROEBUCK'S Christmas catalogue and picking out desirable items. However, I always knew that oranges, apples and stick candy maybe a Milky Way or Babe Ruth candy bar would be the most likely gifts found in my Christmas stocking. Let me quickly add that they were welcome treats which we seldom had at other times of the year during my early years in rural North Carolina.

One thing about growing up without extra cash for gifts was the fact that most all of the families who lived around me were also farm families which struggled to make a living during a period of time when most of our nation was experiencing a prolonged economic downturn. Thus, I had no sense of being poor because my neighbors were also poor. We were rich in other ways. We always had food; much of it grown in our garden or traded for eggs produced on our farm. I had nice clothes to wear as my Mother was a beautiful seamstress. Although all of my family worked hard in the fields we also found some time for learning and fun activities.

I learned to spell the individual names of the states and each of their capitals while working in barns sorting leaves of tobacco to grade them for the market. All of my sibs learned to swim. The first quarter I ever earned came from learning to swim across a stream. Swimming was a treat that our entire family enjoyed together during the summer usually later in the day after experiencing a sweaty workday hoeing or doing other work in our cotton and tobacco fields. Our swimming hole was a wide place in the stream located near a bridge called Cowhorn. The water looked and felt like ice tea, as it had flowed cool out of a thick swamp where the trees shaded the water and their roots colored it. The hot sun warmed the water throughout the day where the area had been cleared of trees to build the road and bridge.

One's feet were always visible on the sandy bottom of our Cowhorn swimming hole. However, we always had to be on the lookout for copperheads and water moccasins, as they also enjoyed swimming in the sun-drenched water.

On evenings when swimming was not an option, we often had foot racing contests. I usually was given a handicap as I was the youngest girl; both slower and clumsy.

Reading was also a pleasant pastime in the summer. A state sponsored bookmobile regularly made stops near our rural home. My sibs and I excitedly checked out the new books during each visit because in the evening there was some free time to read usually between chores and bedtime.

We had a radio, and if there was money for a battery, we listened to the news, and sometimes Amos & Andy and other entertainers. My Father was a licensed Ham Radio operator, and we talked to other Ham operators on his 160 meter-bands. Sometimes we communicated using code as Dad had taught us to send and receive messages in code. Now as I communicate with e-mail on my computer, it sometimes reminds me of my exciting learning experiences more than 50 years ago in my Dad's Ham Shack, when his identifying call letters had been: W4AOJ.

Another neat childhood learning experience was tied to the visits from my Mother's family who lived in a then seemingly faraway place called Cumberland County, Illinois. From time to time, various members of my Mother's family visited us in North Carolina, and I began to think Illinois was a place I might like. When I was five, I rode the train for the first time, which was an exciting trip. I went with my Mother and two older sisters, Pat and Carolyn, to visit my Grandmother Sparks, who was terminally ill in Illinois.

Then I had no idea that I would someday call that faraway place home for more than 50 years and always treasure all of my non-monetary childhood gifts and experiences which had been provided in N.C. by my family and loving parents: Bill & Mary Sparks Hill.

DEAR READERS

Today, I'm using a different format because I want to say THANKS and share some information about THE STEEPLE SCROLL on this my column's first anniversary.

Thank you, thank you for your helpful feedback! You are a great encouragement to me. I have appreciated all your communications, some that you have passed to me by my children, e-mail and particularly the comments you shared with me at the recent Toledo High School reunion (which is my subject for next week).

The first letter I received concerning my columns was from Marilyn Barkley, a gracious lady who is my deceased brother's classmate. It was exciting to have feedback from someone I knew, in writing, much like getting a good grade on a test. I continue to learn from each of you.

In the beginning it took considerable nerve for me to submit my column for publication, although some of my first drafts had been written more than 20 years ago when I was working full time. I have had the desire to write at least since my Mother and Dad first wrote a human-interest column for THE RALIEGH NEWS AND OBSERVER when I was a child growing up in North Carolina.

My daughter Lily said recently, "Mom, although I like your columns, I wonder if other people who read THE STEEPLE SCROLL might think our family is 'kinda' different?" I told her that several readers have shared with me that they are relieved to know that there is another family who has had experiences similar to their family's. I suspect most families are more alike than different.

Now to your questions, where did my title come from? My family moved to Illinois eons ago when I was in high school. We arrived on a beautiful October day in 1945. Uncle Frank Thompson had met the train in Mattoon and then brought us to Toledo. My first glimpse of Toledo was when my uncle had pointed out our Courthouse Steeple when we were a few miles west of Toledo. The October maples had been in full color, adding to the Steeple's beauty on that long-ago day.

The view so impressed me that The Steeple became the symbol of my new home and has remained so for more than 50 years. Whenever I see the STEEPLE, I know that I am truly HOME! The SCROLL merely emphasizes that most of my columns' subjects have had origins in our own beautiful Cumberland County.

My column in similar form is published in Florida under the by-line, UNDER the SUN, because that's where my husband and I spend some time in the winter seeking warmth for our arthritic joints. I have future hopes that my columns will be published in book form.

Now I probably have "over shared" or provided T.M.I. (too much information), both terms that I have learned from you, my Readers.

This column would not be complete without thanking my editor, Billie Chambers, my husband who cooks, cleans and tries to lead somewhat of a normal life when I am glued to my word processor chair, and my sister, Pat, who proofreads and has been my best friend for 70 years. Also, I can't ignore my computer which corrects my spelling even though it also writes me nasty notes and cuts me off sometimes.

Books ~Friends For Life--*August 3, 2002*

"But what is happiness except the simple harmony between a man and the life he leads?" ~~Albert Camus

The thrill of handling a book has never dimmed for me. A book unlocks information and continues to bring excitement and wonder into my daily life. Some people have speculated that the high tech information explosion could render books obsolete. Not for anyone who has lovingly held a book in his or her hand. Or has experienced the thrill of visually processing and storing away its information to claim and use whenever the need arises, will ever stop reaching out to pick up a book to browse. I clearly remember my first reading book, and this week had an unexpected reunion with it.

Recently, I visited my friends, Lawrence and Dorothy Brady, in their beautiful new home in Neoga. I enjoyed seeing how well the rooms, closets and total spaced were organized. There was a place for everything. I imagined how neat it would be to live in such a house as mental pictures of my overloaded and disorganized closets and bookcases flashed on my mental screen. Throughout their new home, the Brady's have ample space to display various items which they have collected, adding both beauty and history to their surroundings while telling much about their life experiences.

When I saw their bookcase, I pulled up a chair. I did not want to move, it seemed as though I was momentarily glued to it. Dorothy shared that many in her family had been lovers of books. Her bookshelves contained many old books. Several of the books had belonged to Mrs. Edith (Buchanan) Bingaman, Dorothy's mother, who, along with her four sisters, had been teachers in one-room schools.

Several years ago, I had become acquainted with Mrs. Bingaman, as she was my daughter-in-law's gracious grandmother. Mrs. Bingaman was a mentor to me when I served on the LLC Board of Trustees, and our friendship continued as long as she lived. One of her sister's sons, Warren Young is a well-known science writer. Earlier he had been a science editor for *LIFE MAGAZINE*.

The first book I pulled from the Brady's bookcase, to my amazement, was a teacher's edition of *FUN WITH DICK and JANE~BASIC READER.* The book contained all of my first reading friends: Dick, Jane, Spot and Puff. Do you remember them? If you don't remember the books, ask your grandma, or maybe, great grandma, to introduce you. My first grade teacher, Miss Nora Blackmore, had introduced them to me more than sixty-five ago, when I lived in Eastern North Carolina. Even with the passage of so many years, my first grade classroom scene clearly surfaced in my mind, with joy, as I turned the pages in Dorothy's *DICK & JANE BOOK*. This book had started me on a life-long reading journey which I hope will never end. I can only guess how many people Mrs. Bingaman and her sisters had taught to read. Perhaps some of you have memories of having been a student in one of the Buchanan sisters' one-room -schools. The sisters' names after marriage were: Marguerite Brown, Blanche Shores, Marie Young and Sylvia Swinehart.

Community Spirit: The Johnstown Celebration--*June 6, 2004*

The Johnstown community, located in the north central part of Cumberland County, was established around 1827, even earlier than Chicago, but it didn't grow quite as fast. It had the Later Mill operating in Muddy Creek, which a pioneer community certainly needed to grind its grain as well as other services including a blacksmith shop, two stores and a school to attract new settlers. At one time, there was another mill named the Tully Mill, which also has a distillery above it. When Muddy Creek is low, the remains of the timber that supported that mill are visible on the west side of the Johnstown Bridge.

Residents of the Johnstown community, some direct descendants of the earliest settlers; plan the Johnstown Celebration. Because of the great response, they hope to make it an annual celebration.

What a fun day. It contained the perfect mix: food, a parade, free rides for the little ones, thanks to Bill Cornwell, plus the opportunity for more than 200 former friends and residents to spend time reminiscing in perfect weather.

Greg and Robyn Morgan, the honorary mayor and first lady of Johnstown, turned their garage into the cafeteria line. Also, many others assisted in making the celebration such a fun day for all. Special thanks go to Todd Myers, Toby Thornton, as well as the entire Thornton family, the Jones Family, Wayne "Bob" Wickersham, Jill and Steve Layton, Larry Hatfield plus many others. Earlier in the week, I saw the Jones family cutting and baling their hay on the "Johnstown Square" to create the parking lot, which served the 201 plus visitors today, (as all did not register).

The best source regarding the history of the Johnstown Community is two volumes in the Toledo Library researched and written by an earlier resident, Freda Misenheimer. Today in the parade there was a car driven by Peggy (Thornton) Kuhn honoring her memory, which was very appropriate as Peggy and her husband Theron now live in Freda's former home.

While enjoying my food, I sat next to Joe Thornton and his wife Marg. Joe at 93 was one of the older attendees. He shared some of his memories of growing up in the Johnstown community and gave me permission to quote him.

When Joe entered the Johnstown School at age five in 1920, there were 61 students in his class. Grover Icenogle, his teacher, was paid $60 a month, which included janitorial duties. He said some of the students were twenty-one years old. Often when they finished shucking corn they often returned to school. They would re-enter the eight-grade class because there was nothing else to do during the winter months.

Joe added, at that time his Great-Grandmother Lavina Thornton had lived in the house across the road from Greg Morgan and that he had another Great-grandmother, who lived in Johnstown.

The parade had sirens, motorcycles, floats, animals and political candidates that included: John Barger, a candidate for Judge, whose family has roots in the Johnstown community, and Golda Dunn; a candidate for Circuit Clerk, all tossing candy.

Also in the parade were my Great-Grandson Logan and his cousin Connor; who are both under five years of age; riding in little cars accompanied by their Grandmother Jeanie (Thornton) Carr. Both boys are direct descendants of Lavina Thornton, who had lived in Johnstown seven generations earlier and no doubt had walked the parade route many times. How it stretched my mind to think of the changes which have occurred in our society during those passing years.

One thing has remained constant: their wonderful community spirit plus the love and caring they extend to each other. How great it is to live in a community that works together and planned this special day, which enabled all of us to think about our heritage as well as enjoy the fellowship of spending some pleasant hours reminiscing with each other. Thank you, Johnstown Community! If outsiders learn what a special place, you are, you may need to install a traffic light.

Encouragement--*January 21, 2012*

"Just don't give up trying to do what you really want to do. Where there's love and inspiration, I don't think you can go wrong." Ella Fitzgerald

Encouragement is good medicine. I want to cite a couple of examples that occurred yesterday that made a positive difference for me.

Last night about dark, my next door neighbors, Stan and Carol, who are Snowbirds and my special friends from Northern Indiana, knocked on my door and asked if I had garbage and recycle material to be put out for collection , as the trucks often come early in the morning before most people are up.

And, yes, I did and I had forgotten about putting it out. I was exhausted as I had shopped for walking shoes yesterday. I remember when shopping was a pleasure, but it seldom is anymore, as I don't enjoy driving in the city traffic, nor coping with the crowds plus lots of walking in the store, trying to locate the items that I need. I think my "mature age" is trying to give me a message that it may be time to even change my Snowbird commuting lifestyle as it is very different now that I no longer have my caring husband Harold to share my life with.

My recycle bin is large and hard for me to handle when it is full, which it was this week as I have been on a shredding binge trying to get rid of old records which are now outdated. Collier County works very hard in order to help its residents recycle, as they provide a larger container than the one used for garbage collection each week to remind residents that they should put more of their trash in the recycle than in their garbage bin. Recycled material keeps the garbage dumps from growing as most papers, plastic and glass discards can be used again. Normally, I have my recycle bin filled; every other week. Anyway, my kind neighbors; each took a bin out of my "cubby hole" storage place that is located off my front lanai and swished them down my sidewalk to the pickup place along the road.

And yes, I heard the start and stop of the Waste Management trucks before daylight this morning, so I was happy that my friends had helped me get the containers curb side last night .

My second encouraging incident came yesterday in the mail. I received a lovely card with greetings written by several of my TOPS (Take Off Pounds Sensibly) friends in Toledo that was heartening to read.

Judy Flake is the treasurer of our Toledo TOPS Club and the one who had mailed the card to me signed by the Toledo TOPS members. Many of you know that Judy is a lover of animals and works very hard as a volunteer to find suitable homes for those animals which are placed in the Animal Shelter.

My Florida Methodist Church, like many other churches, has a group of talented women called "Crafty Ladies" who operate a craft shop where they make many attractive gifts. Before Christmas I had visited their shop and purchased some handmade items for Christmas gifts. I found a crocheted cat on a plastic card, to hang on a door knob to add, a bit of color. The crocheted card made me think of Judy because she frequently sends me notes, even if I forget to answer earlier ones and sometimes, she even calls to update me as to what is going on with our mutual Toledo friends. I had planned to lay the crocheted cat in the bottom of my suitcase to take to her when I returned home. However, I found a large envelope that the crocheted cat would fit smoothly inside a book that would keep the cat from getting bent in the shipping process. After my Florida TOPS Club meeting today, I mailed it to her to express my appreciation because when one is feeling lonely or discouraged, there's nothing as encouraging as a newsy note from friends at home.

Have you encouraged someone today? It could be as simple as sharing some kind words with someone, or perhaps a visit to a shut-in, or helping a child with their homework. Also did you take the time to thank the person who has extended encouragement to you? If not, this may be the perfect day, to do so.

Memories by Association--*March 11, 2006*

A word can be permanently linked to another word, place or action in one's memory. Today at the grocery store I purchased some barbequed pork and smoked turkey. Immediately I began to wonder what the pork would taste like. The carton said it was tangy. My mind raced back remembering all the excitement that had occurred when I had eaten pork barbeque during my childhood. Barbecuing a pig always meant that there would be guests because no one roasted a pig to serve their immediate family.

When I was a child living in eastern North Carolina, having a pig roasted was a way of saying thanks to the neighbors and other workers who had helped to harvest and barn green tobacco as it was a labor-, intensive crop. The pig was put on the grill to barbeque the night before because it was cooked very slowly over an open pit.

Harold and I have had pig roasts or Pig Pickens as they are now sometimes called, at our farm to entertain on special occasion, such as birthdays and graduations.

Back to the barbeque and smoked turkey that I purchased for dinner. The turkey was good, but triggered no memories because I had not eaten smoked turkey as a child. The barbeque was tasty but was seasoned nothing like southern pit barbeque. Southern barbeque is seasoned mainly with hickory smoke, vinegar, pepper and salt. The barbeque I ate tonight had some hot seasoning and mainly tomato sauce.

Another memory trigger was when we talked to our daughter. After dinner, Harold and I called Lily and asked her where she will be working next week, as she travels extensively in her job. She said that she will be driving to Louisville, Kentucky. Lily, her dad and I all began to laugh. Lily added, "I hope I can stay out of the stockyards."

We all laughed because on different family vacations; when Lily was a child, we had gotten lost in Louisville and always ended up in the stockyards. Eventually, when Interstate 64 was completed, we no longer made unplanned visits to Louisville's stockyards, and it became a family joke.

I suspect most of you have had similar experiences within your families which certain reminders can trigger.   Montaigne said it well in 1580: "The memory represents to us not what we choose but what it pleases."

A REFRESHING MOMENT--*August 2000*

Serenity, beauty and peace encompassed my being and surroundings momentarily as I walked this morning. I was immersed in "a refreshing moment." The pale blue sky had small white pillows randomly scattered throughout my range of view. The scheduling for the day that had occupied my mind evaporated, only the beauty of the surroundings remained. I do not know what diverted my awareness and eyes to behold the beauty instead of the ordinary. Was it merely that I looked up?

My eyes focused on the small yellow butterflies flitting ahead of my feet as I approached them. The butterflies would race ahead and then seem to wait until my steps would catch up with them .No doubt they are there every morning as I walk, but my mental eye doesn't take the time to focus on them as it did today.

Tall corn lines my road; usually I think it looks like fences or walls withholding the breeze. Today the rustling of the wind in the drying corn sounded like music .As I finished my walk, the perimeter of the trees in shades of green that surround my house appeared to have been painted by a master artist who had perfectly blended the shades.

While analyzing this phenomenon over my kitchen sink, I decided to peep outside the door to see if this "refreshing moment" of beauty remained. You're correct: it was gone. Did my strident mental examination erase it?

Reason with me a minute. Can you recall times as a child when you could find designs of beauty in the sky? I can. Maybe there are other times that you remember that your environment or your existence was adorned in beauty that was close to perfection. I can recall a few other times that have come without warning. Does happiness or joy trigger a higher awareness?

I am reluctant to spend too much time considering the cause. I am aware that one's mind is occupied with untold stimuli and thoughts each moment. Could it be that the mundane crowds out the exquisite?

My daughter, Lily, gave me "The Serenity Prayer" printed on a billfold size card more than twenty-five years ago. Paraphrasing, it tells us to do something towards changing the things we can and to let the others alone. But the clincher is knowing which things you can do something about.

Thus, I think I'll accept today's gift of "a refreshing moment", while trying to remove from my mind some of the routine useless clutter that squeezes out tranquility, and perhaps my opportunity, to glimpse beauty.

My Christmas Thank You for: 2005

Recently at church my pastor concluded his prayer with this request to the congregation, "Be an answer to another person's prayer." As I meditated on his words, I concluded that I do not know for certain if I have ever fulfilled that role.

However, without doubt I know within my heart that many of my friends and family's actions throughout the passing years have provided answers to mine. If I had kept a list, many names would appear on the continuing record of people who have extended their kindnesses and love to Harold and me.

This year has been different from any other year in my life. You might respond that every year is different. Perhaps I have this feeling because I am approaching my birthday that reveals I have lived on this earth for three-quarters of a century. Harold, for 58 of those years (Christmas is our anniversary) has tried out and modeled each new year for me because he gets there first,; more importantly, he has and continues to share his enduring love and stability with me.

I give thanks for my span of life as I realize that the average time for many people living on our Planet Earth is less than fifty years. Then, I must immediately face the fact as to what have I done with all the years that I have been gifted with?

The Biblical Parable of the Talents comes to mind as I write this. The bottom line is not how long we have lived, rather what have we accomplished! Thus the intent of this letter is to make sure I have not failed to make you aware of my appreciation, love and thanks for the kindnesses you have extended to me personally or to Harold and me jointly and/or to our family.

Because the real gift of Christmas is Love, it seems as though this is the appropriate time for me to send this message to you and pause to ask God above for the wisdom for each of us to best use and share His gift during 2006.

Thanksgiving & Closure--*November 20, 2005*

The following quote is from a letter, which had originally been printed in the *New York Times* a few years ago: *"Today, our most family-oriented national holiday (Thanksgiving) celebrates the generosity of those Americans already (Indians here) towards the newly arrived (Pilgrims)...."Daniel Greenberg President-Legal Aid Society- New York* I kept this letter because it contains a profound truth stated from a very different perspective. The generosity of those long ago American Indians modeled behaviors we have needed in 2005 locally and in Florida's Gulf coast.

I cannot recall a year during my lifetime in which so many natural disasters have occurred. Perhaps it seems that way because each day I see or read something new about the damaging effects of Wilma and/or other hurricanes and tropical storms.

This morning it was an added shocker when the paper's headlines read, "It's not over yet: Here comes Gamma."

After a cup of coffee, I knew I needed an attitude adjustment and reminded myself that this is indeed the Thanksgiving season and I need to be counting my blessings instead of dwelling on possible problems. As I paused to do so, I recalled a vivid scene, which had been printed in indelible ink, on my heart. The event had actually occurred in the aisle of my local grocery store a couple of years ago.

It was a modern day dramatization of our original Thanksgiving story by some of our community's future leaders. It will both warm your heart and reveal that the future will be in good hands:

During that Thanksgiving week, Harold and I had been shopping to prepare for our families' arrival. As we shopped, we encountered six preschoolers and two adult women enthusiastically discussing and then selecting cans of food to go into their grocery cart.

My husband smiled and said to one of the women, "You certainly have your hands full." She responded, "Oh, these are not my children. We are from the day care center down the street. We are shopping so the homeless can have food on Thanksgiving Day."

Perceiving our interest, the teacher shared that all the students at the center had jointly earned one hundred and twenty dollars, over a period of time, by doing extra jobs, in their homes.

Outwardly some of the children's skin displayed their diversity: however the intent of their hearts fully manifested the compassion and substance of that first Thanksgiving scene.

Individually, we cannot feed all of the hungry. Collectively we can make a difference. We can imitate the children, give special thanks and count our blessings, as we anticipate the approaching closure of the 2005 hurricane season.

Do you, like me, find it interesting that it happens to fall so close to our nation's Day of Thanksgiving?

God's Love is Not Denominational--*June 19, 2011*

"Dear friends, let us love one another for love comes from God." I John 4:7 (NIV)

This past winter after the death of my loving husband; returning to my Snowbird home in Florida was a lonely trek, as we had spent many happy years here together, in retirement.

After my arrival in Florida. I met with my long-term friend, Sue, whom I first met when we worshipped together at a small Methodist Church, which has since closed.

Sue shared that she had found and joined the Peace Lutheran Church, which meets in a school, while their new church is under construction on Immokalee Road. She then spoke about some of the many reasons that she felt God's presence while worshipping there. Then she extended me a gracious invitation, to be her guest at their approaching Christmas dinner-party. Feeling lonely, as Christmas would have been my 63rd wedding anniversary, I readily accepted her invitation for an opportunity to socialize with a friend.

At the dinner, I was overwhelmed by the presence of Christian love that was extended to me by those, who were seated at our table, as well as others, who came to our table and introduced themselves during the social hour that followed.

Somehow, I had held a preconceived notion, as one sometimes does about various groups without validity that Lutherans were very formal. Not so!

When I returned home from the Lutheran Christmas party, I then realized, I could not distinguish their warm Christian fellowship from that of our loving small-town Methodist Church here at home.

I accepted the invitation that Sue and others had extended to attend worship services on Sunday and came away experiencing again the same warmth and Christian love enhanced by the presence of the Holy Spirit that I felt in Toledo during worship. And for my readers at home, I need to clarify that the manifestation of God's presence was not related to the physical surroundings, as the services were conducted in a school building, where committed members came early each Sunday morning: to set up folding chairs and a temporary altar in the school auditorium, with banners and microphones. Then, after the service, everything would be removed, so the area would be ready for students and school staff to return on Monday morning. I would learn later that they had been meeting in the school and repeating this labor of love weekly, since organizing a few years earlier.

I am writing about these experiences in my column today for two reasons: first because I have been delayed in returning home, due to my cancer surgery and follow up treatments, and because I was in attendance today at Peace Lutheran's first , spirit-filled exciting service in their new church !

Another friend, Carol whom I had also known earlier, from my G G Women's Club, who lives nearby, has graciously given me a ride to the Church's regular services whenever I could attend. Continuing in worship has been very rewarding and has strengthened me spiritually during this time I have been coping with my health issues.

Since worshiping at Peace Lutheran, I also became excited about their act of faith in building their new facilities, which includes several classrooms to begin providing an Early Christian Learning Center for pre- kindergarten students. They have already employed a Director in order to begin offering these classes for area children on the first of August.

Today was my first time to see and worship in their new church building. Although I am a visiting Snowbird and not a member, I have felt a warm welcome in all their services, including Communion, because I am a person of faith.

As we turned into the drive-way, the parking lot revealed that many had already arrived. The sun shining on the metal roof gave it a sparkling gold color, and the beauty of the church's design was breath-taking. Upon entering the sanctuary, there was a line waiting to sign the guest book. This gave me an opportunity to stand and gaze about at the many ways it seemed to say: "Welcome to God's House."

When I greeted Pastor Liebich, I had to admit, although it seldom occurs; that I was almost speechless at the beauty and results of the Church's act of faith centered in God' Grace that had created this: God's new Sanctuary for His children.

My experiences in worshipping as a visitor at Peace Lutheran Church: reinforces my title: "God Love is Not Denominational".

Good News--*November 12, 2006*

"He who has good health has hope. And he who has hope has everything." Anon

Today, my subject is good news! Some have said it doesn't sell newspapers but it certainly lifts one's spirits.

My first account comes from a front page story in our very own *TOLEDO DEMOCRAT.* In the October 26th edition, I read with excitement the article entitled, "Family Care Center to Open at Health Department."

I have known Janet Stierwalt for a long time, as she had been my daughter's friend since their early school days. I am so proud of her accomplishments. Not only proud but I commend her persistence in achieving her goals. I know first-hand what kind of commitment it takes to commute to college as an adult, as I did. How fortunate for Cumberland County that she has chosen to continue serving our residents. She is proof that one person can still make a difference.

Thus, a big THANK YOU is sent to Janet for her dedication and ongoing goal of making health care more accessible for residents in Cumberland County. I know she is already very busy because I tried unsuccessfully to congratulate her by phone.

No doubt, there are others who helped to make the Family Care Center a reality for Cumberland County. I want to thank them, also.

Additional good news is the fact that Election Day this year set new records in some states for the number of voters who cast their ballots in an off-year election! I had become discouraged by the low voter turnout nationally in some of our past elections.

This year proved once again that American citizens can and do go to the polls when they are dissatisfied with the performances of their elected representatives. Election Day renewed my faith in our constitutional government.

Another source of good news was the U S Marine's Corps' dedication of their National Museum of the Marine Corps on their 231st Anniversary. Jim Lehrer, the anchor of PBS' Nightly News, was the keynote speaker at their ceremony. He shared how being a U S Marine continues to impact his life in many positive ways.

As a child, I had lived near Camp Lejeune a large Marine base in North Carolina. My parents had become acquainted with some Marines and had invited them home to share Sunday dinner with our family on different occasions. Even as a child I had been impressed by their good manners and the interest they took in our family's conversations.

I hope I can visit their new Museum in Virginia and see firsthand some of the items on display that tell the story of the Corps' 231 years of dedicated service to our nation.

All of this good news gives me renewed hope and reminds me that each person has the potential to make a positive difference in the lives of others.

The Gifts That Endure--*October 7, 2004*

This morning, I awoke in the dark around three a m, under the pressure of my unwritten column and falteringly found my way to my computer chair. My thoughts wandered back to some of the events of this week, including the unexpected death of a person who had been my friend for more than fifty years: Jean Hallett.

Now seated in my chair, in front of my blank screen with my pointer showing me where the words need to print, my mind races backwards and reminds me of the many gifts of friendship which have enriched my adult life.

Through the window by my computer, I can view a light in the house across the field. My thoughts go back in time, more than fifty years ago, when the older Gardner Family had occupied that house. The family consisted of Grampy (Allen), his wife Bernice, and their adult daughter Eva.

During the early years of my marriage when I was parenting two children before I was twenty, I discovered what caring and extraordinary neighbors they were!

In my immaturity (married at sixteen), it took me awhile to appreciate the treasure they became.

I now recall, with loving memories, the times I could look out my window and see Mrs. Gardner and Eva walking down their lane, both wearing bonnets, with Mrs. Gardner's dress length being longer than Eva's, giving them a stately appearance. And, oh yes, Eva usually had a basket on her arm that contained baked goodies, in the winter and in the summer they lived up to their name with freshly grown gifts of vegetables and flowers.

Long ago, my first thought at seeing them approaching my house was panic because usually my bed was unmade and all the remains of breakfast were visible on the table as I would be rocking and trying to calm my baby (Roger). My mind first focused on the physical, rather than the enduring gifts of love and care they transported. In time, I fully understood their gifts of love manifested in actions and eagerly welcomed their visits, while learning so much from them.

After the death of my mother, Eva's continuing love and nurturing helped to fill that painful empty space in my life. During Eva's last years, when she could no longer drive, I had   opportunities to repay some of her earlier kindnesses that she and her mother had given to me when I had so desperately needed help and guidance, during the early years of my marriage.

Earlier in the week, as I visited with Jean's family in their home, I could sense Jean's ongoing presence of love and care in the midst of her family as we shared our loving memories about her life.

The enduring gifts of love and care, whether bestowed on family, friends or neighbors, are the gifts that memorialize a person's life in our hearts forever.

What's the Value of a Cup of Coffee?--*October 21, 2009*

I feel as though my husband and I have been on a medical merry-go-around since our skilled and perceptive family care physician, Dr. Perez, wanted to do a thorough follow-up on some questionable results that surfaced during Harold's physical.

Some of Harold's follow-up tests have called for fasting; thus, last week when he had an early appointment, I decided to wait and have breakfast with him after his test was completed.

Besides, Harold makes superb coffee and therefore he is the "designated breakfast-brewer." I didn't want him making coffee he couldn't share. My skills in that arena do not measure up to his; so he usually makes all the coffee. Since our retirement his early morning performance; has allowed me to get forty extra winks of shuteye and then awaken to the wonderful aroma of his fresh brewed coffee. He has even been known to serve my first cup of steaming coffee bedside!

Later that morning, we learned that his doctor was running an hour plus behind. We noticed others who had arrived after us being called in for their testing with other physicians who were using the same outpatient waiting room. I figured that our physician, Dr. Kaplan, needed the added time to meet the needs of her patients; so in due time, Harold's name was called.

I began to fantasize how good a cup of anyone's coffee would taste. My eyes focused on a sign in large print: NO FOOD OR DRINKS ALLOWED, ruling out any nearby coffee dispensers. That was understandable, as at least half of the room's occupants were fasting patients waiting for their procedures.

Many were caught up with anxiety, as they were concerned about the outcomes of their family member's procedures. This led to chit-chatting, as each patient had a designated driver, as I was for Harold. All drivers were given a pager which would vibrate, alerting the driver that their patient would be ready to go home in thirty minutes. This allowed them to leave the office if they chose to do so.

I had been chatting with Sally who was sitting next to me. When the nurse called her mother in for her procedure, Sally decided to use her time to run some errands.

Being aware of our delay, Sally graciously asked if she could get anything for me. Before I considered that it might not be convenient, I blurted out, "Coffee."

Prior to leaving, she asked how I drank my coffee and I replied, "Black," while offering to give her some money, which she refused.

After she left, I put aside my book, which I was having difficulty concentrating on, and moved $5 from my purse to my pocket to pay Sally when she returned. Then, I began to anticipate how good the coffee would taste with a muffin I had placed in the car, thinking Harold might enjoy a bite on the way home. I then rationalized that it probably wouldn't be good for Harold to eat until the effects of his anesthesia were gone.

Soon Sally returned with a large cup of coffee from Dunkin Donuts, causing my mouth to salivate as I anticipated my first coffee of the day.

To my dismay, Sally refused the money I tried to tuck into her pocket. I finally thanked her and headed outside to my car with my pager in hand. She held the door and followed me out saying, "It's rewarding for me, to do something for someone else whenever it's within my means to do so." I thanked her again saying, "I, also, believe in the 'Pass-it-on - Philosophy.'"

While in my car; drinking my coffee and munching Harold's muffin, I had recalled while sitting in the waiting room, the TV had been reporting unending problems from around the world. I knew from instinct that there were, no doubt, other "Sally's" in the midst of those troubled areas who also were sharing "a cup of kindness".

Life in Our Community is Good--*August 30, 2002*

With the hopes and dreams of multi-generations in tow, the Methodist Church in Toledo has a new steeple set in place with a white cross reaching heavenward.

What a gift for each of us to have roots in small town Mid-America. Today was an occasion for everyone to store treasures away in their memory/history book. I'm getting ahead of my story. I should start at the beginning, but I am unsure where it is. Since I do not know the beginning and am certain no one could know, or want an ending to ever occur, I will begin when Florence Marshall, my special neighbor, picked me up at 7:45 this morning.

We went to the Toledo United Methodist for an 8:00 o'clock meeting to plan a service for a Sunday service next month. Florence shared on the way that a new steeple was to be installed on the church this morning. She had scheduled the meeting early so we could also witness the installation of the new steeple.

When we arrived at the church, we saw two men in a basket which had been lifted in the air near the platform where the steeple would be set. People were standing about with their eyes and camera fixed on the action. People on the east side called for us to come and view from that side because the sun would not be in our eyes. I crossed over and called to men above asking what our town looked like from their vantage point. They replied not so different from towns they see every week in their business.

Florence checked in the building to see if anyone was waiting inside for the meeting to begin. Finding no one, she joined the crowd on the east side of the church. I thought to myself about how special our town is and that the steeple installers would know that themselves if they had lived in our community for more than 50 year, as had most of the people gathering to watch the steeple installation. Our town, Toledo, is the kind of town that leaves a positive imprint on your life.

The will of Kathryn Conner Hodges had made the gift of the steeple for the church possible. Mrs. Hodges had been born into a prominent Toledo family during the first quarter of the 20th Century. She had grown up in Toledo and graduated from Toledo High school in 1928. Although she had not resided in Toledo since the early forties, she had not forgotten her hometown and the positive influence it had on her life. Because it was such a magnificent day, combined with the fact we did not want to miss any part of the steeple installation, Florence called our business meeting to order under the shelter of a tree on the lawn.

Two brothers, Ron and Phil Sherwood, pitched in and helped with the assembling of the steeple, while memories about the church were being shared in the gathered crowd. No one was sure how long it had been since the church had a steeple. It was before 1926 because a picture of that date showed the church without one.

Mabel Collier, whose husband, Rev. Clarence Collier, had had been the pastor of the church for 14 years, beginning in 1943, was a wonderful resource for information. People passing by stopped to chat and share some information. There were no speeders because all motorists slowed to a snail's pace to witness what was happening.

In my thoughts today, I recalled the active young people's group that I had been a member of during the middle of the 20th century, along with some of the same people who were in the group today, and my marriage in the church had been performed by Rev. Collier almost 55 years ago. My first view of Toledo when I arrived in 1945 was our Courthouse steeple. It was love at first sight. That beautiful October scene in which I first viewed when traveling east towards Toledo was engraved on my heart and became a symbol of the love and beauty and sense of community that I would share with so many people during the last half of the 20th century in Cumberland County.

My heart can only wonder how this beautiful steeple will overshadow and impact the lives of two young boys Riley and Reid Mathenia, who so intently watch it take its place in our community today. Mrs. Hodges, from another century, has provided this gift of love and hope to guide the pathway of Riley and Reid and all their generation growing up in our community, plus each of us, who will move forward to face the challenges of the 21st Century.

A Surprise Package--*October 15, 2006*

Getting the mail has always been a special event in my day. The mail carrier divides my day in the sense of the things I accomplished before and after the mail arrives. This is a carryover from my childhood. Then, my sibs and I would compete to see who could get the first peep of what the mailman delivered.

No offence meant to Laurie, who is my super carrier at the farm. I'm just not accustomed to saying mail-lady.

I do not know how I became so addicted to the mail. Most of my mail is routine and seldom do I receive packages. Perhaps it relates back to my childhood when I had saved box tops to order some "super duper" gadget or maybe an official "Lone Ranger" badge. I wish I had saved my badge and other gadgets, as some of them are now collectors' items.

When I think of that, it suddenly reminds me of my age, as I use to think that antiques and the likes all came from my grandmother's era.

I was busy yesterday when Harold brought in the mail. I saw a fat brown envelope addressed to me. I immediately put aside my work to take a closer look. Thinking I had not ordered anything, I couldn't imagine what it might contain. I observed it had been mailed at the Toledo Post Office and that it felt soft as I quickly opened it.

Immediately, I remembered ordering the beautiful pillow tops, which I had first seen on display at the Cottonwood Methodist church, as I slid them out of the envelope.

The Toledo Methodist Parish alternates its Sunday evening worship services among its various churches. Last month the services were held at the rural Cottonwood Church, It is the perfect image of the country church from one's childhood memories. Their membership completely restored the church a few years ago, which had included the cleaning and repair of the beautiful stained glass windows that had been donated by the founding members.

While worshiping there I had seen a beautiful centerpiece near the altar that contained a pillow and a candle. The patchwork pillow's embroidering read, "PRAYERS GO UP...BLESSINGS COME DOWN." I figured that Mrs. Esther Padrick had made it as she had made their lovely alter cloths and in the past; I had seen some of her beautiful quilts.

After the service, I spoke with Evelyn Sue Icenogle; the church's gifted pianist; and Mrs. Padrick's daughter. To shorten my story, she confirmed that her mother had made the pillow with her help, as in retirement she continues to use her gifted hands. Evelyn Sue said they jointly were making a supply to sell at the church's annual bazaar. When I told her I would not be there for the bazaar, she agreed to send me the pillow top by mail.

Evelyn not only has her Mother's needlework skills but also is a skilled R. N. who has worked many years as an ER nurse. Thus, she being aware of my lack of skills in the sewing arena, had also enclosed in my package a threaded needle and a small spool of the right color thread for me to close the covers after inserting the pillows.

My lovely pillow is now displayed on the back of my sofa and I have informed Harold that this pillow is not for napping. I have given the other one to my neighbors, Bev & Joe, who are like Evelyn Sue when it comes to being thoughtful. If you would like one of their lovely handcrafted pillow tops, contact Evelyn Sue as I bet she would do the same for you, and the money raised goes to help others.

CHAPTER 4
MEMORIES FROM TRAVELING ABOUT

Over the Hill & Through the Woods--*November 28, 2005*

"Over the hill and through the woods to Grandpa's farm we go,
The horse knows the way, to carry the sleigh; through the white and
drifting snow." Lydia Marie Child: "Flowers for Children" Volume 2 in
1844

Many were on the road during this past Thanksgiving weekend; with the same intent of those long ago sleigh riders: going home. Although their 2005 mode of travel was very different than that of 1844, many shared their forefathers' belief that somehow all will be hunky-dory when we get there.

The need to go home again is a primeval longing within ourselves. It surfaces when we least expect it and is triggered partially by memories, as well as other issues, including the hopes of resolving past conflicts. Thus, by the time Thanksgiving or other holidays arrive, individuals have accumulated a backlog of unmet needs that cannot be resolved by a trip home. When will we fully comprehend that going home cannot meet all our yearnings? Probably never.

Mother can no longer cradle us in her arms, making everything better with a kiss. In fact, before a holiday visit ends, many are beginning to feel they have had too much "quality family time".

Considerable research has been done regarding family relationships and a child's ordinal place in their birth family. An individual's birth order often controls how their sibs feel about them, particularly if you are the oldest or youngest child in a family.

I had a co-worker who shared his disappointing Christmas holiday experiences with me. His experience is the perfect example of this phenomenon. I'll call him Jim to protect his privacy.

Jim, a towering six and a half foot tall, was the youngest of seven children from a military family. He shared prior to going home for the holidays that even when he was in high school and college, his older sibs had continued to treated him as a child, smothering him with their unwanted advice.

He had not been home with all his family present for several years. During that time he had been promoted to a top management position and was held in high esteem by his staff. Jim was anticipating his sibs finally giving him their stamp of approval.

I had tried to clue him in that his family might not immediately grasp his achievements. But his excitement of going home for his family's Christmas reunion seemed to overshadow anything I attempted to share with him on that day.

After the holidays, I asked him about his trip. His downcast expression displayed his dismal feelings before he answered. "My sibs continued to treat me as a child. My mom was the only one who even said she was pleased with my promotion." He added, "We came home two days earlier than we had planned."

Should Jim have avoided going home? Certainly not. There is much pleasure for all of us to gain from sharing the holidays with our birth families. Just don't go home like Jim; expecting specific outcomes. In time, families will take notice of the positive changes in their sibs' lives. It is not that they do not love and care for them. The problem is in families seeing a sib; in a role so different from that, of their memories.

Art Abounds in Our Midst--*February 20, 2006*
True art selects and paraphrases, but seldom gives a verbatim translation.. Thomas Aldrich~ 1903

Anywhere you look in Naples there is art. Many people, including myself, have chosen to live in Collier County because nature's paintbrush has caressed us in splendor from the Gulf to the Everglades, maintaining tropical plants and birds in every nook and cranny that man has not disturbed. Our environment also attracts professional artists, plus many amateurs who create art for their own fulfillment. Then, there is a great number, like myself who just value art in many forms believing that: *Beauty is in the eye of the beholder.*

The Naples Museum of Art is a bonus in our community for all lovers of art. It contains some works of world renowned artists, plus a wide range of other exhibits including the ones they have on loan throughout the year.

My favorite artist in their permanent exhibit is Dale Chihuly. I love taking my out-of-town guests to the Art Museum because it gives me another opportunity to view Chihuly's Persian Ceiling, which is several feet long and consist of many pieces of his colorful blown glass. Each visit, I look upwards at his Persian Ceiling until I get cramps in my neck. The Art Museum is open from 10-4pm on Tuesday through Saturday, and from noon to 4pm on Sundays.

There are several talented artists who live in East Naples. I attended the Berkshire Lakes Art Show last year and was impressed by their displays Many talented Berkshire Lakes artists will be displaying their work this year.

A couple of my neighbors are representative of the talented artists whose works represent a broad mixed medium.

John Pateros, a professional artist who has a studio in Naples, will be displaying his paintings. Also, Cathy Dame, another neighbor, will be exhibiting her work in a show for the first time. Cathy manages an area real estate office and reports that she has had a lifelong interest in creating art. She paints exquisitely using watercolors, as well as painting on glassware.

You can simply enjoy the show as an exhibit or you may find and purchase paintings, prints or sculpture that would grace a wall or special place in your home.

Solitude & Memories--*April 3, 2006*

Memory is the diary that we all carry about with us. Oscar Wllde ~1895
As I reflect, it is apparent that I always had valued and needed an extra portion of solitude in my life. However, I was in my mid -forties before I clearly understood my need for time alone and the disastrous results of not experiencing a minimum amount of solitude.

That was one of those life experiences that we do not clearly understand when it is occurring. However, by remembering and comparing afterwards, earlier events in our lives can sometimes provide meaningful insight. I am sharing this personal information in hopes it will be helpful to you.

When I was a child I loved to hide away from everyone else and read. Sometimes I hid out on a branch of the Umbrella Tree in my front yard. When it had been fully leaved out, it was difficult for anyone to see me perched on an upper limb unless they were standing directly under the tree. The closet in my bedroom had a large storage space below the bottom shelf where I could also curl up and read out of sight, hopefully from being summoned for chores.

When I was in my 40's, my older sisters and I made plans to spend a special reunion week together at the beach. All of us were experiencing the empty nest syndrome and found some time to share with each other. I had thought it would be would be perfect. However, instead, it taught me that the need for solitude in my life was essential and not merely a desirable option.

We didn't want to miss anything at the beach, a place we cherished because we had visited it on rare occasions during our childhood. Thus, all of our time was tightly programmed. After a couple of days, I realized, I was becoming tired and irritable.

My sisters were concerned that I did not want to participate in some of the early morning walks together and other activities. I became a party pooper and poor company. I did not understand it then as I loved my sisters very much and had longed to see more of them. In time, I learned what had happened and understood. I'm sure many of you may have had similar experiences.

I was simply in overload. Because Harold had worked away from home, I was used to being alone most of the day. I often walked a square mile without encountering anyone. I loved the solitude. More than that, I later learned that I needed it. It was when I was in a graduate school and enrolled in a group therapy class, that I fully understood my lifelong need of frequent doses of solitude.

I am very much a "people person" but my system is like my car, in that it runs low and needs to be refueled, with solitude rather than gas.

I now believe that our decisions and actions are derived from issues that we have first thought about in solitude and then stored or recorded in our "memory diary" for future use.

Observations Above & Below--*August 6, 2006*

On my flight to Indy I scribbled several pages of notes including others' comments plus some of my own interpretations and observations.

I enjoyed my flight as all of the plane's crew were-first-rate. The Captain was friendly and informative, much like a tour guide. It was an ideal day for traveling and I always find it interesting to observe how other people react in diverse situations.

Harold and I began our trip with an early ride to the Ft Myers airport; thus, we had time to fill. I didn't mind, as I had a good book, and with the trip's preparation behind me, it simply felt good to relax.

Shortly, my serenity was disrupted by a grumpy man sitting near us who began complaining about kids talking on their cell phones. I gave Harold a look, hoping he would not respond and engaged him in conversation.

A somber moment arose, when I saw a very young soldier take a seat nearby.

His uniform appeared to be an oversized fit. In trepidation, I wondered if I would see his image flashed on my T V screen in a few weeks when The News Hour" silently honors the soldiers that have been killed in action. The agony of knowing so many have breaks my heart. As he left to board his flight; my grandmotherly instincts wanted to hug him and say, "Be safe."

Another flight was preparing to depart from our gate, while the desk clerk was making urgent calls for a missing passenger to return to the gate. The plane was about to depart when a young couple showed up out of breath. The boy gave the girl a lengthy kiss as the girl searched for her boarding pass. The staff waited patiently as the girl finally entered the boarding gate. All of a sudden, the girl looked back, and the boy ran forward and gave her one last kiss. Such is young love!

When we boarded our flight, an attractive young woman and her handsome 7' tall husband arrived at their seats across from me, to find one of their seats occupied. She negotiated the exchange while her husband quietly smiled. I thought she could successfully negotiate any dispute with him at her side.

My attention was diverted to a child exclaiming, "Here are two empty seats; let's sit here." I could understand the child's logic as I heard the mother trying to explain why they couldn't sit there.

Prior to liftoff the pilot introduced his flight team, thanked the passengers and added, "We will be traveling as fast and as we can to Indy today and will arrive 20 minutes early." Then he shared our approved itinerary. He continued to engage the passengers by naming the various cities as they came into view.

When we were in the Atlanta area he reported, "We are traveling at 540 mph at 34,000 feet . . ." Then he suggested that at best in one hour you might have traveled 60 miles in your auto, while our plane was already approaching the hills of Georgia.

Mid-flight a small girl ran down the aisle laughing, without an adult in sight. Shortly, there was a red-faced mother in fast pursuit. An older woman gave me a knowingly smile. I suspect the child had triggered the same empathetic memory for her as she had for me.

My seatmate shared that he was en route to take his grandchildren to Holiday World. I secretly wondered if I could muster the energy to do that.

The Captain's concluding remarks were, "Thanks for flying with us and be careful back on the highway." When I deplaned, he was greeting the passengers. I thanked him for a safe trip and his informative comments. His appearance seemed to fit my earlier mental image of him.

I knew I was on terra firma as I exited the secured area and saw my daughter waving! As I hugged her; I thought her hair now had a bit more salt than pepper. My memory's eye concluded: once she could have been the child who earlier had dashed down the aisle laughing.

Life's Journey is Like Swimming

"Can we live now while preparing for the future?" Brenda Ueland
Carolyn, my older sister and mentor had known the value of each day. Prior to her death, she had suffered from an autoimmune disease in which swimming was one of the few ways she could exercise to relieve or lessen her pain. She tried to swim daily at her local YMCA. She swam early in the morning or when her pain increased. Her principal at Clinton High School, where then she was the much-loved counselor, had permitted her to leave school in order to swim during her lunch hour.

If you read between the lines in my sister's poem, *FOR MYSELF* I think you will realize she was writing about life.

FOR MYSELF
By Carolyn Hill Glasson
Into the water, waves ripple, holding me,
Cushioning, as I begin to trust again,
The goal is to stay afloat, not drown.
Rocking and swaying, unrestrained, I seek a rhythm
To match a most irregular beginner's crawl.

A small tide pushes, washing over-head, as
Muscled, skilled, my neighbor races against himself.
His tide subsides...my strokes fit more easily,
And, soon my lap progress is undirected, effortless.
Over, under, I'm a guest in an undulating, blue-green sea.

Head to the side, breathe, arms over and high, reach.
And over, the back stroke, a bonus one in four.
Ah! New warmth as I catch a smile from another
Whose early morning ritual just now begins.
For the lately arrived, also...a private time...
To sort, to plan, to visualize... to dream.

To exercise by swimming, requires sharing space,
Yet, there is something about the luxuriousness
Of ones own haven, ones private lap-lane.
No matter! Body movement in the water is graceful.
One tests ones present length, reach and breath.

Back and forth, find a center...cushioned afloat.
Afterwards, enjoy the friendliness of lane-mates.
But, let order and simplicity reign through the paces
In the water, as one tests oneself, only oneself.
Thoughts float...time to be... to breathe freely.

Joy is----------?--*March 6, 2005*

I am struggling with defining the word; *joy*. Maybe you can help me
place *joy* in its proper context. Can one experience, recognize and alter
their way of viewing life due to an encounter with joy? Can we create,
store, measure or trigger joy? Below I share how another person's
actions recently brought joy and comfort, in that his kindness lessened
my anxiety.

At times, I do not know how to organize and fully express my feelings in
response to joy. Yet, I know from experience and observation it is a
lovely and often therapeutic encounter in one's life. Thus I am listing
some of my reactions and/or thoughts pertaining to joy. I hope you will
respond and provide clarification and/or your insights concerning this
word. Here is my list:

Joy comes unbidden and is not restricted by place, form or time but is always welcome.

Joy's arrival and/or departure can be sudden although its tracks may linger with bits and parts stored in memory; as certain reminiscences can sometimes trigger its rerun.

Joy is a gift, often spontaneous, which is somehow related to wisdom in its source and perhaps insight.

Joy is usually experienced inwardly but can be shared outwardly.

The Arts, particularly music and creative arts can trigger joy.

Nature is sometimes a way of experiencing joy when:

Taking a walk on the beach,

Viewing a sunset and/or sunrise,

Seeing the sun's reflection on trees, displaying various shades,

Observing animals at play and

Flowers in bloom.

Last night a phone call from my son Roger brought joy in the form of information. Roger shared some very positive information about something that his brother-in-law and my good friend Terry Titus had done earlier in the day. Terry's thoughtfulness and then willingness to share brought some serenity and peace to my anxious heart.

Actions of other people; sometimes friends or maybe total strangers, can and do generate unexpected joy when they do something for others, someone whom you love or yourself, which you cannot do.

Maybe joy is one of those words like love, which knows no boundaries.

An Auction Becomes: A Trip Down Memory Lane--
June 26, 2010

"If you could say it in words there would be no reason to paint." Edward Hopper

Today my plan was to purchase a couple of pieces of my deceased friend's artwork at the Knupp's auction. I already own several pieces but could not pass up the opportunity to view the results of Jan's creativity and talent one last time.

Our granddaughter's mom lives across the street from the Knupp's home and graciously had invited us to park at her house and to come back and rest on her porch and have a bottle of ice water if we got tired or too hot at the auction.

I registered at the Knupp's auction and previewed the sale goods a bit before ten o'clock. I was surprised to see an entire wagon loaded with Jan's beautiful paintings, prints, frames and art supplies, as I had forgotten that Jan had once operated, an art shop, on Toledo's Square. I asked the auctioneer, "What time do you thing the artwork will sell?" He replied, "Around eleven."

As, I was already feeling the heat, we accepted Michelle's offer to sit on her shady porch and rest for awhile.

As I relaxed; pleasant memories of Martin and Jan began flooding my heart and mind. I first knew Martin when I came to Illinois and entered Toledo High School (THS) in 1945. He was a shy, polite but handsome freshman, who always flashed a smile.

A couple of years later when Harold and I were married, I first met Jan at her and Harold's mutual Grandmother Dallas' rural home; as they were first cousins. Thus, our lives and friendships were interwoven with both Martin and Jan, for more than fifty years.

We didn't see much of them during our career years, except; when they came to Toledo to visited family as he work for Caterpillar and they lived in a northern suburb. However, when they retired in Toledo, we resumed our friendship and because we both wintered on the West Coast of Florida we also visited there.

Today, after relaxing in the shade, Harold and I returned to the auction, but it still was a good while before the sale would progressed to the wagon containing the art. So we rested in the shade, by sitting on the Knupp's dining chairs, which were for sale. I again began reminiscing, this time, about the many meals we had shared in Jan's kitchen as she was a wonderful cook. I also could mentally view Martin and Jan's images in their chairs; where others were also resting their tired bodies, as the auction continued through the heat of midday.

Later as, I stood by Jan's bedroom window, my mind wandered back to the day she had died, peacefully, as I held her hand.

John and Barb Knupp appeared to be exhausted as they walked about during the sale. As we visited, I could only imagine how much more emotionally draining it must be for them to see their parents' things sell, as I was a friend and not a loving son like John. But as John said, he had only, so many walls and/or places to store his parents' things.

Also, I'm reminded that many of us and/or our children have gone or will, go through this same emotional process to dispose of loved ones' personal property. As I visited with John, I, also was reminded of how he had cared for Martin when his Dad, was no longer able to care for himself, as many of us have done, for our parents.

When the auction finally progressed to the wagon containing the artwork, I was shocked as to how little many of her beautiful original drawings and paintings sold for! I purchased more than I had planned to use as gifts, as I like John, have a limited number of places to display them. I simply couldn't stand to see Jan's artwork sell for so little.

Then, I realized: the people who were buying her artwork will have a permanent source of beauty and scenes of nature that they and others can spend many relaxing hours viewing during the coming years. By instinct, I knew that would be pleasing to Jan, who always had gone the "second mile" to please and care for others.

The last item I purchased prior to leaving the auction was Martin's *1949 THS Warbler Yearbook(* with fading pictures*)* as it is symbolic of where we first met 65 years ago, reminding me, once more, that the memories of friends never fade.

Two Milestone Gifts--*November 3, 2008*

At times it seems as though I'm forever saying, "Thank you." I don't have any inhibitions about saying "Thank you". In fact, I hope I always remember to do so whenever it is appropriate; otherwise I would be at risk of displeasing my Mother, whose discerning oversight I continue to sense although she has been gone for more than twenty years.

This year 2008 has been a milestone in my life: I have received the life-changing gift of two corneas, from two people who made the decision prior to their deaths to become donors. My first transplant was for my left eye in May and the other in my right eye in October. My driver's license has been marked with my desire to be an organ donor for many years', however; I never thought that I might someday be a recipient. I have difficulty in finding the words to express my gratitude to the families of the donors as well as the skills and talents of many others who assisted in making my successful DSAEK (Descemet's Stripping Automated Endothelial Keratoplasty) transplants a reality. Thus, I want to share some about the remarkable technology of the DSAEK surgical procedure, which was developed by Dr. Mark Gorovoy of Ft. Myers only a few years ago . When I asked him for additional information in order to share with you some details of his remarkable process, he was quick to add that we all build on the shoulders of others and that he didn't want to take credit for the work that had been done earlier by others. Thus, following are some definitions that I have taken from one of his informational brochures and/or from conversations I had when consulting him or his staff that can help you understand this wonderful sight- restoring process.

At one time all corneas were stitched onto the eye; as some still are today. The "cornea is the clear window at the front of the eye that bends and helps focus light onto the back of the eye (the retina). In order for vision to be clear; the cornea must be clean and clear. Corneal disease can cause the cornea to become opaque or cloudy, preventing light from passing through clearly"*… "The cornea has different layers of cells. The bottom layer of the cornea called the endothelium does not regenerate its cells. The endothelial cells you are born with are the only ones you will have during your lifetime. These cells serve to keep the cornea clear by continuously pumping out excess fluid. Endothelial cells that are damaged by trauma or disease cannot be replaced (by your body)."*

I lost most of my endothelial cells (in both of my eyes over a period of time) due to a heredity disease (Fuchs Dystrophy), which clouded my cornea and limited my vision. During my outpatient surgery "with my eye completely anesthetized, Dr Gorovoy removed the diseased Decemet's membrane and damaged endothelial cells. Next, he attached the bottom 10-20% of a donor's cornea that had healthy endothelial cells attached to its Descemet's membrane which (was) inserted through the same incision. After it was placed in position an air bubble was used to hold the (my) transplant in place,"*

I lay still for an hour in order for" the air bubble to press against my tissue in order to secure it in place." Then I went to lunch and back for the Dr. to recheck that my transplanted tissue was securely in place and then went home. The next day I was able to resume most of my normal activities.

Harold inserts two different kinds of antibiotic drops into my eye to prevent infection and will continue to do so for a few weeks, along with a mild steroid in both eyes, which I am to use for a year or so, to help prevent rejection.

In six weeks I will return to see Dr Gorovoy in order to assess my need for glasses. This is a quick overview of this wonderful transplant technology called DSAEK that can be used to replace corneas in eyes that have diseases (like me) or for other people who have injured their cornea.

I suspect many of you already are organ donors. If not and you would like information, you can contact any of the Illinois Secretary of State's offices to receive information on how to become a donor. I can vouch for the wonderful changes in sight that the gifts of donated corneas can make.

*Taken from Dr. Gorovoy's comments or from his brochure entitled: Sutureless Corneal Endothelial Transplant.

Life's Journey From Childhood to Maturity--November 27, 2011

"In a dream you are never eighty." Anne Sexton

Ms. Sexton's quote is correct. However, in real life you can be eight or eighty and continue to have positive interaction with your loving family and/or friends!

Most of the time I don't feel old ,but when I do, I often remember my paternal grandmother who occasionally cared for my sibs and me during our childhood. When I was eight, I had thought she was ancient, as she walked with a cane (as I do, now). However, her mind was quick and able as when she arrived at our home, she always checked to see if our chores were done. If we told her we had already finished, she then would look around to see for herself.   After checking, she often told us to do some of them over, as we had done a "hurry-up" sloppy job, which we probably had, as we were always anxious to finish our chores and get back to reading our latest library book. Thus, whenever I was or am in the "grandma supervisory role," I've tried to be less direct than Grandma Hill had been with me. I may not have succeeded if the opinions of the children were known.

In between my childhood role and now, there obviously have been numerous different stages and roles for me to fulfill. Thus, of late, I find myself moving into the 'mature stage," a role reversal where I'm receiving help from the younger generations in my family.

David's wife, Shirley, recently had a business conference in the Sarasota area and added a few vacation days to visit with me and to relax a few days in the sun,. By the pool. However, I had issues with getting everything turned on and working correctly again. Thus, she has helped me to work through the problems and to shop in order to replace some of the non-working equipment, consuming a lot of her time in resolving my problems.

This was great for me, reminding me of what a gift it is to have a loving family that steps in to help when one needs them most! That reminded me of times gone by, when my sibs and I had helped my parents in like fashion, when they were wintering on the Texas coast. As they aged, some of us would go ahead to help open up or close their homes and/or drive for them, or to accompany them on the plane. This reminds me of the old saying: "What goes around comes around."

Shirley did have an unexpected pleasure on her way home. For various reasons, no one in our family likes to be routed through O'Hare when flying. Shirley couldn't get a direct flight home so she chooses to have a stopover in Dallas instead of O'Hare. Lily flies almost weekly in her work and often has assignments in Texas and is very familiar with the Dallas Airport. On the day Shirley left to return home, Lily called me later saying she had only one appointment in the Dallas area this week and was then sitting in the airport waiting for her return flight to Champaign. I informed her that Shirley was also in Dallas or would shortly be there. Lily was able to contact Shirley via her cell phone and they unexpectedly shared a pleasant meal in the Dallas airport!

This incident reminds me of one time Harold and I were sitting in the Tampa airport watching the plane we were taking home land and deplane following our cruise that had ended in Tampa. I jokingly had said to Harold that I was going to check and see if I knew anyone getting off the plane.

All of a sudden, I grabbed Harold's arm and said that person, from this distance, looks like Roger. I yelled his name and our son stopped and turned around and came over to visit. This was a time that Fritts was racing in Florida and Roger had flown in to help him with mechanical work. So these are two examples that reveal that on any flight, it's quite possible that family or friends may be in the same airport, unbeknown to us.

During our life's journey our roles are constantly changing as we can be on the helping or receiving end. Whatever our role is at any given time, I fully believe that a loving family and friends are two treasured gifts that God has given to all of us, regardless of our age or location.

Sparse or Congested in Sand or Snow~~ Neighbors are Special--March 5, 2006

A neighbor is somebody who lives or is located very close by, literary meaning: a fellow human being. ~~ *Webster's New World Dictionary*

Most of my life has been lived on our Cumberland County farm. On some snowy March days, the mail carrier and the school bus might have been the only vehicles on the road.

In past generations, farm families' livelihood and safety relied on inter-dependency with their neighbors for survival. The age of technology has lessened or eliminated farmers' dependency on each other. Nevertheless, farmers' relationships with neighbors have remained both friendly and stable as changes in farm ownership has often been generational, within the area families.

When Husband Harold and I retired, we decided to spend some of the cold months in Florida. I had incorrectly assumed that the close contact and support that we had experienced with our neighbors would be a thing of the past. I had read stories (probably novels) about people in New York City not even knowing their next door neighbor.

I now know that I had failed to factor in an important variable: many of the Snowbirds living in Florida, like us, were also separated from their families and long-term friends. Thus, our clubhouse dinners and gatherings at poolside were well attended, and soon we were on first name bases with our new neighbors, who were from Canada, the northeastern states plus some from Europe. By the time New Year's Day had rolled around my kitchen was running over with neighbors whom I had invited in to help us observe a Southern food ritual that's derived from my North Carolinian heritage. Southern folklore guarantees good luck throughout the New Year for all who eat black-eyed peas and cabbage on the first day of the year.

As the years have passed, I can fully attest that good neighbors are a vital part of being alive and living life to its fullest. The weather and/or location have little to do with how we interact with our neighbors. Whether we are at our farm home or temporarily escaping to a warmer climate it is part of our humanness that causes us to reach out and seek meaningful and giving relationships.

Being good neighbors does not cause overkill, which can occur in other relationships. Reread Webster's definition above and keep in mind that neighbors do not live in the same household; they separate and go to their own homes.

Do You Have Plans for Today?--*June 26, 2005*

I did. This clear Sunday morning I was driving home from Mattoon enjoying the fact that there was so little traffic. Thus, I was using the time to think about some financial decisions I needed to make next week. Also, I was planning what I needed to do to finish preparing my food to take to the annual Sparks' Reunion today at the Life Center.

About the time I was rounding the curve prior to the Lerna Road exit my life, in a split second was suddenly at risk of ending.

I saw a large deer moving at a fast forward pace preparing to cross the blacktop a few feet in front of my car. A moment more and it was in front of me. I could see its skin flexing as it (a large doe, I presumed, as it did not have horns) moved its hind legs. As fear and anxiety paralyzed my being, I wonder where its mate was as I often see deer moving in pairs.

After I had moved a short distance, without touching the deer or seeing another one: I simply said, "Thank you; God I guess this was not my appointed time." I could feel the sweat breaking out on my forehead, although my air conditioner was running at full blast.

Needless to say, my previous thoughts and planning suddenly seemed unimportant. My mind reverted to an earlier conversation I had had at the breakfast table with my sister. We had discussed what a difference our parents had made in our lives and how fortunate we had been in being born to, and then being raised together, by them.

I share today's happenings with you in hopes that you may pause and reflect on your own life without having to see a deer's eye blinking so close to your windshield.

Are you spending your days, your life, doing things that are worthwhile? Are you accomplishing goals and leaving footprints which are helpful for others? Have you expressed your appreciation to the people who have and continue to make a positive difference in your daily life?

Think about it while time and choices remain. Don't forget to keep a watchful eye out for the deer!

Living in the Present--*August 13, 2006*

"I shut the door on yesterday and threw away the key.
Tomorrow has no fears since I found today." Unknown

Some happenings in my life have given me a new awareness that today is indeed the first day of the remainder of my life and a gift to be cherished. Thus the choices that I make today take on new importance.

We let regrets and/or anger about yesterday, plus concerns about tomorrow consume too much time, thus robbing us of today.

Our thoughts and actions are two of the few areas in our lives that we can fully control. Why waste our precious gift of time regretting happenings from the past?

Today is the moment we can implement change. Admittedly, we may not be able to change everything in one day. However every change has a starting place. It's all right to review and revisit our mistakes and poor choices from yesterdays, as a model of what to be avoided. Simply don't linger there; otherwise one can fritter away their precious gift of today.

How much time do we spend reading the writings of others to receive a different perspective on living our own lives? A person name Leigh Hunt provided this observation, "There are two worlds, the world we can measure with line and rule, and the world that we feel with our hearts and imagination."

I take "the world that we measure with line and rule" to mean our routine workaday world. Perhaps "the world that we feel with our hearts and imagination" is the one that we long to enter but do not know how to do so.

This world is one that we can learn to cross its threshold with practice. Earlier, I stated our thoughts and actions, at least during our non-working hours, belong to us. With planning, there is some time during each day we can use to access this less traveled road.

Meditation is a wonderful way to enter without cost but entails advance planning. Start by reserving thirty minutes of time to spend in quiet and pleasant surroundings. A beginning subject for meditation could be a time or place, maybe from your childhood that you had been very happy. Simply think about that event while shutting out all of your other routine and daily thoughts. Recall what it was that made you happy then and think how you could duplicate that experience. This is a wonderful diversion, much like a mini-vacation and is a start.

Go to the library and check out some books on relaxation, meditation and creative endeavors to learn of other activities. With some planning you could take a night class to study an area that has always been of interest to you, or visit an art museum. These are creative things you can do with family and/or friends.

This brings to mind a reader's group that I participate in during the winter that is without cost (the books are selected one year in advance and can be checked out from your library) and intellectually exciting. There are about a dozen retirees in my group that meet in a public, place but you could begin with three or four. That would mean, you would need to lead the discussion more often.

Each day when the sun rises you have choices. Use them; they will bring new meaning into your life as you enter the world that "you feel with your heart and imagination."

Name Tabs in the File Cabinet

"...For daily gladness; once a man be done
with hunger rich and poor are all as one. EURIPIDES (484-406 B. C.)
Euripides told us about 2500 years ago that when man has enough to eat on a given day, his capacity for happiness on that day is the same as any other man.

There are endless ways to both measure and describe happiness or gladness in our daily lives. Humans usually try to find a measuring stick that is most favorable. Sometimes we call this putting up a good front, or there is more sophisticated terminology we could use to state the same thing.

Anyone trying to find something in my filing cabinet would become so frustrated that they would just sit at the table and eat all day. Of course that wouldn't do much for happiness; while adding unwanted pounds. Recently the name tabs in my file cabinet caught my eye. I need to clarify I have a loosely organized filing system. In fact, most people would not call it a filing system.

In one drawer, there are files Uncle Sam forces me to keep, that is unless I want to go to jail.

Most of my files are not necessarily alphabetical; nevertheless, my hand can reach in and pullout the file I want, that is, most of the time. I kind of group like things. I would be willing to bet most people use a modified filing system ,unless they are just out of school and have not had time to corrupt the system they were taught.

In another drawer, I keep writing stuff, which included incomplete manuscripts, and letters to the editors, some which I wrote and didn't mail. The mere exercise of writing sufficiently lessened my frustrations on some days' thus; I can tear it up and save my stamp.

There are other copies of letters which I did mail, mostly to politicians, and their replies. One thing a person can depend on is an answer from an elected official. Whatever else they do, usually they are quick to explain their actions that are after their vote has been cast.

Before Inside Plumbing

Recently while reminiscing with some friends about childhood memories, I was reminded once again that our lives are more alike than different.

We began by chatting about Saturday night being our weekly bath nights. Yes, you read correctly, I said, "Our weekly bath nights!"

Bear in mind, I'm writing about a time in the 1930's when few rural or small town homes had electricity or inside plumbing. REA (Rural Electrification Administration) brought electricity to my family rural North Carolina home in the late thirties, and Harold and I did not have REA available in our Illinois farm home until after we had been married for two or three years. That was a shocker, as I had been living in town to attend high school, where both, electricity and indoor plumbing, had been available.

But back to our weekly baths, which involved a regular routine for my two older sisters (Carolyn & Pat) plus, myself. During the wintertime a tin tub that was used outside on Mondays for doing the weekly laundry was brought into the house and set by the wood-burning heater in the living room, as there was no central heating, The water for our bath was heated in large kettles on our wood-burning kitchen stove, which we girls had carried in from our outside hand-water pump, as well as the split wood, which was used in both of the stoves.

When the water was heated and poured into the tub, then the decision was made who would be first to bathe. We all wanted to be first because if you were 2nd or 3rd the water would begin to get a soap scum on it from the first bather, as well as being cooled down. Of course, the kettle on the stove was refilled to reheat and the tub could be warmed up for the 2nd and 3rd bather. Also everyone else was evacuated to the kitchen for privacy's sake, maybe to clean up the supper dishes except Mother who stay to wash our backs and to see that we didn't take shortcuts while bathing. After our baths we hurriedly put on our P J's, then paused to kneel with Mother for our nightly prayers, and then quickly got into our feather tick bed, which had fresh smelling clean flannel sheets to get between. If it was extremely cold in our bedroom, Mother would heat one of her flatirons and wrap it in a towel to place at our feet to help warm our bed. As soon as my sisters finished bathing, they quickly got into the same bed creating more body heat that added to everyone's warmth.

After us girls were bathed and snuggly in a clean bed, Mother & Dad emptied our bath water, then poured clean warm water into the wash tub, which had time to heat on the kitchen stove for them to get their bath before retiring for the night. Although, in the winter, we routinely bathed only on Saturday nights, during the summer we took them more frequently.

Dad's home-built Ham radio station (W4AOJ) was located in the corner of the living room so he might check the bands for possible contacts before bathing and retiring for the night. Also this could be a time for Mother to read and relax a bit. At that time, my parents jointly wrote a human interest column for the "Raleigh News & Observer" newspaper entitled "Down Onslow Way" and they might have used some of the quiet time to write, in long-hand. As I look back, this may have been what planted the idea for me to begin writing a column when I retired from work.

Time Marches On & Memories Linger--*May 22, 2004*

Today Harold and I dusted off some plastic chairs and went down to the Toledo Square to watch the Spring Festival parade. We saw our neighbors, Rex and Becky Evans, sitting in a shady spot on the south side and joined them. There was a wonderful breeze, and it would have been a nice place to sit and visit even if there had not been a well-organized Sesquicentennial parade to entertain us. In addition, it was a special treat seeing many friends whom I do not otherwise see very often; among them was Mrs. Esther Hill, who had taught at Toledo when my children were in school.

My mind wanders backwards to other Festival parades. I recalled the Dr. Rhodes celebration of fifty years ago. My mother participated in it because she was a Dr. Rhodes baby that he had delivered in 1907. On that long ago day, I had brought my mother to the parade because my dad needed to stay home and harvest corn. It must have been one of those wet years when farmers were under pressure to get their crops harvested.

That caused me remember a more recent parade, in which Dr. and Mrs. Massie had been honored. I do not remember what year that was, maybe 1987. I just remember I had ridden on a float honoring scenes from Doc and Nellie's life. Of course, there were the other years I attended because my children were participating in the parade via the Cumberland Band, 4-H and/or other activities. In addition, I also have fond memories regarding the years I watched the parade standing on the Square with both of my parents.

I felt a little old last week when I was in the IGA and saw young girls purchasing tickets for the rides. Seeing them reminded me to do the same, as I had done during most of the past fifty years. In the beginning, I had bought tickets for my children, and somewhere along the way; I began buying them for grandchildren. This year I switched to a new generation and bought them for my great-grandson Logan. I have a feeling that job will pass to someone else before another generation surfaces as my allotted three score plus ten and then some (?) will have expired as it does sooner or later for all.

I have just returned home from attending my high school class reunion; a memory-filled climax to a special day. I will save that story for another day when I have had more time to process and sort the emotion-laden details.

In conclusion, I want to express my appreciation to all the people who helped to make this year's Springfest such a special occasion. It is great to be a part of a small town community that works together; maybe that why we are now 150 years old.

Friendship is an Intangible Commodity--*February 9, 2009*
Life is difficult.
Problems challenge us....

Friendship keeps us balanced in a difficult world,
Renews our perspective and enables us to recapture joy. Susan Yates

It is no secret that Harold and I have enjoyed spending the cold months in Florida since we retired several years ago.

When we first retired, we had wondered if it would be hard to make new friends, as we had known many of our Illinois' friends since our school days. We felt anxiety about being separated from our friends and neighbors as they are an important part of our lives.

Quickly we discovered the need for friends is a universal factor. We found a diverse group in our newly developed condo community: there were a few Europeans, several Canadians, and people from a variety of states combined with some Floridians who were still pursuing careers. Yet, almost all of them were interested in reaching out to others and developing a sense of community. Now we feel very close to our condo friends and miss them when we return north each spring.

Today I was reading and sunning at our condo pool, where our unwelcome cooler temperatures have keep all but a few of our hardy Canadians friends out of the pool.

However, because of the warmth of the bright sun we still enjoy gathering at the pool to read, nap, visit and acquire our daily portion of Vitamin D. After chatting for awhile, Ron, another resident from Canada who is chairman of our grounds committee, and a couple of sunbathers, Carole and Lori, agreed to go and pick grapefruit from a tree located behind one of our condos.

Ordinarily, picking a few grapefruit (just like picking apples), would not be a problem but all of the fruit within easy reach had already been picked. Ron had a creative idea that the long handled tool that he uses to trim trees could also pluck the fruit.

It worked! In about twenty minutes Ron and his co-workers returned carrying a grocery bag, filled with grapefruit. The helpers didn't report if they had been conked on the head while filling their sacks.

I commended Ron on his success. Carol, my neighbor, said they had left some grapefruit at my condo door. She knew that I liked grapefruit because a few days earlier when she and Stan had arrived from Ft. Wayne, I had shared some luscious grapefruit with her that I had picked from a friend's tree in the country.

As I was thanking Ron, Lori, and Carol for the fruit, Peggy, another good friend and regular winter visitor jokingly spoke up and said, "I don't know how you could get so excited over a few grapefruit when everything else cost, so much to live here." I replied it's not the grapefruit so much, as it is the sheer thoughtfulness of our friends." She paused for a moment and said, "You could be right." I knew in my heart I was because friendship is one gift that can't be measured with a monetary value.

Throughout my life, friends have been an essential factor in my life, regardless of wherever, I have lived. I like the words of the unknown person who wrote: "Friendship is a sheltering tree."

Socialization: Then & Now--*July 20, 2006*

You have to be a certain age to remember Woolen's Drugstore, which was located on the northeast corner of the Toledo Square. To the younger generation, I'm referring to where the Extension Office is currently located. Well, to be more exact, I need to include part of the current Health Department building. If I didn't, I would be leaving out the very important back room where the high school students of the 40's did their dancing and a bit of flirting.

During the Toledo High School noon break you could easily order your lunch for a quarter at Woolen's Drug Store. Particularly if you thought a Cherry Coke, (5 cents) and 2 dips of ice cream ;(10 cents), plus a nickel bag of chips was a good lunch. As an added bonus Everett Woolen, the proprietor permitted you to run a tab if you were fresh out of your allowance.

Also, if you wanted to eat a bit healthier, he made some cold sandwiches. Husband Harold reminds me that Woolen's, Lime Phosphates were also very tasty.

Then, even the penny had purchasing power. A Baby Ruth candy bar sold for a penny. Now, our government is talking about eliminating the penny because it costs more to produce than it is worth.

I skipped an important part, if you were lucky at lunchtime, you got a ride downtown in Vic Stewart's auto, either inside or clinging to the outside.

And then there was always the possibility that someone had some coins to feed the jukebox and we could listen and/or jitterbug to Tommy Dorsey's; Boogie-Woogie. (I can't remember for sure if my spelling is correct as some things become a little vague after fifty- plus years.) However, I can still hear in my memory what the music's beat sounded like!!

What got me started on remembering Woolen's was thinking about how many of my special friends and family I can see at the Fillin Station whenever I'm in Toledo. There are some similarities between the two businesses then and now:

> Both did or currently serve customers on the Toledo Square.
> Some of the same people who use to drink Cherry Cokes at Woolen's now socialize while drinking coffee at the Fillin Station.
> The ones who might have whistled at the girls, now say, hello.
> The ones who discussed the opposite sex now talk about the weather, the crops or their grandkids.

I must admit there is no comparison between lunch at Woolen's and the Fillin Station, particularly in the pie department. I don't think there is any match for Mrs. Peters' pies. I guess that Woolen's did sell some kind of packaged pies wrapped individually. Also, there would be no free rides to town if gas had cost what it does today. I'm sure most of the students would have been walking everywhere.

In spite of some differences, the socialization and friendliness have not changed as Toledo remains the perfect place to mingle with friends!

How I Knew I Was Home--*May 11, 2003*

On Saturday, a severe storm over Indianapolis delayed our plane's landing at the airport for 45 minutes. It also caused a backup in claiming our luggage as the carrousels were already in use. Having the security of both riding and being with our son Roger as we traveled westward towards home, while viewing the beautiful green-planted fields, soon blotted out the earlier tension caused by our worrisome flight. When we saw the river out in the bottoms on the young corn at the Greenup Bridge, and then the Courthouse Steeple, I knew we were in friendly territory very close to home. We stopped at the "Just for Kids Daycare" in Toledo and saw Jan, our daughter-in-law. She warned us, she had not been able to cross the Bradbury Bridge earlier in the morning.

We did not meet a car after we turned on to the Burma Road, a wonderful reminder that we had left all the city traffic jams behind, another reward of being home in Cumberland County. We discovered Muddy Creek was still out on the east side of the Bradbury Bridge, but we were in # 1 Son's truck, and he and Husband Harold said it was safe to cross the bridge, as only a trickle remained on the road.

It was great to see our neighbor, Billy Scott, waving to us as he walked towards his barn to check on his baby pigs. We felt a few bumps in the road and dodged parts of a tree, which were uprooted by an earlier storm, as we happily complete our homeward journey.

Jan had just mowed our yard a couple of days ago and stocked our refrigerator with food, even had coffee ready for Harold to brew. What a wonderful homecoming! Before long, we collapsed in our own beds.

Sunday morning, Roger came by to take his dad to breakfast and to pick up the Sunday papers. He invited me to join them as a Mother's Day treat. I declined, as "getting the papers had been a Sunday Morning Guys" tradition for a long time. The tradition of going to Toledo to get the paper began many years earlier when our then wonderful neighbor, Raymond Gardner, had invited Harold to go with him. They took time for a cup of coffee and brought all the local news home, along with the paper.

Harold had lost his father when he was a young man. Thus, his regular Sunday morning outings with Raymond were a fulfilling experience for Harold, as he had learned so much from Raymond. One thing he taught Harold was how to cane chairs and refinish furniture. That became a lifelong rewarding hobby for Harold.

After Harold and Roger had left for breakfast, I had some private time to check out my computer and write. Later, I realized I did not have any ice for tea. A light bulb flashed in my mind and all of a sudden, I REALLY KNEW I WAS HOME as a simple phone call to the Fillin' Station could solve my ice problem. Only in small towns do the waitresses pass the last minute grocery lists from spouses to their coffee customers.

A Mix of Surprise & Memories--*February 11, 2007*

How long has it been since you've had a real surprise (an exciting one)? Harold and I had a colossal unexpected one on Wednesday.

I need to back up to set the scene. Thursday, the eighth of February was Harold's eightieth birthday. Our son Roger had arrived on Tuesday from Indy to help his Dad celebrate. On Wednesday afternoon he said he was going to North Naples to visit with Amanda Meyers; a friend, who formerly lived in Indy. Before leaving he said, "I will return before dinner." I assured him anytime would be fine as I planned to serve leftovers for dinner. He called later to say he was caught in a traffic jam in North Naples and would be delayed.

To shorten my tale, he returned later after he had pick up Lily, whose flight had been delayed for an hour in Indy. She had wanted to surprise her Dad on his eightieth birthday. She was so successful that at first I doubted my vision until I hugged her!

Needless to say, we didn't eat leftovers as I rushed over to Publix's to get filets of flounder, her favorite fish. On Wednesday, as we celebrated Harold's birthday, our children were as happy to be out of the Midwest's single digit temperatures as we were to have them in Naples.

During their short visit they found time to tour Naples in their rented red Mustang convertible (with the top down) revisiting childhood memories from earlier trips to Naples. They visited the beach, the pier, saw the alligators sunning on the banks south of Naples (instead of visiting Jungle Larry's; as we had done years ago) and ended with a sightseeing visit to Marco Island. Our "post 50" children returned north, with warm red faces and abundant new memories to share.

While there they had reminisced about their earlier childhood Christmas vacations that we had spent in Florida. Being avid swimmers, they would always swim in the Gulf during our holidays, whether or not the water temperature was amendable to such actions. They had thought vacationing in Florida was synonymous with swimming in the Gulf. During the chilly holidays, I had been content to walk barefooted on the beach while keeping an eye on the children. We recalled seeing the natives, all bundled up while walking on the beach with looks of disbelief as the children frolicked in the Gulf. Now Harold and I are the "onlookers" with sweaters.

During the winter of 69/70' Harold worked in Naples for the Geitz Construction Company. We then lived in an apartment building on Alamanda Drive located behind the strip mall that contained Naples' first Publix store, which remains there today.

Lily had completed one semester of college in Illinois and had happily taken that winter off to join us in Naples. She worked in W. T. Grant's Bradford House Restaurant, which was located on the Trail, north of Publix's original store (about where Linen' and Things is now). She earned pocket money to spend, which left considerable beach and pool time during the day. She was and is a good communicator, thus she had enjoyed chatting with her customers in the restaurant.

At first Lily was unaware that one of her customers was a generous benefactor whose gift continues to serves all Neapolitans. He was a polite 0gentleman who was a regular   customer of the Bradford House's weekly $3.99 "All You Can Eat Special." His wife often accompanied him. Lily soon learned he was a native of Indiana, and they often chatted about the Fighting Illini and Indiana Hoosiers. Some time had passed before she learned that her regular customer and Hoosier fan Mr. Lowdermilk, had given "a beautiful strip of white sandy beach: her favorite place to swim in the Gulf" to the city of Naples. No doubt his generous gift is worth millions of dollars, today!

Memories and real life continue to reveals how others' lives can impact ours in so many positive ways.

CHAPTER 5
THIS AND THAT

Be Thankful for All the Gifts you Have

"Life is a succession of moments. To live each one is to succeed." Corita Kent

Harold has had a hacking cough that he had been treating with drinking lots of liquids and cough syrup with me contributing the proverbial chicken soup to his diet. We had hoped it would soon run its course as he did not have a fever or other symptoms. I took comfort in the saying that most colds dissipate in seven day regardless of what you do.

A couple of mornings ago, I stumbled out of bed, wondering if this would be the day that Harold's cold would go away. I found my usual cup of steaming water and the newspaper waiting on the table, thanks to Harold's morning routine of thoughtfulness. Usually, by the time I've read the front section of the paper and sipped my water, I'm ready to think about breakfast.

Casually Harold said in his usual stoical manner, "I'm having trouble seeing." I screamed, "What did you say?" as no one has ever accused me of being stoic. He responded, "I can see pretty good without my glasses but when I put them on, there is a black or blurred spot in the center of things," and added, "I've already tried cleaning them a couple of times; without any improvement."

I tried to control the sense of panic that was consuming me as I thought this surely doesn't have anything to do with his cold and coughing as I tried to decide what we should do next. I took some encouragement from the fact that he could see without his glasses.

I envisioned all kinds of outcomes, none desirable, as my stress level continued to rise. We decided to quickly get dressed and go for help. To make a long story short, when I began to look for my glasses I couldn't find them. I suddenly remembered the night before I had placed them on the dresser near Harold's glasses instead of putting them in their usual place.

What a wonderful sense of release to find Harold's glasses instead of mine!! I immediately took them into Harold whose vision problem was immediately corrected. I put on my thoroughly cleaned glasses as tears of joy streamed down my face.

The mix-up was an understandable mistake. Our glasses are the same color and both made of the flexible framing. Harold usually arises before me and out of consideration; he collects all his portable parts without turning lights on in our bedroom.

The remainder of the day we counted our blessings and realize all of our ordinary problems were not worth complaining about. *"Every good gift and every perfect gift is from above.' James 1:17*

Learning at Toledo High School (THS)--*July 30, 2006*

Last week I wrote about socialization activities associated with THS. Afterwards, I thought about the lasting effects that THS has had upon my life. The combination of my teachers, classmates, family and the total secure learning environment all played a significant role in my life. I don't think I comprehended the importance of these combined elements when I was experiencing them. Rather, most of the time I thought growing up was an O K time in my life. Yet, I can look back now and wish I had spent more time applying myself academically and a little less time socializing!

As a teacher, I learned that moving to a new school can be unsettling for students. My sister and I had previously attended a large school in Virginia where each of our homerooms had more students than all of THS combined.

There were no school buses during the 40's in Cumberland County. Thus, it was necessary for us to room at our aunt's home in Toledo during the weekdays to attend THS.

We had never been separated from both of our parents. You can guess what an adjustment that was for us, not to mention cooking and doing our homework without their supervision.

I had wonderful teachers, but being self disciplined and knowing how to take full advantage of the learning opportunities,, was another story.

Miss Katie Foster was both a good teacher and very personable. She was not much older than some of her senior students as THS was her first teaching job.

Mrs. Norma Kelly was my Spanish teacher. She had both high expectations and a twinkle in her eye. I babysat some for her son Mike and dearly loved her. I can't count the times during my adult life that I have wished that I had paid more attention in my classes. Two times come to mind: when as an adult I took classes in Mexico City and in retirement when I have volunteered as a tutor for Hispanics who desperately wanted to learn English.

A funny story comes to mind when I think of Mrs. Elizabeth Light, who tried desperately to teach me how to sew. She thought it was important to use a thimble, when doing handwork. Thus I would quickly take it out of my sewing box and put it on my finger when she came near me. She deserved an A+ for effort. Before her, my Mother, who was a talented seamstress and my 4-H leader, had about given up on teaching me to coordinate my left hand at the sewing machine.

Also in my typing class, I never fully learned the touch system. It also involved coordination. So now, as I'm working at my computer, I use the hunt & peck method. As other lefties know, we still live in a right-handed world.

Rev. Collier was also a respected teacher at THS, as well as the pastor of the Toledo Methodist Church where I attended Sunday school and the Sunday Night Methodist Youth Fellowship. The church and the many friends I made there were another important link during my school days. Rev. Collier was the minister who officiated when Harold and I were married.

Friendships established long ago with some of my THS classmates have endured throughout the passing years and remain very important today. Now, I often see Vera Scales, Oma Layton, and Maggie Venetta, Wilma & Jr. Clark, Vic Stewart and other THS classmates in Sunday morning's services.

Many cherished memories and learning experiences from my years at THS continue to both play a role in my life and reside in my heart.

Living and Dying in Grace and Love—
September 15, 2002
"Wise and faithful people count the days and make the most of every moment." Rev. Alice Shirley

Death is a natural rhythm of life: even as is being born. Following birth, eventually, physical death becomes a reality for each of us.

In last week's column, I shared how birth and death define our earthly time. They are the natural borders of our life on earth.

I am discussing death because a beautiful friend, Jan Knupp, has shown me how to both live and die with courage and dignity. There is a quote that states: *A coward dies a thousand times while a brave person* dies *only once.* Jan was in the brave category. Her body was returned to earth today, in the presence of a multitude of people whose lives had been enriched by her love and grace.

Returning to my opening question: is it the fact that we don't freely talk about death that adds to its mystery? Obviously, none of us wants to bury our children or die prematurely. Aside from these fears, then, is death an unnatural occurrence for our parents or for us; somewhere beyond our allotted three score& ten years? Is there pleasure or quality in life for anyone being kept alive by artificial means? Is remaining unconscious with a lung machine breathing for you, living? I think not.

Jan did not readily accept death's bidding. About ten years ago, her pulmonary specialist told her that she had a deadly lung disease for which there was no known cure, and further, she could not expect to survive for more than five years. Did she give up? No, she resisted death through living each day to the fullest and received the gift of five bonus years beyond her predicted life expectancy.

Jan found joy and purpose in life by loving and caring for her husband and family, entertaining and loving her friends, traveling, enjoying the arts and trying to meet the needs of others, particularly helping her Aunt Hazel.

She successfully met the challenges that each new day presented. Through it all, she never lost her sense of humor nor resorted to the poor me syndrome or withdrew from living her life to the fullest.

A couple of weeks ago her pulmonary specialist; said that there was absolutely nothing remaining that he could do other than helping her to die free of pain. Jan had told me, he sat on her hospital bed for two hours talking, because both knew that would be their last visit. Her physician had discovered, like so many of us, that simply knowing Jan was tantamount to friendship.

Upon returning home, Jan, with the help of her husband, chose to receive care from Hospice. She courageously chose the terms to accept death, even as she had done in deciding how to fully live all her allotted days. She wanted to remain in her home, surrounded by her husband, family and friends, which she did.

The first time I visited with her after Hospice has began its services, she asked me to read a book which they had given her on dying. After I read the book, she shared in a matter-of-fact way that she knew that she was progressing toward death more rapidly that she had thought she might. Not too long before Jan stopped breathing, her husband and I prayed the Lord's Prayer, at her bedside. I think it was more for us than for Jan, as she was already at peace.

Do You Live in a House or a Home?--*July 14, 2012*

I have lived in both, as, my needs have been different at various times and stages during my life, thus far. I have found there are some significant differences as well as some similarities between a house and a home. Because words often have many meanings, I once again verified their definitions by checking my old standby: *Webster's Dictionary*. Also I have checked their meanings with others sources I'll start with *Webster's* definitions. I found for *house*: shelter, a building human beings live in, living space, a place where things are stored, a building occupied by a tenant or family. And to continue with *Webster's* definitions for *home*: a place where one likes to be, the place where one was born or one was reared, a restful or congenial place or thought of as the center of one's affections, it is at the center or heart of a matter. Then it adds the meaning for *at home*: comfortable, at ease, familiar: a definition that I really like and can verify from experience.

One could wonder if it matters whether we live in a house or a home as they have many commonalities that provide for one's physical needs, as both usually have roofs, doors, windows, a variety of furniture; including appliances, beds, various types of flooring, etc. Thus, I don't think the structure or furnishings makes   significant differences between the two or is what sets them apart.

Also, one can rule out finances and/or the amount of money that the people earn who reside in both houses and homes. I recently read where a New York woman, who had given up her U S citizenship in order to move to Europe, had placed her New York apartment house on the market for a multi- million dollar amount.

Following are some quotes from writers that put into words the benefits one can receive from living in a home:

The good, the true, the tender,
These form the wealth of a home." Sarah J. Hale
"Home is not where you live, but where they understand you."
Christian Morgenstern

"The home of everyone is to him his castle and fortress, as well for his defense against injury and violence, as for his repose." Edward Coke
Plus, I collected these responses from friends and family at the Fillin' Station this morning: "A house is a structure-- a home is an emotion", "You live in a home and could have many houses, but you only live in your home." My next response was almost identical to the previous one; "You live in your home but a house is a building," and one more who said, "Love prevails in a home."

As I stated earlier, I have lived in both. I had a very happy home life during my childhood even though, I was born during the Great Depression of the 1930's at a time when cash was short. The children worked in the fields along with the adults as my family then lived on a labor-intensive tobacco farm in the rural South.

However, my parents also found time to co-mingle learning, fun, games and swimming in the creek with our work. Whenever we had footraces I was given a handicap, as I could not run as fast as my older sisters. Also, as we chopped the weeds out of the tobacco fields, my Mom, an ex-teacher taught us to name and spell our than 48 states and their capitals, as well as other skills such as naming all the members of President Roosevelt's Cabinet. I still remember that he appointed the first woman ever to serve as a U S Cabinet member: Frances Perkins, Secretary of Labor, from 1933-45. Perhaps this stored knowledge played some minor role many years later, when I ran and was successful in becoming the first woman ever to be elected to Lake Land College's governing Board of Trustees in 1975.

In the early 1940's my family moved to a naval housing complex in Norfolk, Virginia during WWII. The important thing was that our family was together again, which quickly turned our apartment into our home. My family then moved to Illinois in the mid 1940's after my Dad had been discharged from the U S Navy. Here, I met and fell in love with Harold Dobbs, a mid-western farmer who became the love of my life. I soon dropped out of Toledo High School to marry and moved into Harold's Cottonwood farm house, which became our beloved farm home: where we raised our three children and continued to live and love for more than six decades.

I now am a tenant in an apartment house that meets my physical needs at this stage of my life. However with loving memories in my heart and having mementos from my happy past scattered about in my apartment, it sort of, if not completely, turns my apartment into a home.

Life is Like a Lawnmower; Sometimes--*June 7, 2002*

Making too much of life, Like it won't come around again.--James Kavanaugh

Watching Husband Harold slowly circling on his mower cutting a fresh swath of grass with each rotation is hypnotic. Overcast skies foretell more rain and tell me repeated mowing is on the way. The mower's constant hum seems to remind me how much cutting the grass is like life, in that there are many cycles in life that we repeat over and over without conscious thought. Nevertheless, the most important decisions need our undivided attention.

The learning cycle, like mowing, is one that we repeat over and over again. When we are exposed to new information we first examine it and then make a trial run for fit. Finally, if we think the new information is meaningful or useful, we proceed to internalize it for future use in our lives. In time, with repetition and practice the information is stored in our brain cells for instant recall as needed.

Learning who we can or cannot trust is another ongoing cycle in our lives. Your system may vary somewhat from mine. By and large, my system is to trust everyone until a person gives me cause not to do so. This system works in most cases. The first time someone betrays my trust, I credit it to "A bad hair day" as everyone has a day when they get up on the wrong side of the bed. If betrayal occurs a second time, I'm inclined to think life is too short to spend time trusting that person. I repeat this system as needed. Thus, I do not need to reinvent the wheel each time I meet someone new.

Shopping is another cycle much like lawn mowing in that it repeats itself in a habitual manner. There are those tried and true brands that one picks up in the store without thinking, for the most part. Can you think of other tasks that you perform in a like manner?

We would be dizzy all the time if we had to think about every task in life each time we performed it. Habit takes over and automatically performs those routine daily tasks, much like it does for Harold when he is mowing the yard. It would be tedious and stressful if he had to tell himself each time he cuts a new swath of grass that he must not leave gaps, etc. It is good that he can use that time to plan or think about other things.

Are there ever times that one needs to give conscious thought to every action?

All will, no doubt, reply in the affirmative. For example, we want our dentist or surgeon to be alert and concentrating on the tasks at hand every moment we are in their chair. We have that same responsibility many times in our lives also.

Most important, the gift of life itself is so fleeting that we should never let habit dictate its use. It is too <u>precious</u> to not live and savor each moment in full awareness.

GET THE ERASER--*June 2000*

My children often take care of some odd jobs about the house when they visit. (I remember when I did this for my parents. It doesn't seem so long ago.) My husband and I are thankful for their help.

On one occasion, David, our carpenter son was hanging a door. My three-year-old grandson, wanting to be entertained, asked his dad to draw him a truck. David told him to ask me to draw for him. He added, "Grandma drew animals for me when I was your age."

My grandson brought me his paper and pencil. I drew a cat as I had drawn for David many years ago. I used circles for the body and head. I added the cat's facial features including whiskers with pointed ears on the head. I then completed my project by adding a long tail. My grandson took one look at the picture and yelled, "Dad, get the eraser!"

Personally, I did not think my cat looked all that bad. However, my grandson was use-to his Dad, a good artist, drawing sixteen wheeled trucks with many details. Needless to say, my grandson has not asked me to draw for him again and I have not volunteered.

The above incident reminds me of my relationship with my computer. I often must erase and try again. What is more damaging to my ego is when my computer sends me nasty authoritarian messages, such as, "What's this?" Or "You have shut down inappropriately and may have damaged your computer. We are scanning for errors." Occasionally it tells me," You have made a fatal error and the computer is shutting down." The computer policeman gives the errors numbers. I have thus far received error # 651. I do not know how much higher they go. No doubt, I will find out unless I give up and call it quits.

Prior to my retirement, I had a wonderful secretary, Linda. I could give

Linda a few written notes. Using her computer's word processor, she could turn out a well-written letter without mistakes the first time. I never heard her threaten or talk back to her computer like I do sometimes out of total frustration. I did not know then how difficult it would be for me to learn a task she did with such apparent ease. My only contact with the computer at that time was to enter my password to receive or send a message from my boss who was located in another city. I had no responsibility for turning the computer on or getting on line and certainly had no typing skills. Now, I wish I had paid more attention, or better yet, had taken lessons from Linda. That is hindsight, which is always 20/20.

I have a love-hate relationship with my computer. On those times when I can surf on the web, locate information, and send my e-mail, I love my computer! When I get messages from the e-mail postmaster telling me there was an error and my letter could not be delivered, well, that's a different story. What's most discouraging is that most of the time I know the problems belong to me, the operator, instead of the computer or some problem out in cyber space. I have always believed that I could learn any task if I work at it long enough. I hate to now admit I was born fifty years too soon and give up. Thus, I do plan to take additional classes. By the way, maybe I should take classes from my grandson who recently finished kindergarten. He operates his computer with skill when playing games. The only game that I have played on my computer is Solitaire. Of course I already knew how to play it. Everyone needs a role model, even a sixty-nine year old grandmother who is trying to master her computer.

Maybe I can yet disprove the old adage," You can't teach an old dog new tricks."

Can We Choose Between Old and New--*September 16, 2006*

Some things you keep. ...They're good for you, reliable and practical... . So you hang on, because something old is sometimes better than something new. Anon

How do we choose between the new and old? Or is this one of those "it depends" decisions?

When I was a child, a bookmobile made regular stops at a crossroads near my rural home. I always looked forward to its visits and checked out as many books as possible, as reading was my favorite pastime.

I found it exciting whenever there were new books on the shelf. A new book always had a special feel, scent and look all its own, besides the anticipation of discovering the excitement, which any book's pages might reveal. Without doubt there would be no handprints or tears on the new book's cover nor folded corners that had marked some previous reader's place.

Opening the cover of a new book continues to arouse my curiosity. However, with the passing of time, I have learned to love and equally value old books. I'm reminded that ideas written about mankind by Plato, Aristotle and other Roman and Greek philosophers before the time of Christ are applicable today.

When I read a book that was first published a hundred years ago, I think of the authors and the time that they had lived and written about. I try to imagine how different their world was from mine.

I wonder about the people who had owned and/or read some of the old books before me. Did they enjoy reading the book? Maybe the book had merely collected dust in someone's bookcase.

Growing up, I was the third daughter in a large family. So guess what: I wore a lot of "hand-me-downs" until I grew taller than my sisters. My Mother was a talented seamstress. She made my hand-me-downs fit and often she had been able to disguise their earlier appearance.

I always loved wearing a brand new dress even if it had been made from printed sacks that had once contained flour or chicken feed.

For special occasions such as my birthday and Easter, I was permitted to select my fabric and buttons from the Sears & Roebuck catalog for my Mother to sew. The catalog contained real sample pieces of material in several different colors, thus adding to the decision making and excitement of choosing the yard goods. I fully understand the meaning of "wish book," as I spent many hours looking at the new fall catalog when it had arrived in the mail.

In time, I learned that clothing tailored to fit was more attractive than ready- made clothing. Now in maturity, I continue to wear some of my old favorites, both because they feel comfortable and I have developed emotional attachments to some pieces hanging in my closet.

Today I asked my husband if he liked new things better than the old. He replied; "I like you best and you are old." After I got over the resentment, I decided it was a back-handed compliment and truthful. At the very least he must think, like the above quote, that I am "reliable and practical."

I think deciding whether the new or old is best surely needs to be left, in the "it depends" category.

Blackboards and Winter--*October 17, 2003*

There is a direct relationship between blackboards and winter, that is, if you use your imagination a bit.

Think way back to grade school. For some of you it could be a "one room fits all" building. However, it isn't necessary for you to share that information to participate. If you are currently in an elementary school, I think you can also visualize my connection.

I haven't been in an elementary classroom lately, and it's possible a high tech method of cleaning the blackboards, which excludes children from washing them, has been developed, and/or maybe electronic equipment has completely replaced chalkboards. But I doubt it.

To get on with my story, the combines are sweeping the fields clean of living vegetation, and Mother Nature's winds are stripping the beautiful fall colors from the trees in preparation for winter's barren look.

Even though we want to stretch the beauty of fall, past seasons prove that Mother Nature cannot be deterred from her yearly assignment of delivering winter.

Now for the analogy: as a child and continuing through the years that I taught in a 6th grade homeroom, students enjoyed washing the blackboards. Perhaps it was because it provided a change of pace from studying or maybe they simply enjoy helping the teacher. I did.

The killing cold and sweeping winds of winter, like washing the blackboards, prepare for a clean start. Both are changes: what was isn't anymore. Many of us have trouble adjusting to changes, but in time, we do and often feel, in hindsight, the changes were good for us.

Throughout the winter, Mother Nature is always working hard behind the scenes. She even lets the crocus flowers come up while the frost is still shining on the ground and remains busy behind the scene, preparing the spring bulbs and seeds to flower, once again, at the dawning of spring.

And who knows, on the clean blackboard the teacher may write NO HOMEWORK TONIGHT instead of a full page of assignments.

Let's all take more time to anticipate and enjoy the gift of clean starts in our lives, when or wherever they appear.

Beauty & Serenity Prevail--*May 30, 2004*

"I can look at life through the windshield and not the rear view mirror."
Anon

These words are not original with me, but they help me to keep my life focused. Each of us can choose where we want to be in most aspects of our life: even if you are now working or living in less than ideal surroundings.

Eleanor Roosevelt was the wife of our 32nd president, who had served longer than any other president. At that time, she wrote a column entitled, "My Day" and traveled extensively for several years in order to be the eyes and ears for her crippled husband. That, then, was an atypical role for a first lady although she is now remembered the world over for her humanitarian work. She was subjected to negative reports for her actions. She wrote these profound words, "No one can make you feel inferior unless you let them."

Let's think of what these words mean and how we can apply them to our own life. The key is "unless you let them." We control how we feel about our actions and behaviors and do not need to let others superimpose or dictate how we feel about ourselves. Others can and may say hurtful things, but that does not make them true. When others have said or have attempted to plant untrue information about another person, time usually reveals the truth.

Political campaigns are an excellent example of this. Polls tell us that Americans do not like negative campaigning and often those candidates who pursue it are defeated at the ballot box or have problems governing if elected.

Last night I was awakened in the night by the activities of my previous busy days. There was no returning to sleep in spite of the fact that I tried some of my usually successful methods to induce sleep. It includes taking ten deep breaths and recalling my favorite and most relaxing mental images, such as strolling through beautiful flower gardens, sitting near and/or wading in slow moving water while listening to or watching birds and recalling music that I love.

I got out of bed, looked out my west window, and saw a magnificent view of the moon. It was a partial moon displaying the most beautiful shades of orange, perhaps because in was in a lower western position and I was viewing it through a hazy atmosphere. Its beauty and serenity cleared all other thought from my mind and made me happy that I was awake to view such a gift.

Beauty and serenity are present everywhere if we have the frame of mind to perceive them. It reminds me of the psychological principle that states our minds cannot concentrate on two thoughts at the same time. When given a choice, choose the positive.

AN ODD MIX

Retirement and ageing cannot be mixed in life as easily as I am doing in this sentence. They simply do not mesh without friction. Regardless, life normally deals them out in the same hand.

One lesson experience has taught me is to play the hand that life has dealt in the best possible way. Life is change.... period. Opportunities available today have no guarantee for tomorrow.

Remember when you were a child and thought there were ages and ages between your birthdays or other special holidays? The reverse is true for retirement, particular in the ageing segment.

I have an aversion to the fact that when I was younger; retirement was painted as a dreamland experience. No one mentioned the hidden word named ageing and its consequences.

Could it be that I did not have ears to hear anything which would mar the beautiful expectations I had mentally painted for my retirement? The instructions I heard were," Save sufficient money and all will be great when you retire".

Now that I look back with" a mature perspective,", I discover there had been red flags along the way. Incidents that could have told me that retirement wouldn't be a second honeymoon. Such as when my parents were touring Mexico by train and my Mother had to use a wheel chair because of unexpected health problems. Another clear reminder was when I had gone in the ambulance to meet my Father's plane in St Louis after he had experienced a stroke while on the Texas Gulf.

My husband and I have been retired seven years. It is an unmatched passage in our lives. Like a less traveled road, there have been curves and potholes we did not anticipate.

On the other hand, freedom at this stage of our lives to invest our time doing things that are important to us is a gift we cherish. Prior to this passage in our lives most of our days were filled with routine schedules containing little flexibility.

The positive factors certainly outweigh the limitations that have come with ageing. Only a few days ago we spent some unforgettable time on the Gulf of Mexico. The calm and blue of the water as it blended with the sky painted a scene of total serenity.

Recognizing that life is full of changes and not being afraid to meet them head on is a key to coping in any stage of life particularly in retirement. Ageing sometimes causes one to spend more time in stressful environments, such as hospital waiting rooms. When my children and I waited anxiously in an innovative new hospital, a runner would come from the operating room every hour to report to us on the progress of my husband's lengthy heart surgery. What reassurance having people around that are responsive to one's anxiety and needs. On the night before Harold's surgery, his nurse pulled down a Murphy bed and ordered dinner for me so I could remain overnight in his room.

Thus, in retirement's difficult times there are people who smooth out the roadblocks even as others have done in all chapters of my life. The best way I know to say thanks to these gracious people is to pass their unanticipated kindnesses on to others whenever the opportunity presents itself.

Here is my statement on retirement and its odd mix of freedom and ageing,

"It isn't necessarily a fairy tale time of living happily ever after"; quickly, I must add, "when has life been that way?" Ageing is another stage in life that calls for courage and the ability to accept each day with strength of mind and plans to make the best of it. I remain an optimist. When the morning's sunlight comes into view; thankfulness and wonder continue to inspire me on most days.

Adapting--*September 2, 2012*

My *American Heritage Dictionary* says it a verb that means, "To adjust to a specific use or situation." My subject: *adapting* comes to mind because this is what we have been attempting to do in relationship to our extreme weather during this season!

This morning I awakened to the peaceful sounds of a steady rain falling outside. I call it peaceful because my childhood home had a tin roof and I learned to love the sound of summer rain falling on it. Perhaps, I liked the rainy days because they pleased my Dad, who was a farmer, but also it meant that I wouldn't have to work: hoeing in the fields on that day. This was a plus because it meant there would be some time to finish reading my library books, before my state's (N. C.) Mobile Library Unit, returned to a nearby crossroads for me to select new ones.

As a child, I recall my Dad standing on the porch, early in the morning with a troubled look on his face, scanning the sky for any hint of a rain cloud. Bear in mind, we did not have the sophisticated weather reporting technology (that predicts accurately, part of the time) in the 1930's, that we have today. I have shared in an earlier column about being caught at school in the 1940's by a damaging hurricane in Norfolk because no one knew how to predict its routing or landfall. Not that it's a perfect science today, but enough is known to close schools that might be in a hurricane's path. However, during Isaac, our most recent named hurricane, we now know its actual path was much different than the predictions, which had been given a couple of days before its landfall. Adapting to the extreme heat this season, plus the lack of rainfall, has taken its toll on our lives as well as our environment in many ways including: hardly any fresh veggies and/or flowers, trees and shrubs dying, along with a serious reduction and/or losses in farm production that will impact the income of many grain and livestock farmers. The harvest will reveal the facts; but simply driving through the countryside, I've observed that some farmers have already mowed some of the fields that had been planted in corn; I could only guess what their planting cost losses were. These costs, in time; will reflect indirectly on others in our community. Also people relaxing, from children playing, to adults walking, jogging, shopping or socializing with friends, have all adapted their routines to cope with this season's intense heat.

In conclusion, I'm reaching for a ray of hope. Can the three inches of rain that has slowly fallen thus far this weekend from Isaac's remnants give us any evidence? Although we have adapted to one of the driest and hottest seasons on record, will this storm; Isaac, who created havoc in other parts of our nation be our helping hand?

Yes! "Yesterday is gone, tomorrow is uncertain" and I CHOOSE TO LIVE IN THE NOW and read my book today, and listen to the harmonious sounds of falling rain.

A Slice of Life Without Boundaries--*May 26, 2005*

"The future is not some place we are going to, but one we are creating."
John Schaar

A few weeks ago I had an occasion to visit Golden Gate High School (GGHS) in Naples. I was thoroughly impressed by its lovely entryway, wide hallways, and its total campus, although its population somehow seemed younger than I had been in high school. At first glance, I could see little in common between it and my small town high school.

GGHS' Campus seemed to be a better match to the small college where I had completed my undergraduate work in Illinois (EIU). My high school was on my mind because a few days earlier I had received an invitation to its annual reunion.

Many of you who are past thirty have or will receive an invitation to your high school reunion this summer. It would be interesting to know what makes some people attend while others toss it into File 13. It seems that that graduates who reside closest to their school are less likely to attend. Maybe distance truly makes the heart grow fonder. After experiencing several reunions, I have some unofficial observations, which admittedly are colored by emotions.

Until this year, I had been uncertain why attending my high school reunion was such an emotional event. I do not mean to imply it had been a bad experience. No one made me go; to the contrary, I had looked forward to attending.

A couple of years ago, there was a young professional woman who lives in my condo complex that I began seeing at the pool doing daily laps. She shared that she wanted to shed several pounds before she attended the 10th anniversary celebration of her graduation class. This made me wonder if reunion-emotions are a girl thing.

My husband and I attended the same high school. He graduated a few years before me and doesn't seem to experience any reunion upheavals. However, he is stoic about most things; we are truly an example of opposites marrying. When I attempted to quiz him about his feelings, he said, "People can look at things however they want to."

Our school no longer exists. Several years ago, the schools in three neighboring communities consolidated, creating a larger high school which could offer more diverse curricula.

My high school enrollment total was less than a hundred students. Part of the original building remains as it now serves as the home office of a former student, Burnham Neal's multi-state corporation (BEN TIRE).

Last Saturday, my husband and I attended our school's multi-class reunion, as due to dwindling numbers all graduates and attendees of Toledo High School are invited to one annual celebration. The oldest living graduate will turn 103 this month and the youngest graduates are all fully mature, whatever that is.

All of a sudden light bulbs began to flash in my mind as I shared both dinner and hugs, while reminiscing with most of the 80 people present. High school is such a formative and life shaping event in each of our lives! Of course, revisiting those memories is emotional, as we had formed lifelong friendships. Some of you like me had made career decisions together. That was a time our peers had more influence on our lives than our parents, molding our self images and life styles. Shared conversations confirmed my long-held suspicion: jointly my classmates have left indelible prints on each others' lives!

Some of the students walking the hallways who appeared so young to me at their sparkling new GGHS will at some future date share these same emotions when a committee of their former classmates mail them invitations to their high school reunion. .Even today their bonding, which is occurring, is not any different than it had been for me.

In the meantime, you who have been tossing your former classmates' invitations into File 13 should reconsider. There are some revealing facts in store for you. The glamour girl or guy who made your heartthrob may have lost their curves and/or hair. The student who helped you pass advanced algebra or the bookworm may now be the president of his/her own High Tech Corporation or an institution of higher learning. More important, you will come away with a greater awareness and appreciation of the earlier environmental and humanistic influences which are now an integral part of your life.

Maintaining Our Comfort Zones--*September 11, 2003*

To function effectively, our bodies and minds need a certain comfort level.

I awakened at 3 am this morning and began tossing in my bed, hoping to go back to sleep. The more I twisted about, the wider-awake I became. Additional thoughts began surfacing, which lessened the possibility of my returning to sleep as all the unresolved issues from yesterday began competing for my mind's attention.

From experience, I have learned that sleep can be an eraser of ideas but not of unresolved stress. If in the night; I come up with ideas or workable solutions, I need to record them before going back to sleep, or else they vanish before day-light. Sometimes a few ideas scribbled on my bedside notebook clears my mind and lets me go back to sleep.

Meeting our emotional and inter-personal needs has some things in common with keeping our financial accounts in order. To stay in an emotional comfort zone, unresolved issues need our attention and some kind of resolution; otherwise we end up with a negative balance, which interferes with our daily living.

I can usually assess and resolve most of my financial needs using my calculator and checkbook, as the same bills reoccur each month.

Emotional concerns are often more difficult to keep in balance than financial ones because they are not usually routine issues. At times, we ourselves are unsure of what we really want and nearly always, there are others involved in any resolution of emotional problems.

Some emotional issues are beyond our control. There is a saying, "If the solution is not yours, then the problem is not yours." That is not always the case. After we have done everything we know to do, we must decide if we can tolerate the problem for a while. We usually can tolerate some emotional discomfort if we know it will end in a reasonable length of time. If not we need to distance ourselves from the source of the problem. Admittedly, this is easier to say than to do and sometimes we need to seek qualified help.

Many solutions to inter-personal concerns can readily be discovered through communicating and networking with others. We do it all the time, often around our dinner tables. Sometimes, because of our roles, we become facilitators. Each week, I have an open house dinner for my grandchildren. Last night at dinner, my "bride to be" granddaughter shared a concern pertaining to her wedding day: she needed to find someone to play at her wedding because the regular organist at her church will not be available on her wedding day. I contacted some friends who were able to give us several names and one has agreed to play for the wedding.

Support groups like Alzheimer Caregivers are another way Americans as a society have learned to restore a measure of comfort and emotional balance for families, which are dealing with the same problems. Today on the anniversary of the 911 tragedies, many people gathered at the site of the Twin Towers to comfort each other.

Often when we reach out to assist others, it is restorative for us. This brings to mind the well-known Bible scriptures, "Do unto others as you would have them do unto you" and "To love your neighbor as yourself."~~~

From time to time, we need to take the time to balance our emotional needs just as we do our checkbooks in order to prevent overdrafts.

If we do not work to maintain a reasonable balance in our emotional comfort zones, we will have no resources to help others or ourselves.

Is Change A Gift?--*May 21, 2001*

'Continuity gives us roots; change gives us branches, letting us grow and reach new heights." Pauline Kezer

How, when and where are unceasing questions which surface for me at this time of the year. Don't turn me off. I'm neither a theologian nor a person who writes a code of conduct for others (doing that for myself consumes enough time). You may have guessed I am a social worker. Like you, curiosity and wonder fill my thoughts at times.

I think the signs which announce the coming of spring, each winter, are similar to the messages in our life that foretell a change is on the way or that one is needed. Our intuition reveals this to us. I do not mean some mystical presence when I say intuition. Rather, I am referring to a body of research which claims our intuition is nothing more than all our senses collectively giving feedback to our minds.

Every year I am overwhelmed with the beauty and promise of spring. It reoccurs without explanation. Nevertheless, there are signs, which tell us winter is leaving and spring is on the way.

In Illinois, the daffodils and other early flowers blooming in beds of sleeping brown grass and leaves are "change messengers" reporting that more beauty is on the way. These changes occur while the tree branches continue to resemble dark sticks waving in the March wind sprinkled with traces of snow.

In our lives, boredom is a change signal. When routine tasks no longer hold our attention, sometimes we can change the order in which we perform work. In other circumstances, boredom may mean we need a major change because we are missing opportunities that could enrich our lives.

Life is a precious gift. Much of it is consumed in sleeping, earning a living and other essential work. At best, our discretionary time is limited.

Some people think change implies failure. I think the opposite is true. Even small changes can bring new perspective and insights into our lives.

Long-term relationships may be an area where change is needed. No, I do not mean your family! They are very special relationships which may well benefit from changes regarding how we interact and support each other (they are not the ones to whom I am referring in this instance). Are you always the one who must do the calling to maintain contact in other relationships? I'm not suggesting that anyone should terminate friendships that they enjoy. Simply re-evaluate those relationships that have become a chore to maintain because you no longer have anything in common. Friendships need to be nurtured in some way by all involved parties.

Are you attuned to the signals of change which inform you that you are missing out on events or meeting people that can enrich your life? Maybe it is time to be a mentor, take that trip or class you had planned.

Listen to your intuition and branch out.

Change in the New Year--*December 22, 2012*

... God grant me the courage to change the things I can.... Reinhold Niebuhr

At this time of the year, we usually think of changes in the form of New Year's Resolutions. However, I'm struggling to find the words to share some community changes I have in mind. A few nights ago, I went with my Granddaughter to see my Great-grandchildren's Christmas Program. As they sang, tears moistened my eyes as I thought of the Connecticut Families who would never see their children perform along with the families of those adults who valiantly gave their lives trying to protect the children.

Do I have all the answers that explain why another human goes on a mass killing spree, taking the lives of others human beings? No! Do I think it's time for all caring citizens to say, "We have had enough and let's work together to do whatever it takes to stop the killing?" Yes! We all can ask for legislation to prevent guns of war, which often are used in the mass killings from being readily available to the public. I do not hunt but am not an anti-gun person as I know men as well as women, among my family and friends who enjoy hunting. I tend to believe deer playing in the distance is a lovely sight. However, I did not particularly like the one who came into my car via my windshield a few years ago, turning my car into salvage, clearly revealing there were surplus deer roaming in our area.

Today, I write as a parent, grandmother, great-grandmother, former teacher, counselor, social worker and Sunday School teacher who spent most of my adult working years interacting with children and their parents. Some were troubled children, as some had abusive and/or neglectful caregivers. These were some of the children that I worked with as a counselor and/or a social worker.

Of course, most of the children that I taught in the classroom were very normal children who were eager to learn with loving and caring parents. But there were some exceptions who didn't know how to fit in.

The human elements are what I want to share some thoughts, suggestions and potential changes, which we could enact as a caring community. Sometimes, as a teacher, when I had duty supervising on the playground, I would encounter a child standing alone that caused concern, as the others children were involved in games or huddling with their close friends. If it was a child from my class, I would quietly ask other students to include the child in their games. I avoided this isolation in my classroom by choosing the work or study groups.

Children who are poor mixers are sometime troubled children who might be slow learners, have a speech impediment or simply be from poor families that prevented them from participating with others in activities outside of school. Social cliques form early in school, as they did among the students' parents. It is not uncommon for children with lesser mental health issues that spring from the home to be magnified in a school setting. Also the same children may not get help early on .If they do consult a counselor it becomes a stigma if other children, learn about it. Many students, unfortunately quickly arrive at the stage in life where peer approval is the most important thing in their young lives, creating lasting problems for the most vulnerable. I want to cite three incidents from my own life, which I eventually adjusted to, that were very troubling as a student. They were: having a very bright sister, my height and moving to a different culture during high school.

My sister, Pat just older than me, whom I was very close to was intellectually gifted. In my small southern school, I would have her same teachers who would question why I didn't excel in all subjects as Pat had. Also, my parents had high intellectual expectations for all their children but seemed accepting if they felt we were fully applying ourselves. But how did I accept the fact that I believed that my teachers thought; that I was the "dumber" sister?

By the time I was in the sixth grade, I had fully achieved my adult height, causing me to soar over all my classmates, boys as well as girls, and even some of my teachers. This was very troubling and the students gave me undesirable nicknames over my growth in height that I had absolutely no control over.

Later, I moved from a large city school in a Southern beach town, Norfolk, Virginia to Toledo and had to board away from home to attend school. But more troubling; the culture was different and I spoke with a Southern accent and felt that students were making fun of me, because they encouraged me to speak, then would smile among themselves. I didn't understand then, that they had not previously heard a classmate speak with a southern accent and just found it interesting.

Next week I want to continue by sharing some thoughts that come from my professional training, work experiences plus my troubling childhood experiences.

The application of the Advent Candles of Hope, Peace, Joy and Love that we have been lighting and reading about each week together in worship, during December could benefit our society all year long. We could share more love and compassion with the students who are trying to cope with various disabilities and /or differences which currently result in them being shunned by their classmates. That possibility could cause them in the future to become troubled loners in our society.

Checking Things Out: in Our Garden of Life

The Times They are a Changin'. Bob Dylan

Throughout my marriage one of my husband Harold's favorite pastimes had been planting a garden as soon as spring had burst forth in Illinois. Gardening was relaxing for Harold, but not for me as I grew up on a

Labor- intensive farm where I often had a hoe in my hand and found it anything but relaxing.

The arrival of springtime weather was his clue to migrate north, as the birds did. Last year we had a magnificent clue as hundreds of robins preparing to migrate assembled in our yard for a fuel up~~ literally striping the holly trees of every red berry in sight.

It may be a bit early to plant in Illinois. Nevertheless, it's not too early to scan the new varieties in the seed catalogues as you sip a cup of hot tea in Illinois or during a relaxing day at the beach in Florida.

Harold and I developed a habit of daily walk-around to check out the progress of his newly planted garden. Admittedly, the first day after you've planted, it was highly unlikely that you would see any evidence of having doing so. An unexpected positive side effect for me was nature's creative environment to analyze mental changes that I want to consider for my life. There needed to be a beginning, or planting time, for those changes even as there had been one for the garden to thrive.

On our daily walk we often had seen other things, perhaps the red bud tree sending forth buds and bits of color, along with the returned robins, hopping and then pausing to unearth a worm for their hungry chicks, or even a proverbial dandelion sneaking a bold display in the newly mown and weeded lawn.

And likewise, when I was working to change a poor habit or trying to establish more effective mental processes, other ideas might surface that could be equally as important, or in some occasions more so. For an example I'm sharing an idea that I've really worked on that won't be embarrassing as some of the others haven't met with too much success in changing poor habits. A positive one is learning to handle incoming paper the least amount of times; preferable once. I've learned to make one of three choices: toss it directly into the recycle bin, put it into a predetermined appropriate file such as: to pay, tax records, letters to answer etc., or my third choice is to place it into a maybe box if I needed time to reconsider..

Unexpected disappointments crop up in the garden walks as they do when implementing carefully thought-out mental planning. One year when Harold's rows of extra-sweet "Sugar & Cream" roasting ears were about ready to harvest, we decided to wait one more day before preparing them for the freezer. A bad decision, as the coons thought the corn was just right for harvest that night!! The next morning the corn was either stripped, exposing the bare cob, or spoiled with the shucks partially remove and imprinted with little paw marks that made it unsafe to eat. A recent example of a poor mental choice was waiting too long to sell financial stocks.

Change is ongoing, whether we call it global warming in nature or encounter it as a result of our own poor judgment. One of life's profound ongoing lessons is learning how to cope with it.

Honor & Exercise; Your Right to Vote--*October 22, 2006*

Voter registration and turnout in the U S remains the lowest in the industrialized world. In 1988, 37% of potential voters failed to register and barely 50% (of them) bothered to vote in the presidential election....George H. Bush became president with the support of only 27% of the people. Webster's New Universal Encyclopedia,

October is the month that the press and citizens begin to take serious note of candidates seeking offices in the fall elections. The candidates, themselves, have been trying for months to convince voters that they are the ones deserving of the public's big X on Election Day. As Election Day approaches, history and memories of people seeking to vote in past elections flood both my mind and heart.

Yesterday, my son called me to discuss some of this year's candidates. As it was in my birth family, the importance of being informed and voting has passed to my children. They recall meeting candidates, helping to hand out cards and putting up posters; even for their Grandfather; now deceased, Dad and me; as all of us had been candidates at separated times in the past.

When I was a child growing up in the segregated south my Dad had served as a Voter's Registrar in North Carolina. At that time, people wanting to vote had to prove they were literate. This was prior to the great Civil Rights Movement, when whites had easier access to schools than black people.

Long ago, my Dad had a simple test for literacy, which he administered equally to everyone seeking to register. He handed each of the potential voters a current copy of the local newspaper and then asked the applicant to read him a paragraph. At times, he had been pressured to be more lenient towards whites, who could not read, but he did not yield.

After many years of struggles and confrontations, all literacy tests and poll taxes were finally declared illegal in 1964, with the ratification of

the XXIV Amendment to the U.S. Constitution,
Women had struggled and protested for many years prior to winning the vote.

Above my bed, I display a lovely handmade friendship quilt in place of a headboard. I cherish the seventy-five year old (plus) quilt which was given to me a few years ago. It holds many loving memories for me as I personally had known many of the women who so long ago had pieced the quilt blocks and embroidered her name on it to honor a special lady: Miss Eva Gardner. She then had assisted the women of her community; in their homes during childbirth and times of illness. Later in her life she was my loving neighbor.

It makes me count my blessings when I recall that most of the women who made the beautiful quilt. As, some who were my relatives, did not have the right to vote when they were born.

The XIX Amendment to our U. S. Constitution, which was ratified on August 18, 1920, finally had given women; who were citizens and of legal age, the right to vote.

In total, great sacrifices have been made through the years by untold numbers to give all citizens of legal age; the right to vote.

Every time I cast my ballot, I am remind it is a privilege, as women and many others had entered the 20th Century without voting rights.

Keep in mind as you vote: millions of people from around the world would like to exchange places with you.

Exercising our right to vote now can help our democracy to be there for our children's children.

Animals Homes are Also Caught in the Meltdown—
July 3, 2009

Today I sat on my screened porch, reading an article about the housing meltdown, when a small bird caught my eye. It appeared to be flying into the screen wire and then disappearing. Shortly, it returned and I laid my paper down to observe it more closely.

I saw it landing on the outside of screen and literally walking up the screen the remaining two feet or so to the top and then hopping into the roof enclosure near a rafter. I also noticed a stem of what appeared to be dried grass trailing behind, much longer that the length of the bird's body. As the bird made trip after trip carrying bits of straw and dried grass, I knew it was building a nest to house its unborn babies.

After reading the article about the crash of the housing market in the United Sates, I thought about the many families who had worked as hard as this industrious little bird to provide a home for their own families, then losing them during our nation's ongoing financial downturn. This reminded me that the animal world is not immune to losses either. Weather conditions, as well as animals of prey, can destroy their homes which they have instinctively created for their families.

Humans have been given the power to reason and think. However, we do not always fully exercise this gift, and it often does not serve us as well as instinctive guidance does for animals. There is strong research that indicates humans have been using their powers to build, create and market products that harm other species in the animal world as well as themselves.

Every living thing on earth shares earth's air and water. Tobacco is one example of a product that man has marketed around the world; no one any longer has doubts about its being hazardous.

Global warming, which many believe has been enhanced by man's use of fossil fuels, along with other man-made problems, is destroying the habitant for many animals. Some scientists have reported that the warming in the arctic areas has the potential to eliminate polar bears and some other animal species during the first half of this century.

The good news is: mankind, who created some of our world-wide environmental problems, has the potential to do an about-face and to begin cleaning up our environment. Sad to say, earlier, our country had not been the world's leader in promoting "greener standards." Perhaps that is because we are the world's second largest offender (next to China) when it comes to polluting, even though we are not the second largest in population.

Some major greening legislation is now in our U S Congress, as the House of Representatives recently passed legislation on greening our schools as a start.

There's a vital role that each one of us can play in the greening of our earth by beginning in our homes and community. Our environmental changes can certainly impact our children's lives as well as those of our animal friends.

Circumstances Impact Time--*May 10, 2007*

Before you judge another --- just to lay him on the shelf, It would be a
splendid plan to take a walk around yourself. -- Helen Welshimer
When under stress, normal niceties do not always suffice or fill the gap.
Time and value are words that we could readily define under ordinary
circumstances; however, there are instances when these seemingly
simple words do not necessarily mean the same thing to everyone.

Take time -- it's a piece of cake to define an hour as 60 minutes, a day as
24 hours and a week as seven days -- that is, if things are going
smoothly.

We find entirely different experiences when we spend these same lengths
of time in pain, grief or fear. In some of these circumstances, time seems
to be without end.

Many of us do not know the value of the time our parents had or
continue to invest in us. They began lovingly providing for our needs at
birth and no doubt will continue as long as they have breath.

Some of us who now have children understand why parenting is a loving
time commitment without end. Our parents persevered in caring and
loving us long after we thought we were fully in charge of our lives.

Defining this kind of time commitment brings me to the term 'value,'
another word with diverse meanings. One meaning of value is also
closely associated with and somehow conveyed to us by caring parents.
The simplest definition of value may be monetary; however, that's not
always a correct assumption. We know the value of $1 or $1,000 but do
we know the value of one million dollars? Our government sometimes
tosses the word millions around as we might handle loose pocket change.
If you are like me, dreams have been my main connection to values in
the millions.

But I want to discuss values that do not have price tags, yet have
profoundly influenced our lives and determine how we resolve issues.
What is the value of friends? What is the value of loving parents?

The value of friends might best be realized in their absence. I can't
imagine what my life would have been like without friends and loving
parents! Although I have experienced times of separation from friends,
and my parents died more than 20 years ago, both collectively have
given me the gifts of love and stability.

Memories of my parents continue to provide love and guidance. When I currently have difficult decisions to make, I recall and draw upon their loving examples, which are stored in my heart.

Friends and parents have in the past, present, and will continue in the future to influence how we utilize time and apply our values. Thus, let's remember these positive influences in our lives whenever we are tempted to judge others who do not have them.

After Three Score and Ten--*July 20, 2003*

Why is it that we do not freely talk about the priorities and needs that exist for people during their post three-score and ten years of life? I have named this period: The Third Stage of Life. It is a well-known fact that preparing for any endeavor increases its chances of success. Statistics tell us that many Americans will live the last 1/3 of their lives after age 70. Thus, early on, it is important for us to gain insight and knowledge as to what will become critical needs during The Third Stage of Life, a stage, which we all hope to live and enjoy to our maximum potential.

Our society spends enormous amounts of time learning about and preparing for: career choices, marriage, parenthood and all the child rearing stages; pre-school, adolescent, teen and etc., but little on the years past age seventy. Sometimes, I think society as a whole labels the Third Stage of Life as the, "Waiting to be planted time," while putting their head into the sand and refusing to acknowledge that the frailties of age will ever come down the pike for them or anyone they know.

Considerable information is now available on how to prepare for The Third Stage of life, both financially and medically, although it is not accessible in a uniform manner. However, there is little preparation on how to cope with the psychological and other normal aging changes that confront people as they enter The Third Stage of Life, which some have erroneously called "The Golden Age."

Research and technological advances have extended Americans' life expectancy well beyond that of earlier generations and now predict that many born in this century will live to be one hundred years old; meaning that more people will experience the Third Stage of Life than have ever done so in past generations.

The Baby Boomers generation attracts much attention as they continue to advance through the various stages of their lives. This generation has made its needs known due to the large increase in our nation's population, which they first created in the post-WWII era. Now they are again in the news because they will begin creating greater demands on our government's dwindling Social Security and Medicare Trust Funds. The *AARP Bulletin* reports one in four Americans will be in the 65 or older age bracket later in this century.

What is wrong with teaching the needs and special requirements of The Third Stage of Life, even as we now teach parenting, money management, career choices, and many other subjects that impacts students' future lives? Gaining realistic knowledge of future needs can help each citizen to be prepared for the time when they can no long work and become more dependent on the services that others provide. Our society can rise to the challenge as it has, in the past.

It is conceivable that during this century a married couple in their forties will be caregivers for three generations: their children, their parents as they reach the age of 75 as well as their grandparents who may be coping at the same time with the unique problems that come with being 100 years of age.

My granddaughter reported to me that she has recently put into effect several new ways of saving money that she learned last semester in a college Consumer Ed class, because the information applied to her life. Children and young adults who today see their parents trying to cope and assist with the problems that their aging parents and grandparents are experiencing, could also benefit from factual knowledge, teaching them how to manage more effectively when like experiences occur in their lives.

We've learned that advanced warning and training in how to prepare for a tornado or a hurricane increase the survival rate. Thus, it seems that early training and preparation in coping with problems relating to longevity would help families do the same.

As I continue to research this topic, I would welcome your input as to the areas and issues that have given you or members of your family the most difficulty while trying to maintain the maximum quality of life during your or others' Third Stage of this journey we love: called life.

A Man Who Never Forgets his Roots

September 3, 2003

Burnham Neal like many of you; grew up in Toledo. Throughout his life, he has never stopped caring about his home area; although his successful business endeavors have been far reaching.

Burnham's parents were Edgar and Lora Ann Neal. His father was a local businessman selling gas and serving his community, on the local school board. Mr. Edgar Neal established the Neal Oil Company more than 75 years ago. Mrs. Neal had been a kindergarten teacher at one time and she maintained a lifelong interest in education.

Burnham, a 1940 graduate of Toledo High School and his only sister Rosemary, graduated in the Class of 1943. He joined his father in business in the 1940's. In 1967, Burnham purchased and remodeled the Toledo Grade and High School, using the building for the tire store, office and warehouse. This decision enabled the Neal family to maintain the corporate headquarters of their business in Toledo.

I first knew Burnham when my family resettled in Toledo after WWII. Then, I was a student at Toledo High School and Burnham was a handsome bachelor who all the girls admired. It has been during my tenure as a member of the Neal Foundation Board that I have learned how much he cares about our community and the many ways in which he has given back to our area in leadership and financial resources, without display.

Burnham along with his mother and sister organized the Neal Foundation in 1976 "for educational, charitable, and community development purposes designed to promote the welfare of central Illinois."

The successful fulfillment of the Neal Foundation's goals during the past quarter of a century have touched the lives of many people in a positive way and will continue to do so because when you help students and others organizations to achieve their goals, they are enabled give back to our community. Yearly the Neal Foundation has awarded scholarships to students attending both, Eastern Illinois University and Lakeland College. In a further effort to promote education, the Neal Foundation yearly honors an exemplary teacher, giving a teacher selected by his//her, peers a financial stipend to use as he/ she chooses.

The Neal Foundation has and continues to supports many facilities which daily serve our community. They donated the land for the Cumberland Life Center; the Neal Park, which has tennis courts and other equipment for community use. The Neal Park now has an attractive entrance on Rte 121.

The Foundation has given to The Sarah Bush Lincoln Health Center, including the Toledo Clinic, The Sumpter Township Library and many more community projects, which have improved the quality of life for area citizens.

Burnham and his wife Nancy had been long termed; anonymous supporters of Eastern Illinois University's Foundation, in 1997 EIU honored Burnham and Nancy by naming their annual awards: The Burnham and Nancy Neal Philanthropy Awards. Since then Nancy and Burnham along with Burnham's sister Rosemary; now deceased have given the funds to build The EIU Welcoming Center, which serves students from throughout Illinois.

Many people, in our community and beyond have been and will continue to be the recipients of the gifts and services, which the Neal Family quietly chooses to give back to the community where, they first established their successful business.

Taxes, Possessions, & Death--*April 17, 2006*

"Death and taxes are sure things. " Anon

We have survived tax season one more time; hopefully we can find ample reasons to remind ourselves of their value in a civilized society as we take a breather and move on to other issues. Today, I want to explore the impact of possessions on our lives. They have a grip similar to that of death and taxes.

What are possessions? Webster is not much help as he lists everything from property to wisdom as possessions. At one time, I had naively thought my children were my possessions. However, only through independence, could they or anyone have matured and become contributing members in our society.

This topic came to mind recently when a person told me about her friend who was stressed-out and depressed, as she prepared to move into smaller quarters, which allowed her to keep only a small part of the items that she had collected during her lifetime. That is a happening which many of us may face sometime during our lives.

It is good to think about what it means while we are acquiring "VIP stuff (at least to us)." I used to collect Fiesta Ware and could write a book about the impact of collecting as a hobby.

Whatever your age, give some serious thought about what you now choose to collect, as acquiring and caring for possessions will consume valuable time and resources throughout your life, which might otherwise be put to better uses.

As an example, let's look at books, a possession, which most of us have in our homes. Did we have anything to do with their creation? Probably not, would be the average person's response. We bought the right to read it and learn something from another person's labor and data. Is there value in possessing the books, which our taxes give us, free access to at our local library? Probably not, with the exceptions of references material and/or those books which have special meaning. A bottom line test of a book's importance could be similar to one used when you are cleaning out your clothes closet. Ask yourself how long has it been since you had an occasion to wear or in the case of books, to use them. Passing books on gives others the opportunity to read and learn, plus lessening the need for us to dust and secure more bookcases.

Examine your major possessions, which have been labeled as necessities. We gained legal possession or title to our homes or other property when we made the final payment. However, I'm sure that you like me, receive a yearly tax statement and will continue to do so as long as you possess the property. In addition, there are other ongoing payments such as utilities, insurance and upkeep.

Thus, we must conclude there are few physical things which any of us truly possess without some restrictions. Reality teaches us that whenever our heart ceases to beat we will not possess any physical property.

Is it a good thing to strive and use our numbered days to possess those things, which are beyond what we really need and actually enjoy?

A thought to ponder: there are no penalties or taxes on the happy memories that we gathered during our sojourn. They do not consume space nor create extra chores, thus leaving us with more time for living when we learn not to let our possessions possess us.

LITTLE WORDS, WHICH COMPLICATE--*September 5, 2004*

A collection of dwellings becomes a neighborhood when people talk to one another. Dr. Ellsworth Kalas.

Words are the basic transportation vehicles in our communication system. But not exclusively, looks, body language and touch are also integral parts. Early on, I recall my mother sending clear messages with a stern look and/or placing both hands on her hips. Equally important, I remember her loving approval when she gently touched me with her hand.

As a reference source, for additional insight into understanding the meaning of *word*, I switch from WEBSTER to my ROGET 21ST CENTURY THESAURUS to look at its synonyms. At first glance, I noticed *word* was separated into six different categories: discussion; statement; unit of language, the one I have chosen to explore; command; promise; and password, which I immediately associated with security on my computer.

Roget defined units of language as: concept, designation, expression, idiom, lexeme, locution, morpheme, name, phrase, sound, term, usage, utterance and vocals. Needless to say, some meanings are clearer than others.

The above research is to share with you the many usages which the word UP has in our daily communication. A friend sent me an e-mail about this versatile two-letter unit in our language. She did not know its source. The title is:

DID YOU EVER STOP TO THINK ABOUT UP?

It's easy to understand UP, meaning towards the sky or at the top of a list, but when we waken in the morning, why do we wake UP?

At a meeting, why does a topic come UP?

Why do we speak UP and why are the officers UP for election and why is it UP to the secretary to write UP a report?

We call UP our friends, we use it to brighten UP a room, polish UP the silver. We warm UP the leftovers and clean UP the kitchen. We lock UP the house and some guys fix UP the old car.

At other times, the little word has special meanings.

People stir UP trouble, line UP for tickets, work UP an appetite, and think UP excuses. … In addition, this UP is confusing: A drain must be opened UP because it is stopped UP. ... We seem to be pretty mixed UP about UP.

To be knowledgeable of the proper uses of UP, look UP the word in the dictionary. In a desk size dictionary, it takes UP almost 1/4th the page and definitions add UP to about 30.

If you are UP to it, you might try building UP a list of the many ways UP is used. It will take UP a lot of your time, but if you don't give UP, you may wind UP with a hundred or more.

 One could go on and on, but I'll wrap it UP, for now my time is UP, so I'll shut UP.....

Clarity is up to each of us. No wonder we sometimes misunderstand the message another person is trying to convey and vice versa. Let's keep trying to achieve clarity. Could you imagine what our world would be like without words?

Living Creates Stress--*October 9, 2005*

Stress is a signal that we are alive. If we were not experiencing any stress, there would be no activity not even a heartbeat. We do not want to eliminate all stress-simply learn how to reduce it when it becomes unmanageable and harmful.

Eons ago, when I was in the midst of my career as a social worker, I had a poster on my bulletin board which showed a zebra losing his stripes and his legs becoming entangled in them as they fell around the zebra's hind feet. On the poster the zebra is looking back helpless, not knowing what to do about it. The caption at the top reads in large letters, *I'M HAVING STRESS.*

That's the way it often is with us.   When we are in the midst of stress, we can diagnose it without knowing how to manage it.

I find preventive planning is one of the best ways to lessen stress. Admittedly, that is not always possible but it can work in coping with those situations that we know in advance will create stress. When you have choices, do not plan those events back to back.

Relaxation is the enemy of stress. Every day find some time to engage in activities such as walking or whatever forms of exercise you do. Spend some time reading, meditating, and journaling or allow time for crafts or whatever is most relaxing for you.

When unanticipated stress surfaces, rely on brief intervals of mental imaging by focusing your thoughts on past pleasant events. Store your favorites and then you can mentally recall them when the need arises. I've shared many times my favorite way of reducing stress: walking on the beach and hearing the rhythm of the waves as they dissolve on the sand, or I also tune in some of my favorite music. Another favorite mental imaging technique from my childhood is hearing rain falling softly on a tin roof.

Many times, stress arises from being an adult caregiver for someone in your family, whether it is a sick child, spouse or parent.

You may be the child that your parents or other family members have always looked to for help, in the past. Do not assume that responsibility alone.

When it is a parent that needs extra care, involve everyone in your family from the beginning and work out a plan to share the responsibility. If other members of your family live away or have a job which prevents them from giving hands-on care, let them help pay for adult day care or for someone to come in and give you a time off, or they could plan to provide the weekend care. <u>Don't hesitate to ask</u>. Accept offers of help from friends and neighbors join a support group. There's much to learn from others who are experiencing a similar situation.

Prolonged, unrelieved stress can be very damaging to your health. Consult with your doctor or a counselor if you are not able to work out a plan to control or lessen the stress in your daily life; otherwise, you may become the one needing the caregiver.

Ageing & Change--*June 29, 2004*

"Ageing has not changed how I feel on the inside as there; I am the same person I always was." Judge Wm. J. Hill~ 1982

Now that I have passed my own "three score and ten" benchmark, I am actively reviewing how my family and others before me had dealt both with and modeled growing older. I am discovering there are some issues in my life that age definitely does change while others remain constant. The above quote was my father's response to a question as to how age had affected his thinking at age 77 after he had experienced a crippling stroke, which fortunately had left his mind intact.

When I h asked my father the above question, I had been preparing a speech on ageing to present at a national convention of the Community

College Trustees Association. The Illinois Community College where I then served, Lake Land Community College (LLCC), as a trustee, had an outstanding program, which served its 15 county rural district's seniors. At that time, I did not understand how my father could have responded in such a positive manner; however, now I clearly understand. Ageing was then and is yet today a very difficult stage of life to define, as it is fraught with ongoing changes, both voluntary and involuntary.

My view as to who is old has also changed. When I was in grade school, I thought anyone a few classes ahead of me was old. I also remember a bit about longing to be older (not lately), even when I thought if I ever reached age sixteen, it would be the perfect grown-up age. Not so long ago I had the illusion of still thinking I was middle-aged; however, having two children past fifty burst that bubble. Now on some days when I first awake in the morning, arthritis makes me feel old. After I move about a bit, that notion usually disappears, and I again think as I did as a child, that anyone older than I is old.

Character and values are two issues which ageing strengthens. My former ambitions and goals are now modified. Achievement and success take on different meanings, particularly in the area of competition, which is for the greater part non-existent. Co-existence seems to be more the norm, with a strong desire to reach out and assist my peers.

Conformity and freedom of choice are two important issues which have changed me in a positive way. In retirement, I no longer feel any need to conform to the expectations of my working years. I now have more freedom of choice, even regarding necessary tasks. If I am in the midst of a good book, I can finish reading it if I so choose. Another plus is my husband and I can take vacations without planning in order for them to fit into both the children's and our own schedules. Most days, I do not think having accumulated more years is a big thing, as I always prefer it to the alternative. I am keenly aware, and logic confirms, that more of my life's days are behind me than ahead. This awareness has given me a greater appreciation for each new sunrise and I give added thought as how to best use the gift of each new day. In total, I find this stage of my life less stressful and more enjoyable than my teen years and give some credence to the thought that "The best may be yet to come." Of course, there is always the slight possibility that memory has dimmed my perceptions

CHAPTER 6
FAMILY = LINKS OF LOVE

A Bit of Family History--*October 23, 2011*

Occasionally, when people ask why I write my column, I often respond, 'Probably because both my parents had done so." When I was a child living on our bright leaf tobacco farm in Eastern North Carolina (N C), where I was born, and my parents jointly had written a human interest column for *The Raleigh News and Observer,* which was published in our state capital. Post WWII, when my parents had settled on their farm in Cumberland County my Mom had written a column entitle, "Down Cumberland Way" for the *Journal Gazette* in Mattoon.

Recently, while trying to sort through old boxes of "stuff", which I had saved during almost 63 years of marriage, I ran across one of my Mom's columns that was "heart rendering" as it was written in 1954 shortly before my Dad , William J. "Bill" Hill, was first elected Cumberland County's Judge . He was re-elected and served continuously until retiring as a Associated Circuit Judge in 1966. Dad was the last Lay Judge (not an attorney) to serve in Illinois. My Dad had no formal degrees in education as he was self educated and never stopped learning. He had helped to organize the Illinois Farmer's Union and served as its first acting president in 1968. Earlier he had served as Spring Point's Supervisor.

A few days before his death, we had celebrated his 77th birthday, with friends and extended family at a Pig Roast held at my farm home.

On the night, my Dad lay dying in the hospital, the staff moved him into a private room so my two sisters and I could remain at his bedside and talk with privacy. His mind was clear as we reviewed our past life as a family, and he shared some of his goals for our future! My older sister said, "Dad, I need to hear you say, "I love you." Dad was astounded and replied, "Your Mother and I have worked to provide food, clothing, shelter and education for you, plus fulfilled our goal of helping all seven of our children to attend college. Isn't that saying I love you?"

Dad had given his body for medical science education and research to be a learning tool for students.

Billie will print Mom's column next week as I thought you would find it interesting. Thus, I am sharing some background information this week for clarification.

Dad had enlisted in the Army Air Force in the 1920's. He was stationed at Chanute Field in Rantoul, Illinois in 1925; where he had met and served with Oakley Cutright, who was dating Lois Huffman, of Toledo, who was my Mom's cousin. Oakley brought my Dad, a native North Carolinian to Toledo as a blind date for my Mom when she was a senior at Toledo High School. They instantly fell "head over heels" in love and were secretly married after a few dates; unbeknown to my grandparents as Mom was a cherished daughter. My Sparks's grandparents and Mom then had lived on their farm located in the north edge of Toledo where John Wilson's barn now stands.

Although married, Mom graduating from the top of her THS class in 1925. Mom took some training classes and began teaching in a one room country school until my Dad was discharged from the Army.

Dad was born and had grown up on a farm in N C. but after his discharge, he   had tried working awhile, for Lou Barger; a Cumberland County farmer.

Then my parents returned to N C where my Dad was more familiar with farming and purchased a bright leaf tobacco farm. Our family lived and worked there for several years, until Dad voluntarily joined the U S Navy during WWII; although at his age and having 5 minor children, he never would have been drafted. He felt that he could not live with himself unless he enlisted because of Hitler's invasion and atrocities in Europe. He was assigned to serve on the training staff at the Norfolk Naval Training Station, where our family rejoined him. After WWII our family returned to Illinois.

My Dad, who had enjoyed reading and learning all of his life, wanted his children to develop and share his interests. He had a particular love for history, geography and government and wanted my sibs and me to be well-versed in these areas. I guess he succeeded, as after college, I had taught elementary Social Studies, for awhile. Thus, even as we(my sisters, Carolyn and Pat ,and I) worked as children, hoeing in the fields, as growing tobacco and cotton were labor intensive crops during the 1930's We practiced and learned the names of all the counties in N C, our presidents, the names of our states and their capitals, plus who made up President Roosevelt's cabinet and what their duties were. I still recall that he had appointed the first woman ever to serve in the position, as the Secretary of Labor.

Dad's hobby was building and operating his "ham" amateur radio station; and he used it to expand our understanding of geography. He operated both on the code and speaker bands. Dad let us children, speak to his contacts on the 160 meter broadcast band and we could ask the operator questions about where they lived and then we would have to get out the atlas and/or our geography books to find where the ham operator lived on our maps. Any time we had homework, we got a waiver from our household chores and we probably took advantage of that privilege, particularly on the nights, it was our turn to clean up the kitchen.

I hope you enjoy reading my Mom's column that she had written almost sixty years ago, that will substitute for mine next week. You'll quickly note that she was a better writer!!

Birthday's Markers Along Life's Journey--*April 10, 2011*

I've recently experienced my 80th birthday with flowers and being a special guest at meals, plus a surprise party with a cake and all the trimmings hosted by my friends and neighbors. It was a pleasant occurrence that left me speechless. I had gone to a friends' home for dinner and when we had finished eating and having coffee, I heard a commotion and in came a house full of neighbors carrying a huge cake made to look like the numbers: 80.

The following day my niece, Gale Titus Quinn, and her husband Jack drove down from the Sarasota area, where they have recently retired and took me to a delicious seafood restaurant overlooking the water. Thus, my birthday celebrations continued for two days. Needless to say, I enjoyed turning 80, but had not expected all the attention.

I guess that turning 80 is a bit of a landmark like it had been when I had reached the age of fifty. As I'm a "saver of stuff". I looked at some of the cards and paper from past birthdays that are beginning to turn a bit yellow with age. I inwardly tried to measure some of the many ways my body had aged in the, same lapse of thirty years. I decided not to go there. Nevertheless, you who have already travel this same journey know and I don't want to frighten my other readers who are on the road.

One thing I found, when looking back, was a poem my older sister Carolyn Hill Glasson had written for my fiftieth birthday. Some of you will remember Carolyn, who is now deceased, as she had taught English at Cumberland for a period of time. Here's her poem written in April of 1981:

Repeat Celebration

By Carolyn Hill Glasson

This sister of mine is straight and tall,
 Said to be square,
but a glint in her eye that allows for
some speculation.
Mary 'Liza is a combination. Well, that she is!
A product of a mixed marriage. What do you think of that?
Her pappy is a rustic charming cuss, a
Southerner from eastern North Carolina,
Where cotton and tobacco and moonshine were
What the gentle men talked about
during those warm,
moist and fragrant hours
of youth.
Then her pappy skipped that country
ran away from home
To wear the Army Air Force khaki,
Goggles and all.
Soon, he. being stationed at Chanute
In Illinois,
Was invited by a local lad to Toledo, and
There he met his match,
A bright and beautiful, tall and adventuresome
        daughter
of a conservative,
very particular
Cumberland County farmer and his equally particular
family adoring wife.
William and Mary, from opposing fields,
 Across the Mason Dixon line,

Had grandfathers who faced each other where some did not survive
        the nation's battering Civil War.
Mary 'Liza being the third girl born to farmers,
who thought they needed
A big strapping son, to plow that field
        harrow again.
And tote that tub of just pulled tobacco plants,
Was called by her gentle man, Grandfather John,
Re-Peat, meaning another one!
Little that bothered Mary 'Liza and she grew
        straight and tall,
        anyhow,
And learned quickly, helped along by having
two older sisters to observe as they
thrashed their wings
seeking longed for adventures
And depleted their energy tangled in the undergrowth.
Mary 'Liza being down the line.
took her time.
spotted daylight
In the distance there
And avoided the tangles encountered by the older two.
Such success she had, one becoming aware of her qualities
        of mind
And come to expect astuteness, as routine.
Somehow, the picture with Mary 'Liza as Chairman
        of the Board of Directors,
        all men.
Most quite prominent,
And her centered just so
        is natural,
like that's what she was trained to do.
This third daughter of a considerably mixed marriage
        between the youngest son
Of a North Carolina "Southerner" gentle farmer,
        and the bright-eyed apple
        from the eye

Of a careful, proud and ambitious, mid-west farmer,
Mary 'Liza will continue to ladle the gravy she chooses
        As she has already
Carefully seasoned and exactingly baked her main course
        during her first half century! (end of quote.)

Keep in mind, this was written by my loving oldest sister who was no doubt a bit prejudiced, as to my skills.

Carolyn's Birthday--*August 9, 2013*

Today is Carolyn's birthday. If she were living, she'd be eighty-six. I wish I could send her a card. I guess I can in my heart. Perhaps that's why I recently discovered the witty and interesting 50th Birthday package that she had spent considerable time assembling along with writing the poem for my first half-century birthday . However, I know as a fact when she had a goal her poetry flowed freely, as when our Dad died she wrote a lengthy informative poem about Dad's life in less than a week because we read it at his memorial service. I loved it so; I had to split it up into two separate weeks, when I shared it with you a few years ago, in my column.

Today and during the next few weeks, I want to include some happenings that occurred during the first fifty years of my life that Carolyn had listed in my 50th Birthday big collection of stuff.

Many of her writings include historical and political dates, plus some grim realities of the Depression Years. Plus a few humorous stories thrown in, that had significance for our family. Carolyn hadn't listed any sources so I can't credit them other than to general knowledge. Many of them will be known to you also, if you had been as interested in governmental events and history; as our Dad was. He had continued to teach us, as we worked in the fields. I've shared before, that when my sibs and I were children, we had to exercise our minds and kept them busy learning subject matter appropriate for: History, Poly Science and/or Geography 101. Perhaps that was why Carolyn includes dates and names of governmental reps and their actions, in my birthday package, maybe as a bit of satire.

First, I want to relate a story Carolyn loved to share about her first date in high school. One might entitle it: "Sometimes: Families Teach Their

Children Dissimilar Things."

Carolyn shared that she had been careful to listen to the evening(radio news) the night before, with Lowell Thomas and H. V. Kaltenborn reporting, to be updated on current events and what was going on in our capital, as well as checking out our daily paper The *Raleigh News and Observer.* Then, she thought about what she would wear and how to fix her hair so she would be fully prepared, both physically and mentally, for her first big date. She said after the young man picked her up and they were driving towards town, she began to bombard him with the national news out of Washington and how N C. reps had voted on recent legislation. She said he didn't reply and looked at her like she was from "Outer Mongolia." She didn't know what the problem was but perceived she had not said the right things and she didn't initiate any more conversation. Needless to say, that young man didn't ask for another date.

Later, when she discussed the situation with her girl friends, they said for a starter, you should have discussed what was going on in sports and had shared the latest scores to have impressed him! Of course then Carolyn didn't know anything about national sports or who sports teams were other than some boys who performed on her local high school teams. This was when families were still coping with the effects of the Great Depression and there would have been no funds or time for extra curricula events. Perhaps, our family's early teaching on historical and political issues is the same reason that I have little or no interest in national sports today.

I did pay attention and attend when Roger played football at Cumberland High School. In fact, he lectured me about not coming out on the field if he was ever on the bottom of a pileup, as he thought that would be the height of embarrassment if I did. (And I probably would have, especially, if he had been slow about getting up)!

Here are some average US yearly salaries from the 1930's that Carolyn included in my 50th Birthday package:

Pilot $8,000.

Coal miners $723.

Maid $260. (Yes, women's wages were at the bottom.)

Hired Hand $260. (I think some kind of housing and a hog to butcher were included as fringes for most tenants.)

Lawyer $4,218. (So what else is new?)

More next week from the happenings that occurred during my first 50 years of life on Mother Earth, according to my sister, Carolyn.

Subliminal Journey

"The seed ye sow, another reaps...." Shelley

Revisiting the messages, both psychological and intellectual, that have shaped my personality is an emotional trip down memory lane. I can clearly recall some of them today.

My Father's cardinal rule was, "Don't be dumb and do stupid things', always think first." Of course, he kept repeating it, as I never completely met his standard (still trying).

Mother's was "Do your best and be patient, loving and kind, then things will work out in time." Time has proved her message to be comforting and good advice in spite of the fact I was then seeking immediate answers.

My Grandma Hill taught me her dictum of being frugal by example." A willful waste makes a woeful want" was her favorite saying. As a child, I never quite understood the "woeful want" part other than it didn't sound good. She demonstrated how to avoid "the willful waste part" by the chores she assigned me.

In season, Grandma sent me to the orchard to pick up a bucket full of the wormy fruit that had fallen on the ground. I always wished I could pick the fruit off the tree, before it fell, but that was never my assignment. Thinly and with patience, she peeled each piece of the fruit cutting out the decayed and wormy section with her trusty pocketknife, often cutting away more than she kept. I devoured the salvaged slices of fruit until she thought I had enough, and then the remainder went into her blue granite pan for the next meal. I then carried the scraps to the chickens. Today, I am reminded that Grandma was an "early environmentalist" faithfully recycling everything. Grandma had impressive proof that her thrifty ways paid off as she always had some greenbacks hidden in an inside pocket on her underskirt.

My Grandpa Hill's message was "Too bad you were born a girl." Previously I've shared why he named me Pete (because he wanted a grandson). I suspect he unknowingly helped me to develop my feminist attitudes. I regret that his lifespan did not prevail permitting us to fully know each other. I'm sure we could have discovered redeeming graces in each other.

My sister Carolyn's hypothetical response was "I'm wondering if you have thought about...." and then go on to suggest some workable choices to my current dilemma, in such a subtle way that I sometimes thought the resolution was my own idea.

My "city" aunt worked hard all day cooking and cleaning in her boarding house. She then enjoyed relaxing and visiting in her swing under the magnolia tree in the cool of the evening. Even now I can still hear her melodious laugh which pealed forth as I played "hide n seek" with my city cousins, during my families' evening visits into town. I reasoned that working all day wasn't so bad if you could enjoy the evening. More impressive was the fact my cousins had lovely "store bought" clothes and even an inside bathroom in their home.

These early childhood memories which played a role in shaping my behavior and values may bring to mind for you some of the people, ideas and incidents that molded your outlook and behavior.

Remembering Childhood Chores: Blended With Fun
Activities--*May 2, 2010*

As I was searching for a topic to write about; I made a list of some things that I recalled doing as a child for fun as well as field work and chores that many kids don't do today.

I need to explain that one of the reasons was because I grew up on a bright leaf tobacco farm in Eastern North Carolina. I'm sure many of you might reply that you also grew up on a farm. Then life on a tobacco farm was very labor intensive involving the whole family and different from the Midwestern farm lifestyle, where we raised our children. Now, as in Illinois, machinery does some of the farm jobs which were once done by hand, but then, there was jobs for everyone including children by the time they were old enough to enter school.

One of my first jobs was being the "water boy." That involved carrying quart or half-gallon mason jars to workers in the fields. This is one job that my kids also did for their Dad.

Another job was sitting near the yard pens that contained small chicks in order to scare the hawks away as they would swoop down and quickly select a small chick for their lunch. And of course the chickens had to be fed and provided water, So the younger children who didn't work in the fields had the job of turning by hand the corn Sheller, which removed the corn from the cobs in order to fill the chicken feeders, plus filing the water pans. Later in the day we gathered the eggs.

Then, there was the never ending job of keeping the wood box filled in the kitchen and the one by the living room stove during chilly weather, as this was before electricity or gas was available in the rural areas.

One of my earliest jobs in the field was searching the leaves of the small tobacco plants, both front and back, for worms in order to kill them. This was a job I hated most because tobacco worms were long and green, looking much like the tomato worms in today's gardens. This was before DDT and other chemicals, so it was necessary to pull their heads off. If you just threw them on the ground, they could return to the plants.

When I was old enough to handle a hoe, I went to the fields like my Mom and older sibs to chop the weeds out of both the tobacco and cotton fields.

When school was in session, immediately after getting off the bus we changed out of our school clothes to work in the building where the dried tobacco was sorted and tied in bundles in order to be sent to the market. Even though our hands were busy at work tying the dried tobacco in bundles, we used our minds to learn to spell the states and their capitals or to discuss other things we had learned at school that day. Some afternoons we also picked cotton and were paid a penny a pound. I assure you it took awhile to pick one pound of cotton! But it always was fun to have a penny to buy a Baby Ruth candy bar at the little store that was opened at school during my lunch hour. Of course, now there are no penny candy bars.

During the summertime after work, fun times included going to a nearby swimming hole to swim and play. Also the traveling bookmobile from our town's library came once a week to a cross road about a mile from our house. We walked there to return the books that we had read and also to checkout any other books which we had not read. I recall the excitement of occasionally finding a brand new book that had not been checked out! They always had a nice slick cover with a clean smell. Some summer mornings, when there were no chores, I would climb up into the Umbrella Tree in our front yard to hide and read my newest book while watching for our rural mail carrier in order to be the first to get the mail. My folk's subscribed to the *Saturday Evening Post*. I liked to be the first to get it and read the most recent chapter of the mystery serial novel, that all my family read. We would discussed it during mealtimes. Thus, I enjoyed being the first in the family to learn and tell "who done it"!

Also, in the fall when my Grandmother's grape arbor was fully ripened, we would go after our evening chores were finished and eat our fill of luscious grapes. Sometimes, I still can recall the luscious flavor, of the Scuppemongs. If we had to work very late, we couldn't go to eat grapes because the mosquitoes would eat us up.

When swimming and grapes were out of season, we often had foot races after working, which were enjoyable. I usually was given a handicap because I was the youngest and slowest participant.

Most of my classmates also lived on farms and had similar jobs at home. Thus, I never have felt that working as a child was out of the ordinary, but a good training experience as I learned early on many lessons which have proved helpful to me throughout my adult life.

Love Keeps on Giving--*August 21, 2001*

"What really matters is what you do with what you have.", Shirley Lord
Death is a subject we are reluctant to discuss. Our society provides us little training in how to cope with it in our loved ones' lives, or our own pending death, for that matter.

My secret heart was drained of understanding when my oldest sister Carolyn and my youngest brother Frank died. Their August birthdays have again caused memories of joy and sadness to swirl in my life, as I have reexamined the void created by their premature deaths.

Passages in living become easier for us when we are able to observe how others we love have successfully navigated them before we do.

Earlier in SISTERS, I shared with you what a profound influence Carolyn was in my life. Through her courageous living she was a strong influence and role model which helped me in my early childhood and continues yet today. Recently as I meditated on Carolyn and Frank's life and death, I learned new insights about death.

First I need to share some information about Frank's half-century sojourn on earth. He was stricken with schizophrenia during his last year in college as he was looking forward to a career in teaching. Then little was known about this damaging disease. It created havoc in Frank's life. My parents were devastated trying to find treatment for him. No one in my family was untouched by the ongoing struggle to find help for Frank as well as how to cope with his symptoms. At that time, there were no known support groups or little research. Over time, research has made a difference in treatment. His disease, with medications, was stabilized for longer periods of time and he experienced some return to normalcy. When my Father experienced a crippling stroke, Frank provided loving care for him at home. Frank's gift of care to my Dad was a vital one which none of his six sibs could provide. When my Father died, Frank assisted in Mother's ongoing care.

Frank often expresses his joy of being able to give back to his parents the gift of care which they had extended to him during most of his life.

Later, Frank became a leader in the group home where he lived the last years of his life. He served as editor of a supportive newspaper published by Effingham County Mental Health Board and taught self help classes, giving hope to his peers and their families.

Carolyn was the counselor in her local high school when a painful autoimmune disease struck her. During her sick leave she discovered her pain was more bearable when her mind was occupied helping her students. Swimming was the one exercise that lessened her pain. Upon her return to work. her principal consented to her using her lunch hour each day to swim at her local Y. In return, she worked overtime assisting seniors in locating and enrolling in the colleges which would help them achieve their maximum potential with scholarships or grants when eligible, while fulfilling her other counseling duties. All her life, she reached out, in her gentle but determined way helping others (from all walks of life) who crossed her path resolve conflicts or secure needed resources.

Thinking of the lives and the deaths of Carolyn and Frank has given me a new understanding.

It is: Dying successfully means living your life to its fullest and sharing your gifts of self throughout your allotted days, regardless of what kind of hand you have been dealt.

"Peace is my parting gift to you... ." John 14:27 -NEB

December's Enduring Gifts--*December 17, 2006*

December is a month of wonders, hope, and love, both temporal and holy. Nevertheless, it is easy to get entrapped in the stress of things we perceive to be necessary and end up with the feeling of never quite meeting one's expectations.

I'm sure you know the saying, "Something good can come out of everything." Being involved in a near fatal accident one week before Christmas when I was a young mother; etched this truth on my heart and forever changed how I celebrate Christmas. Since then Harold and I have not felt a need to exchange material gifts with each other, instead we share gifts of the heart.

My story begins long ago at our farm home, on a stormy night one week before Christmas. I had decided to make a quick trip to the then Hickory Corner store to pick up some items for Christmas baking. I bundled up Lily; my two and one-half year old daughter in her bright red wool coat and securely tied her matching red bonnet. I loved that coat that my cousin Olive Wilson had passed along to Lily when Alice had outgrown it. Roger being independent, grabbed his coat and raced us to the car. There had been a cross between rain and snow falling on my car as I turned on the wipers. Then my road was graveled and didn't seem slick. As I stopped to cross the Burma Road, I discovered too late that it was covered with a glaze of ice.

Monetarily, I collided with a car and began spinning out of control. Next thing I knew Lily was thrown from the back seat (before seat belts) head first breaking the windshield. My car turned sharply; throwing Lily on the floor board instead of through the broken windshield.

As I lay by Lily en route to the hospital, I could hardly distinguish her flesh from her red coat as all was soaked with blood as she lay very still in shock. Ed Lashment, who drove us to the hospital later, told me that he wouldn't have bet any money on Lily's chances of survival. Roger was not hurt and I had briefly been knocked unconscious and was hurting.

At the hospital, good things began to happen. The young doctor(who later became a surgeon) did a wonderful job of stitching Lily's face and neck back together, which when healed left little scarring.

Being a person of faith, I prayed while Lily was in surgery and the nurses were putting me in a hospital room and preparing a crib for Lily by my

177

bedside. I soon felt calmness within my heart and believed that Lily would live. I promised God anew that I would work to help others, in thanksgiving for Him giving the doctor wisdom to spare Lily's life.

Years later when I became a teacher and a child welfare social worker, I felt that I was given opportunities to work towards fulfilling that promise made long ago.

Harold, in a state of anxiety, soon joined me as he had come upon our wrecked car on his way home from work. I told him I knew that Lily would be o k. He thought I was still in shock from the collision.

Much later, the nurses gently laid Lily in the crib with her head bandaged and hooked her to support equipment and kept a close vigil throughout the night. (Today, Lily is a geriatric nurse.)

Dr. Supple shared that he had keep her anesthetized for repairs as long as he could safely do so. He reported that it took more than a hundred stitches to close the deep wounds on her face and neck and added, "She is very lucky to be alive as the deep cuts were near to her jugular vein." One week later on Christmas Eve, Lily and I returned home. Never had home looked so good!!! Somehow, it didn't matter that much of the hustle and bustle that I ordinarily had done to prepare for Christmas went unfinished.

The ultimate gift was awakening on Christmas morning, which was also our seventh wedding anniversary, with all of us together surrounded with the love and help of friends, neighbors and family.

I had learned and have not forgotten what gifts are vital.

Memories of Mother That Continue to Live--*2006*

For me, maturity means reacting, during a day, with calmness, consideration and friendliness to all the people with whom I come into contact. Frank Hill~ THEN-N-NOW

The only way I could communicate with my mother today is via memories and her love which I try to regenerate from within my heart. Heart-generated actions are easier to experience than to live and/or explain. I think you will understand as you recall your own mother's love if you like me must communicate today in memories.

My mother had taught by her actions.

At times, I was a slow learner when it came to actions from the heart. In fact, I was well into maturity (the gray-headed stage) before I discovered how to put into action some of the behaviors that my mother had lovingly demonstrated to all of her children.

I suspect as you remember your mother, in your heart, you carry a similar list of her strengths. Here are some actions that my mother practiced in daily living:

> Put others first.
>
> Don't think God has authorized you to judge others.
>
> Give anyone the benefit of the doubt:
>
> Love, teach and share.
>
> Don't do things for rewards. Let the fact that you have been given eyes to see and abilities to fulfill the needs of others be your reward.
>
> Don't be offended or feel slighted by the actions of others as one cannot ever fully know what another person is experiencing within.

Mother instinctively knew that you can accomplish many worthwhile things if you do not find it's necessary to claim credit. Now as I am searching for words to describe her actions, the idea … that she tried to fulfill the Golden rule fits…best.

I have three sibs who like mother no long reside on earth: Carolyn, Pat and my youngest brother Frank. As I think of their lives, I'm reminded of how well they modeled our mother's teachings. Carolyn was trained as a teacher/counselor and Pat as a teacher/librarian; both were employed in public schools for many years. Frank also had been preparing to teach when he had been stricken with schizophrenia during college.

In retirement Pat helped to establish and operate the PADS homeless shelter in Mattoon. Carolyn's counseling skills had reached beyond the school to friends, extended family & to her community.

With the help of medical advances, Frank had eventually become more stable. He learned to live with the devastation of his disease. He helped to care for both of our parents, enabling them to remain at home until their deaths. That had given Frank a sense of satisfaction, as the family had spent several years caring for him (primarily inspired by mother's love) when there had seemed to be no hope of recovery for him.

At the time of his death Frank was living in a half-way house where he had helped others and their families to cope with the damaging effect of schizophrenia by example and writing. He had served as editor of *THEN-*

N-NOW CLUB NEWS; a publication of The Heartland Human Services in Effingham.

Now that death prevents me from thanking or doing for my mother in person, I can continue to thank her by reaching out and sharing her teachings of love. I'm a strong believer in the "pass it on theory."

LEARNING TO WALK AT SEVENTY-EIGHT—
June 2000

Father's Day is a time most of us give extra time and attention to our Dads. Perhaps you're like me and can only honor your Father through memories on Father's Day this year.

However, separation by death and the passage of time does not lessen the love and respect one has for his or her Father. Sometimes those feelings increase because we do not have the ability to visit and release emotions through a hug or shared time.

One visit clearly emerges when I spend time reflecting on my life with my father. That event occurred a few months prior to my father's death in 1982.

Earlier my father (Judge Wm. J. Hill) had experienced a stroke, which had left him physically incapacitated while leaving his mind intact. He had worked hard in therapy at a rehabilitation center with little success. He knew his quality of life had been permanently impaired, with little hope of any future changes. During that time my family had tried to spend as much time with Dad as possible. My brother Frank, along with my Mother, provided daily loving care and therapy.

One night, I had been in Dad's room giving him his medication and tucking the covers under his feet. When I had turned off the light and bent down to give him a goodnight hug he pulled me closer and whispered," It is hard to learn to walk at seventy-eight."

I was glad that I had turned off the lamp .I sat on the edge of the bed and held his hand as hot tears streamed down my face. Tears were not strangers. Tears had fallen unbidden many times since my father had been stricken. The anguish of seeing his body so damaged and the boundaries of his life narrowed to four walls became unbearable. Prior to that evening, I had managed to do my crying in private.

Memories of times past, in which I had walked with my father flooded my heart as I sat on the edge of his bed that night. I had clearly remembered the thrill it had been, as a child, in learning to walk physically with my dad. In the early thirties, most people I knew walked wherever they went. Then, dad was six foot two with broad shoulders and he had a rapid stride. Thus, it had taken me some time to match his pace.

Throughout my life, whenever I walked with others; they would frequently say," Slow down! Do you think you are going to a fire?" I would answer that I was only trying to keep up with my dad. Because I had learned to match my dad's pace as a child, I had been permanently programmed with only one walking pace--fast forward. At least that's how it was until my joints began to show their age.

The above relates to walking physically with my father: there has been many more important journeys in life, which he taught by walking them before me.

One of the most important journeys which he modeled was the thrill and joy of ongoing learning. Thus I have not had to walk in constant unawareness of all the wonders which constantly surround me. Another crucial thing my father had taught me was when I walked through life and saw others exposed to prejudice and injustice: I should not close my eyes and look the other way.

Back to that night long ago: I finally regained a speck of courage which helped me to respond. Courage was another gift that Dad had given by example .I said," Dad, I know that it is hard to learn to walk at seventy-eight, but I will help you even as you have taught me so many different and valuable ways to walk in my life".

For Dad--*May 21, 2006*

It's post tax time and I have been cleaning and sorting papers. Because I'm a "hopeless saver" I tend to save more than I shred.

When I was storing papers, I came across a file that contained poems;, which had been written by my sister Carolyn Hill   Glasson.

One poem entitled *Repeat Celebration;* was written on the occasion of my 50th birthday and another one entitled *My Dad* had been written, at the time of my Dad's death. It was read at his memorial service on July 10, 1982, which was held in the Court House where he had been elected and served as Cumberland County's Judge.

This poem, which is historical and biographical, is about Judge Wm. J. (Bill) Hill's life, which spanned much of the 20th Century (1905- 82). The inserted brackets are mine for clarity. Quoting:

FOR DAD
By: Carolyn Hill Glasson
As a child, I heard about how it was
for this adventurous Southern man,
how it was early in this century
for a country boy growing in eastern North Carolina.

To his mom, he said, "There is more than this.
There has to be! And I think I shall set out to see.
Picking cotton, hoeing tobacco
shall not be all there is for me."

"Hush, Buddy," she answered...
Your daddy's old, can't work hard.
Tobacco must be planted,
mules fed, chickens tended, cows milked.
Hitch the wagon, Buddy.
Cream and eggs must go to town...
And do practice your singing,
You, my little seven year old,
are chosen to do 'Jesus Loves Me' in church on Sunday."

Running, out of breadth, "Ma," he said,
"I saw old Doc's new car...so big..
and bright lights it had... coming straight for me.
I had to jump in the ditch, Ma."

"Little Buddy, that could be the Devil's work...
Not for the likes of folks here-abouts..
Don't go getting idee-as,
watching that new fangled buggy-machine."

In 1917, "Goodbye," he said,
and headed out to sea.
Brother Rex was s-ent to retrieve him

from his job as ship's cook. He was twelve.

...cooling his heels,
He tended the grape arbor,
learned to graft fruit trees,
read all the books in the one room school,
and bided his time.

In 1922, after almost a year in the army,
he was sent home again.
Too young, too much in a hurry!
At eighteen, he was in again, the Air Force.

In an open cockpit, he hurtled across the sky
from Washington, D. C. to Chanute.
He caught pneumonia and more, but an admiring Cumberland
County soldier(Oakley Cutright)
brought this daredevil flyer home
to meet his family and friends.

Bill's mind, clear and strong,
instinctively knew
when he saw the lovely farmer's daughter.
University bound was Mary, but soon
she changed her mind.
Children of opposing forces, Yankee and Confederate,
they met and married here,(Toledo,5/4/1925)
this county seat.
Muddy and rocky were the roads,
Frozen were the winters,
The warm season short, and the crops were not in demand.
Two became three in 1926.
Back to North Carolina, by the- coast,
A track of land, a mule,
Old Galem swapped for a truck,
And soon a sister 1929.

Experimental learning we call it today,

As you go, hands on, farming skills, fertilizer use, bee culture,
cultivating, seed beds, curing, , husbandry, parenting…
Also, he found the time to wind coils,
To build a radio,
And talk around the world with code.
Fluorescent lights blinked from a top antenna poles
And frightened natives walking late.
At days and labors end,
He grabbed his towel, and walked the dusty road
To swim in the snake and weed lined creek,
As neighbor children asked their parents about this tall,
This unusual man,
Who was a little different from the others, thereabouts … .

Another daughter, 1931, and soon to try Illinois.
The winters still were icey, the crops not selling…
And again, the Model T was swapped for a truck to travel,
Three girls and Mon, furniture, special Bard rock chickens,
Our Boston bull, Lady, with her pups.
Settling, growing roots,, Onslow county, became our home.
He led us in hard work, deprivation, perseverance…
We completed, planned, dreamed… and heard stories
of great grandpa, Civil War, England,
What was and what just might be…if you thought it through,
Worked 16 hours a day…and had it written in the stars.
Productivity was the order of the day,
Unless of course, there was school lesson.
Books always came first…
So we learned to bring home a large stack… .
First there was food, then shelter, then learning…
That is how it was…
World War II came and went.
A bit over draft age at 37, the father of five
(now two very special boys),
He knew his obligation to his country.
He very patriotic, had learned skills
He wanted to share,

An early believer in equality for both Blacks and women,
He had no doubt that Mom could handle the farm.

Soon there was seven children,
Which meant nine to feed, clothe and shelter,
With whom to counsel, share love and discipline,
And he struggled for patience in the planning,
The caring, and found it difficult.

He organized foot races, ping pong tournaments'
word games, and told stories of other days,
yesterday sand tomorrow... lots of fantasy
to relieve the burdensome sameness
Of how it was.

As small children, we enjoyed the family rule
Of all of us being home together,
but that same old "home by dark" philosophy
Did not please us as teenagers.
Younger brother allowed as how
Dad and Mon struggled and fought
To change each other in little ways,
And neither ever did,
Each remaining true to self,
each knowing the other worthy of changing still.
He had a way of becoming quickly angry
And just as quickly, feeling foolish and saying so.

At war's end, he said good-by to life
as a U. S. Navy Chief Petty Officer
and headed his family west to Illinois.

Settling in with seven young ones,
the older one off to college,
left little time for anxiety,
and the neighbors proved they were.
After the first crop was up,

Charlie Tarble, farm advisor, brought folks out to see,
what some said couldn't be done,
fertilized corn, growing thick on the row.
A first in Illinois,
a first by an Eastern adventurous country boy.

Family, farming, public service,
electrician, policeman, athletic director,
sailor, bee keeper, sportsman, grower of fruits,
ecologist, lover of nature, teacher of amateur
radio, 4-H club organizer, soil conservationist,
politician, questioner, student, husband, father,
citizen...through it all, an inquiring,
a searching , a wanting to know... and seemingly,
limitless energy to seek his truths...

In November of 1953, by a slender margin,
Cumberland county folks, who knew him well,
voted him a new hat, a new opportunity to learn,
and Mom went home with Cumberland County's new judge.
Countless ways of learning crammed into forty eight years
prepared him to listen, study, and see justice done...
for rich, poor , competent, ill, or wanderer...
He rose to the challenge of a new opportunity
to hear and find the truth
for himself and his contemporaries.

An old dream... to own and pilot his plane
Began again in 1963.
Patchett from Casey became his mentor...
he went up again and again.
Another goal realized in April of 1968.
He was a licensed pilot and
with the excitement of one ten or twenty,
he took his thoughts into the clouds,
soaring with the wind, the birds and fantasy...
remembering still to dip his wing

to the special girl, his partner, his anchor
on Bluebird Farm.

Searching still, night found him peering through his telescope
checking scientific reports of constellations,
stars to steer by.
One son-in-law taught him about
surf fishing and Port Aransas.
He loved testing his vigor with the Pompano or Flounder.

His last solo flight was September of 77 at 72.
His last big challenge came in 1978
with a massive stroke.
Learning to be an invalid was a hard fight,
Made a lot easier by the loving patience
of his youngest.

A rarity, the earth's eclipse of the moon...
Could be the Heaven's marking the universal calendar
for this special, this inquiring, this adventurous,
courageous, truth seeking country boy, our pilot,
William James(Bill) Hill.... 1905-1982

POMEGRANATES, PECANS & FIGS—
December 12, 2005

What do these three foods have in common? For me they all
grew in my Grandma Hill's costal Carolina yard.

Last night I served a dish of bright red, juicy pomegranate seeds
to my dinner guests. Bev; one of my guests, who had never seen
them before asked me to tell her something about them. I told
her the first thing that comes to mind is how difficult the seeds
are to remove from their orange size rind without splashing juice
everywhere.

Webster's exact definition reads: 1. A round fruit with a red
leathery rind and many seeds covered with red juicy edible flesh.
My Grandma's lone pomegranate bush bore a limited number of

fruits on it. Early on my cousins and I would try to decide who would get to pick and eat them. Grandma settled that. When they were ripe she picked it, took her trusty pocket knife from her apron pocket and sparingly divided one among us. Grandma had told us if we picked the scarce fruit too early, it would be wasteful and they would not be fit for anyone to eat as it would be too sour. I didn't know until I was in high school that the saying about "waste creating want "was not her original expression. Of course, we didn't heed Grandma's advice and we all had to individually discover firsthand how sour they were. This reminds me of another time I secretly sampled a teaspoon of Mother's vanilla even though she had repeatedly told me it would not taste good. Bev loved the pomegranate seeds I served last night and said she will be looking for them in the market. There is a limited time they are available fresh. You can buy canned pomegranate juice on the shelf which, like the fresh fruit is very high in antioxidants especially polyphenols, which early research shows may reduce cholesterol and have other health benefits. The pecan trees provided nuts for Christmas goodies, including our stockings, shade and a limb to hang our rope swing on so Grandma could keep a watchful eye on us from her front porch. Grandma's fig bushes formed a row outside of her kitchen window. Her fig bushes bore more plentifully than her lone pomegranate bush, but like it, the fig fruit turned your mouth wrong side out if you attempted to eat them before they were fully ripened. Again, I can attest to that! You may be more familiar with Fig Newton Cookies than the fresh fruit, as figs are not a native fruit of Illinois. Here is Webster's exact description for Figs: The hollow pear-shaped false fruit of the fig tree, with sweet, pulpy flesh containing numerous tiny, seed like true fruits. My memories date back to a much earlier time than the "freezer era", when Grandma canned her figs as sweetened preserves to eat with her hot biscuits at Christmas time. She also served them at other times. Sometimes she served them a as a snack after my cousins and I did chores for her such as picking up the fallen apples or following the turkey hen to learn where she had hid out her nest. My childhood memories of my Grandma wander much like her turkey hen did through Grandma's orchard when the hen sensed I was trying to discover her nesting site.

History & Heritage--July 31, 2005

History is intertwined in my heritage as it is difficult to talk about my life without reviewing the historical events which have shaped it.

Each time I work at my computer I can view the portraits of my great grand-parents, Samuel and Jane Sparks, which are displayed on the wall, above my computer. An older cousin gave me both of their stress-lined 2x2' framed images when I had expressed an interest in my family's history. I never want to forget how their sacrifices made in the 19th century; have, and continue, to positively impact my life in this, the 21st century.

Family records show that Samuel and Jane were married in Terre Haute, Indiana on July 26, 1849(156 years ago). A historical event which occurred the next year had considerable to do with the fact I am now a resident of Cumberland County.

The U.S. Congress on September 21, 1850 created a land grant to build a railroad from Chicago to Mobile, Alabama. An Act of the Illinois Legislature approved on February17, 1851 made a donation of these lands in central Illinois to the Illinois Central Railroad (ICCR). Many sections of land were given to ICCR to help build the railroad. In addition the grant included land which the ICCR could sell to encourage residents to settle and begin farming in the fledging state of Illinois, which had , been admitted to statehood only thirty years prior to Samuel's and Jane's marriage.

In time, Samuel and Jane found their way to Cumberland County and purchased some of the land which had been given to the ICRR. My mother Mary Sparks; later to be Hill, was born on this land 98 years ago, because her father had purchased the land after Samuel and Jane's death. Events which occurred in 1925 made it seem unlikely that I would ever live in Illinois or see much of it. My mother met, and after a whirlwind romance, married my dad to be; William J. "Bill" Hill. Because he was a native North Carolinian who had been in the Army stationed at Chanute Air Base, he soon took her to live in eastern N.C. My grandmother Sparks never forgave my dad; as if my mom played no part in the marriage.

Thus, I was born and grew up in N.C. I only knew that Cumberland County, Illinois was a faraway place where my mom had grown-up and that my grandmother didn't care very much for my dad.

History intervened once again and changed my life in a way which I had not expected! World War II began and my Dad enlisted into the U.S. Navy. My parents had sold our farm in N.C. and we were living in Virginia during the war. My grandparents in Illinois had died and some of their land which had once belonged to Samuel and Jane became available. My mom and dad both agreed to purchase the land because they knew if he did not survive the war it would be best for us to live in Illinois near mother's remaining family.

The rest is history. In time, WWII finally ended in 1945, and when I was in high school, my entire family; moved to Illinois. We began living on the land Samuel and Jane had purchased so long ago.

My happy ending to this story is that 57 years ago, I met and married another Illinois farmer named Harold. Now, when I look up from my computer at Samuel and Jane's picture I sometimes thank them for settling in Illinois and tell them that we are trying to be good stewards of the land they had the wisdom to purchase so long ago. Once in awhile, I whisper "I hope some of my great-grand children will someday own and love their land."

Important Perspectives--*October 3, 2013*

"To have a short winter, you need to have a note due in the Spring."
Frank Thompson, former A C Dealer on the Square

A few days ago at the Fillin' Station, my cousin John Wilson overheard me chatting with a friend about wishing for a short, mild winter. He then shared the above wisdom from his Grandfather Thompson, was also my Uncle Frank from whom my sister Pat and I had rented an apartment from during our high school years. He had a wonderful sense of humor and usually spoke: when he had something to say. Thus, I've decided to write about Uncle Frank and his wife, my Aunt Bess, who was my mom's older sister.

I smile whenever I recall that: the Fillin Station(F S) now occupies the same spot that had been The Diel & Thompson Allis- Chalmers Dealership (AC), that had been owned by my Uncle Frank and his family.

Now people meet, greet, eat and exchange information at the F S, on the same spot that farmers had done, earlier when it was an AC Dealership. My dad, who had been a frequent participant, called it "Chewing the Rag." And yes, in the Fall season they also ate, as Uncle Frank purchased peanuts by the 100 # burlap bags full for area farmers and loafers to munch on. And if my memory serves me right, I think they also had access to pop and/or coffee. My dad would sometimes share information with our family that he had heard there.

Long ago men talked about women getting together and having a "Hen Party" so I guess, staying with farm language that could have been labeled a "Rooster's Meeting Place".

My first memories of Uncle Frank go way back to when he and Aunt Bess had visited us in the 1930's when, I was a grade-school student growing up in Eastern North Carolina.

The next time I would see Uncle Frank was in 1945 at the close of "The Big War." After my dad was discharged from the U S Navy in Norfolk , Virginia my family had ridden the train to Mattoon as my folks had made the decision to resettle on their Cumberland County Farm where my mom was born. Thus, Uncle Frank had picked up our family at the train station and driven us to his home in Toledo.

En route about five miles west of Toledo, he pointed out our Courthouse Steeple a beautiful sight as we looked East down the road seeing fall colored trees in between. I stored that view in my heart, as it was my first glimpse of my new Illinois home. That long ago vision also provided the name for this column when I began to write about 20 years ago! Also, it became a land mark for me, because whenever I could view our Courthouse Steeple through the passing years, I knew I was almost home.

When we arrived in Toledo at Uncle Frank's lovely Victorian style home on North Meridian Street, they graciously let our family reside with them, until our furniture moving van arrived from Norfolk so my parents could move into their farm home near the Fairplay School, in Cottonwood Twp.

Because Norfolk was a beach town, with Virginia Beach near-by on the Atlantic Ocean and Ocean View was a beach on the Chesapeake Bay, I had thought nothing about walking on the town's streets in my bathing suit. One day after school, I had been swimming at the Toledo Rez , and

I walked to Woolen's Drugstore on the Square, wearing my bathing suit and was dancing in the back room where Mr. Woolen kept his jukebox and allowed high school kids to dance and drink Cokes for a nickel . Aunt Bess got word of my unheard -of transgressions before I got home and about threw me out, which would have meant I couldn't continue going to high school... At that time; in the mid 1940's, there were no school buses, nor roads to support them! Needless to say Aunt Bess relented and let me continue going to school, but I never wore my swimming suit to town again and learned a lesson about Toledo's cultural values being very different from those of Norfolk!

I gave my Aunt and Uncle Frank Thompson lots of headaches when I lived in their home in order to attend Toledo High School. But now, as I look back with embarrassment in hindsight, on some of my "growing up antics," I realize, I also had learned a lot from both of them due to their strongly developed character and Christian values.

I believe my Aunt Bess had been the first woman ever elected to an office in the Courthouse, when she served, as Cumberland County Treasurer in the 1930's. Years later in the 1970's, I became the first woman who was elected to Lake Land College's Board of Trustees. I suspect knowing and learning from my Aunt Bess's strength of character and the fact that she had been successful in her election endeavors; may have given me courage to seek the office. My success gave me the opportunity to work towards fulfilling the many demanding responsibilities: involved in governing and providing for the educational needs of LLC; which was still expanding in territory and building its campus. Later in 1984, I was elected to represent all of our Illinois Community Colleges Trustees at national meetings, as President of the ICCTA. Sometimes, we can live and learn from others!

Holidays Traditions--*November 1, 2006*
To everything there is a season.... Ecclesiastes 3:1
My husband and I are "morning people" and thus early risers. However, our internal systems can't adapt to rolling back the time as quickly as it jointly took Harold and the mysterious satellite to change both our atomic and regular clocks.

This morning we were chatting while trying to catnap and remain in bed the extra hour so our morning paper would be available to digest with our first cup of coffee.

Harold causally said, "This is the first day of November." All pretense of sleep evaporated as my mind began to commingle the blessings and tasks of the approaching holidays as though I was viewing them through a kaleidoscope.

To slow the tempo; I began to think about the fun jobs November ushers in, well, at least prioritize them in declining order of necessity.

Baking fruitcakes can head the list, with cleaning the catchall drawer of unfinished tasks and sorting out the tax records, falling on the downside. Our traditional fruitcake recipe contains predominantly: dates and pecans. We bake early in order to observe the "Treatment" tradition from my southern heritage.

Having grown up playing under pecan trees in my Grandma's front yard makes me particular about the kind of pecans I use in my fruitcake. I want light colored new crop pecans, as using dark colored, year old nutmeats diminishes the flavor of the cake. We have not been able to find new crop pecans in our local grocery store.

We bake two or three batches, as we use small fruitcakes as gifts during the holiday season and want the table cakes to last through New Year's Day.

Some of my earliest memories involved my extended family gathering in our house for syllabub and fruitcake on Christmas Eve. My Dad's sister came and made the syllabub. There always was a separate bowl of flavored with vanilla for the children. The Christmas I was married was the first year my cup was filled from the adult bowl.

Writing Christmas cards falls somewhere in the middle of my holiday agenda. I have shared in the past about my lifelong love of receiving mail. I continue to look forward to opening Christmas mail. Somehow, it is a letdown when the only personal message on a card is the sender's signature. Thus, when I send cards, I usually try to write a note and/or include my Christmas column.

The job of updating, or better yet, replacing my address book is begging to be done. As you fully know, after so many scratched-through changes the addresses become illegible. With new addresses on holiday mail; it is the ideal time to start a new book.

The sad part is removing the names of the departed. Somehow, it seems if I do not delete their addresses, their loving presence will linger a little longer.

Shopping doesn't consume much extra time. Long ago to encourage my family to save, we began giving saving bonds and/or cash as gifts .Doing so simplifies things for all and certainly eliminates the need for anyone to stand in exchange lines.

There is indeed a time and season for all things. Necessity will take over in '07 and insist that I finish cleaning the catchall drawer of all tax records. The good news is: I was able to go on line today and order new crop pecans, which are ready for shipment.

My last planning job involves facing reality. I will simply mark through the remaining non-essential tasks on my 2006's "to do list". Then I will have ample time to give thanks, meditate and fully share all the blessings of this holiday season.

Childhood Memories of Growing Up on a Tobacco Farm in North Carolina--*June 20, 2005*

I grew up on a labor-intensive farm. Translated into ordinary words, that meant in order to survive there were jobs for every member of the family except the baby. It was a survival way of life for families during the depression laden years of the 1930's. Early on in my family, one's age determined their work assignment. However, having job assignments for all members of the family were not peculiar to my family, as neighboring families out of necessity, also had similar work routines.

Before mechanization, both growing and harvesting bright leaf tobacco involved a lot of hand work which included everyone in the family plus trading off work days with the neighbors.

As soon as a child could hold a hoe, there were weeds to be chopped out of tobacco, cotton and corn fields, not to mention the family garden. The garden provided much of the food that families ate during the summer with the excess being canned for the winter months.

When I was too young to hoe in the fields or garden, my first job was to assist my grandmother in caring for my younger brother, Jim at the house, as my mother also worked in the fields during the growing and harvesting season. The child next to the baby was often called the "knee-baby." These are some of my earliest memories from that stage in my life.

When the sun was high in the sky, my Grandma Hill filled a mason jar with cool water so I could carry a fresh drink to the rest of the family working in the fields. She admonished me not to dilly-dally en route to the fields as the water would be hot before I got there, even though she wrapped it in a towel to protect it from the sun's heat. There were other jobs, such as filling the chickens' watering fountains, feed pans and pulling the bigger weeds out of the garden. Shelling peas and breaking green beans were jobs for smaller hands.

Once in a while there was treats. Occasionally, my Grandma purchased fish to fry for dinner (which was always cooked in the middle of the day) from Mr. Hood. Mr. Hood came along the road hollering, "Fresh fish," as he was selling fish packed in tubs of ice stored in the opened rumble seat of his Model T Ford. If I stood close to Grandma, he would give me chips of ice, while she checked to see if the fish looked and smelt fresh. I don't recall if I washed the fish taste off the ice before licking it like a penny sucker. The traveling fisherman was available because we lived fairly close to the coast. This was before we had our first kerosene operated refrigerator.

Also, if I was careful not to lose any of it, my grandma would let me stand by our rural mailbox and wait for Mr. Trott to hand me the mail. Somehow, that seemed like a special treat because when older family members were at the house, they usually got the mail. On the day the "Saturday Evening Post" came in the mail grandma would let me carefully leaf through it, that is, if my other jobs were finished.

Another job, I didn't mind was churning the butter. I guess it was because the cream finally separated and turned into butter. When Grandma took it out of the churn and patted it into her butter mold, it always looked the prettiest in its final stage giving me a sense of accomplishment.

Today when I occasionally see a butter mold selling for big bucks in an antique shop, it takes me back to these my earliest pre-school childhood memories when I had been , too young to work in the fields.

Although I probably would not have agree with this statement as a child: learning how to work early in life has benefited me in a positive manner throughout my life. It has given me the satisfaction of knowing that I can. accomplish almost any goal.

Grandma Hill's Pockets--*January 24, 2001*

Grandma's pockets tell the story of her life. They were two, one attached to her apron and the other hidden on her underskirt. Her apron pocket was on the right side on her butcher style apron made from bleached flour sacks, as grandma didn't waste anything not even flour sack cloth.

Her reasoning was "a willful waste makes a woeful want." If any item did not have a truly, utilitarian purpose, you didn't find it in her home. . Grandma kept a hankie and a pocket knife with black sides and a sharp blade in her pocket. The knife was off limits to kids or anyone. At that time she was no longer the chief cook in her house as my uncle's wife; Aunt Sophie did most of the cooking as she had three children whose father was grandma's son. Of course, grandma didn't hesitate to: provided supervision as she did for my Mother, on her frequent visits. When my sisters and I visited grandma's house, in the late summer, she took all the kids to pick up fallen apples in the orchard behind her house. She thought "idle hands were the devil's workshop". I did not know those words were not original with grandma until I was grown. as I'm remembering these glimpses of my grandma, from memories of my childhood .

Her chicken house was located in the orchard, as land was too precious to waste an inch. Most of her food was produced on her subsistence farm or bartered in return for farm produce. Grandma would gather up the edges of her apron to make a bag for us to pick up the "knotty" apples from off the ground; ones no one would bother to pickup today. The "good" apples on the trees were saved for canning. If the chickens had eaten half of a dropped apple, we usually left the other half for them to finish. That was not waste, it turned into eggs or eventually into Grandma's yummy chicken and dumplings. Our reward came when we returned to the porch (grandma called it the piazza) with her apron full of apples. She then took out her knife and began to peel razor thin. The apple peel wound off in one continuous strip. As the flesh of the apple could not be wasted away with thick peeling. At times we would catch the peeling to play with; as it unwound like a streamer. Grandma was immaculately clean in everything she undertook and had washed the apple. Hopefully we has not ingested; any chicken manure. When there was no apple flesh left after she peeled, cored and deleted the worms, we took turns eating the thinly sliced bites. When grandma decided another bite of green apple would give us a belly ache, she then sliced the remainder in a kettle to stew and then we kids carried the scraps out to feed the chickens.

Grandma's Secret Pocket --*February 8, 2001*

Grandma was a survivor. I do not mean of some T.V. show. I mean of a hard and difficult life even as many of you are. Words do not come easy for me to explain. A survivor is a person who does whatever it takes. At different times, different skills are required. Even we who have not been put to the ultimate test can detect survivor skills in others.

During the Post Civil War era in the rural South. it's economic structure had been devastated as some of their towns had been occupied by Northern soldiers. There was little domestic stability or order. Certainly no schooling was available for a poor female. Scratching out a living consumed everyone's time and energy. Grandma fortunately was able to marry a man who could provide a home for her and she bore him three children. He died young and grandma was left again to fend for herself and try to earn a living.

She later married my Grandfather Hill and they scraped together a minimum down payment to purchase a small subsistence farm. They secured a cow, a sow and a few chickens. Eventually money was saved from selling eggs and butter to the people in the nearby village. This is the same town I would ride a Model T school bus: to attend elementary school in the 1930's. They planted an orchard which included a variety of fruit and pecan trees, plus a grape arbor. The fruit, eggs and milk supplemented their diet and also generated cash income. My Grandma knew more about scratching out a living than my Grandpa as prior to the Civil War he had lived comfortably on a slave plantation, as an educated son, of the Overseer. However this was after the War and the South was occupied by Northerners. Grandpa was more successful at telling stories than he was at eking out a living during the difficult economic times, in which they lived. Grandma loved him anyway and always called him Mr. Hill.

I do not have any memory of him as he died when I was a very young child.. I only knew him through my father's stories. Grandfather gave me my nickname, Pete, which my family continues to use. The story as to how I got the name "Pete" gives me a clue that he wouldn't exactly have been for women's rights. Who knows? My mother was a strong woman and modeled positive traits for all her daughters too.

You may have guessed by now that Grandma was the family banker and the secret pocket on her underskirt was the place she kept her money.

The only paper money I ever saw as a young child had "Washington's" picture on it. You can imagine the shock one day when Grandma turned her back, lifted her dress tail and pulled a $20 dollar bill, out of her secret pocket. I thought Grandma must be rich. I began to believe her when she told me if I worked hard, fed the chickens, looked for the turkey's nest, picked up the dropped fruit without whining and did my homework, someday, I might even have a bicycle.

Cues From Mom--*September 12, 2007*

It seems of late that I have been writing about serious subject matter such as love, learning, sharing, and responsibilities. Maybe that's because our daily life is so impacted by these values.

We can face life head on, ignore it, or live in denial. The first choice is extremely difficult, the second we can tolerate, for awhile and the third gets us nowhere; other than buying a little time.

Facing up to the hard issues of life is the most difficult, but at the same time it is necessary if we want to keep some normalcy and sanity in our lives. Our relationships with others, both past and present, are strong supports.

How often do we fail to reach out and grasp opportunities that can enrich our lives or extend assistance to others? Are we in tune to these occasions, or perhaps are we too wrapped up in thoughts and activities that are self-serving?

On Labor Day, I had lunch with the Johnstown Ladies, a group of friends that has met monthly for many years. One of my tablemates shared that she had left home without making her bed. She added, "This morning I visited with a neighbor and the time just got away."

I replied, "Don't sweat the small stuff."

On busy days, I've crawled into an unmade bed without consequences. I'm sure she made better use of her time.

In today's busy world, funeral home visitations are often one of the more likely places to encounter friends from out of town. It was on such an occasion that I saw a couple of women who have been my friends since high school. It was wonderful to visit with both of them. I recognized one friend's voice before seeing her face. It seemed as if I had spoken to her only yesterday.

Our high school years hopefully exposed us to new intellectual skills but equally important are the bonds of friendships we established that have supported and nurtured us through the passing years.

A few Sundays ago at church, I saw a couple whom I had not seen for awhile. We exchanged greetings and when I asked about their family the wife responded, "I know about your family because I read your column." Later, as I thought about her comments, I wondered if I write too much about my family. Of course, that's the subject I know most about.

I thought back to the time when my mother, Mary Sparks Hill, wrote a column, primarily about her family. It was entitled, "Down Cumberland Way." As teenagers, my older sisters and I created plenty of subject matter. When writing about our antics, my mother used the pseudonyms of April, May, and June for the three of us. Some of my friends enjoyed calling me June in a teasing way.

Apparently, I had no permanent damage from her columns, as I am following in her footsteps. Perhaps the secret is in not saying anything hurtful about others. One of my mother's favorite sayings was, "If you can't say something good about someone, don't say anything."

Her words found lodging in my thinking as I now say the same thing to the younger generation in my family. I also, try to adhere to her rule in my own writing.

Our environment already contains ample pain and suffering from causes we can't control and we must learn to tolerate them in our imperfect world, thus all positive actions that we can generate and share are welcome.

Next, I have inserted one of my Mother's columns that I discovered in a box of saved stuff. It's a sampling of her values that have shaped my life!

October 1954
Down Cumberland Way

By Mary Sparks Hill

Bill says he was born lucky with a hoe in his hand. Maybe that's why we are still diggin'. The other day when he entered in from "diggin'" Soybeans with a combine, he was barely recognizable.

Down in eastern North Carolina where Bill was born and raised, nearly everybody was his cousin. So one year after a poor tobacco crop the mayor of Richland's persuaded Bill to become the town's only paid employee for the sum of $100 a month(during the depression era of the

1930's).

He read the meters, collected the taxes, paid the bills and policed the town. Nearly every time that Bill had to lock up a guy for disorderly conduct the fellow would say, "You can't do this to me. I'm your cousin Charley." But Bill would only grin and say. "Tomorrow when you sober up and pay your fine, we will be cousins again."

When the war broke out (WW II) Uncle Sam started building two camps in Bill's home county. Bill got a job as an electrical inspector paying $100 a week, but all the while Pearl Harbor kept bearing on his mind. Here he was with a wife and five children to support, yet he could not bear the thought if Hitler won. I rolled all the stones in the way that I could, but Bill had the courage of is convictions and enlisted anyway. Somehow the cows and chickens kept us going until he was promoted to CPO, and then we were all together again. We lived in a naval housing Project (Merrimac Park) at Norfolk, Va., where Bill had shore duty as an instructor.

Jane and Frank were born in naval hospitals and being there besides the wives of sailors and marines who would never see their babies, I gradually understood how Bill could not have done any other way and lived with himself.

We went to Sunday School in Merrimac Park's community building where every denomination attended and nobody cared what your creed was. Somehow what you are fighting for gets awful close to home when all of your neighbors have someone in the service. Those telegrams "wounded, missing, killed in action," came fast in Merrimac Park~~~ and then the news that, "it was over."

We were rootless then, with seven children. What to do? A retirement in the Navy? A civil service job? Farming? It seemed important to live where people knew each other, as they passed on the street and it was memories of people back in Cumberland County that decided us. We liked the way you played the game. We had set up housekeeping as Lou Barger's hired hand 25 years ago and 8 years ago(1945) we came back the second time and we knew we couldn't have chosen a better place for a home.

Political news attracts Bill like a magnet. We take two daily papers and lots of magazines and yet he comes home with more for me to dispose of. He can not only name our 96 senators but can tell you how they voted. Bill feels deeply his debt to mankind and I know he has the talent and ability to be of service.

We are a healthy and well fed family and we are not seeking personal gain or glory. Win or lose it has been a wonderful experience,(Dad was elected Cumberland County Judge on the 2nd of November in 1954)the confidence of old friends and the trust and faith of new ones, has made it both humbling and challenging. We will never forget it, because the priceless things in life: money doesn't buy.

Lily's Love Endured--*August 1, 2007*

Love is slow to loose patience -- it looks for a way of being constructive. It is not possessive. It is neither anxious to impress nor does it cherish inflated ideas of its own importance.

Love has good manners and does not pursue selfish advantage. It is not touchy. It does not keep account of evil or gloat over the wickedness of other people.

On the contrary, it is glad with all good men when truth prevails. Love knows no limit to its endurance, no end to its trust, no fading of its hope: it can outlast anything. It still stands when all else has fallen. 1st Corinthians 13:4-8

In May, my nephew Tim married Anna, a creative and talented young woman. A few days ago, I received a thank you note from them.

As I did not attend their wedding ceremony, they included a copy of their wedding program. It is unique, containing many lovely sections, which they had jointly written specifically for their wedding ceremony.

I particularly liked their version of First Corinthians, which is quoted above. This chapter has always been my favorite in the Bible.

Its message remains an ongoing challenge as it shares the essence of perfect love in action. I have not achieved the level it portrays and I suspect it may not be humanly possible for me to do so.

However, it's good to be reminded to strive in the right direction. The Love Chapter is kind of like the voice on the GPS Navigational System -- telling you to go back when you've missed a turn on the road to your destination.

Another section of Tim and Anna's wedding program shared the names of close family members, now deceased, who had helped to shape their lives in a positive way.

Immediately, I began to think of names from my past that I might honor in a similar manner. My parents were obvious choices. However another name I would choose to acknowledge would be Lily, my husband's mother.

Lily was a person I never met. She died when my husband was only ten years old. Nevertheless, her influence and values have profoundly impacted my married life. We named our daughter, in honor of her. Harold has extended love and consideration to me throughout our half century-plus years of marriage. The act of always putting someone else first is not a normal human trait; he had to learn it from someone, who modeled that behavior.

Lily's love and guidance bestowed upon her young son, so long ago, multiplied and spilled over into my life and the lives of our children, as well.

Lily's influence has proven the words from the above scripture: *Love knows no limit to its endurance, no limit to its trust, no fading of its hope; it outlasts everything.*

Here We Are--*December 18, 2011*

Here we are fast approaching the most Holy Season of the year! What thoughts occupy your mind?

Is it last minute shopping, traveling plans, or maybe preparing the Christmas dinner plus all the other remaining tasks? In the past years these would have been my thoughts. Now in my "mature stage," whenever I take the time to pause, often beautiful memories of Christmases past flood my mind.

I've read that many people become depressed during the holidays and one might think that would happen to me because, having lost my husband a year ago and my oldest son three years ago during the holidays, plus I am alone and do not have family nearby; but for the greater part of my life, I was very happy and am blessed with happy memories.

I am and have been a person of Christian faith during most of my life. Thus, when I think of Christmas I think of the Joyous gift that was first given to all mankind at Christmas.

Today, I have singled out four Christmas holidays to write about; that were forever imprinted on my heart, .in happiness and love.

The first happened during the Great Depression of the 1930's.

We had never been used to getting lots of gifts because of the great financial black hole that consumed our nation's economy during my childhood, that some people think resembles today's economy .

My two older sisters and I would hang our stockings on the fireplace and our usual gifts in the stocking were English walnuts and oranges that we did not have at other times of the year and sometimes included school supplies and bright colored socks. My Dad had extended family who grew oranges in Florida and often mailed a sack to my family during the holidays. My family had received the Sears catalogue in the mail around Thanksgiving, which we called the "Wish Book". I had worn it out, looking at the dolls and had one in particular picked out that I wanted the worst way. My Mom had tried to discourage me because she obviously knew there was no money available for dolls from Santa, whom I still wanted to believe in when Mom told me it took all of Santa's money to provide things like fruit and pencils for all of the other children, on his long route.

And Mother had been correct because when I awakened early and went to look under our tree in the living room tree, there was no doll but my stocking did have two oranges plus a tangerine as an extra treat.

Later in the day we went across the field, to my Grandma's home for our Christmas visit, with them. When I arrived my Aunt Sophie motioned for me to follow her to the room where they stored and cased eggs to sell and dug down into an empty egg case. There, lo and behold, lay my doll from the Sears wish book! She quickly added "That Santa had left it there for me because his bag was getting heavy." My Aunt knowing what poor crops my parents had and no doubt had purchased the doll for me when she had bought one, for her daughter! That was one of my happiest childhood Christmases.

The next special Christmas memory was a few years later in the 1940's; when my Dad had enlisted in the Navy during WWII. We thought it would be our first Christmas without him as he had been denied leave and Mom had little cash to spend on Christmas gifts, so we were prepared for a wartime holiday without Daddy present. Then at Christmas Eve there was a knock on the door and there stood Dad with a sack full of Christmas gifts that included a nicely wrapped gift for each one of us! But the greatest gift was having Dad home for almost a week. Another special Christmas happened in 1947, as that was the year that Harold and I were married on Christmas Day. Our marriage lasted for almost 63 loving years; with our love growing stronger during each passing year until Harold's death last year. Our union of love continues alive, in my heart.

The last special Christmas season that I want share about happened during 1955. It was a bit like the first one I had written about , when it comes to being prepared with gifts for all as I was unable to purchase or wrap anything, but it taught me that the gift of a loving family is the greatest gift of all. One cold rainy night about a week before Christmas, I had bundled up Roger, who was five and Lily, who was two and one-half years old and driven over to Barger's Store at Hickory Corner to get some supplies to make Christmas cookies. Unbeknown to me, when I approached the Burma Road it was slick, Soon I was hit by a sliding car and knocked into the ditch. This was before seat belts and Lily was thrown into the windshield and her face was badly lacerated, However, the swerving of the car threw her back, on the inside floor of the car, instead of out on the road which no doubt spared her life. Nevertheless her face was a mass of blood, glass and open flesh, soaking her clothes with blood. Dr Supple told me; it took more than 100 stitches on her face to close the wounds and he reported, he keep her out for repairs, as long as her young body would tolerate.

She had excellent care as her young doctor later would specialized in surgery and through the night caring nurses stayed nearby. Later the ambulance driver told me he had not expected Lily to survive the trip to the hospital.

To make a long story short Lily and I returned home on Christmas Eve. Never did home look so good even though my Christmas shopping had not been completed and our car was wrecked. It didn't matter my loving family was there to help and Lily had escaped near death and Roger had not been seriously hurt. Lily is now a teaching nurse helping others. I often wonder if that terrible incident so long ago had something to do with her career choice? Ever since then, I have known that God's gifts of His Son, love and family are the Christmas gifts that really matter.

Why Snowbirds Go Home--*May 29, 2009*

Springtime, is a special event in my rural Illinois community that draws me homeward .

Going home has always held an emotional significance for me, even as I suspect it does for most people. When I combine these moving feelings with springtime flowers in full bloom; I'm left without adequate words to express my inner feelings. Nevertheless, I shall try.

Although flowers in Naples, which I love, are ablaze with vibrant colors during most seasons of the year. Florida does not have the cold climate to nurture spring bulbs nor to accentuate the changing seasons.

When we arrived home a few days ago the irises and early day lilies, plus my old fashion climbing roses were in magnificent bloom. I gathered, the overflow of rain, which has caused headaches for our area farmers had something to do with the beauty and intensity of the blooming flowers. Thus, reminding me once again, that something good can come out of occurrences that seem to be problematic.

Another positive factor in coming home could be labeled "friendship." It's such a positive uplift to see so many people that not only know your name but who takes the time to stop and say hello and ask you how you are! It doesn't matter whether you're shopping, eating, at the post office or maybe parking the car; people pause to greet others. Some people think this is a Midwestern trait. I think in part, it is a small town attribute. Of course, growing up near a small town where many people really know each other or at least some member of one's family accounts for some of the familiarity.

Having recently attended my village's Spring Festival and my annual high school reunion was responsible for part of the social interaction. As I had walked through the carnival rides a few times, in hopes of seeing some of my grandchildren or great-grandchildren, I was reminded that I'm not as young as I once was and looked without success for an empty bench along the way. Long ago, I used to wonder why someone would come to the festival and sit on a bench to visit. Passing time often supplies answers to many questions, as it did in this case, for me. Nevertheless, it doesn't deter the excitement I felt in simply being home. I think there is a relationship between the beauty of the spring flowers and the spirit of our local people. Perhaps it because both are gifts from God.

I can't comment about the joy of returning home without mentioning the importance of family. Our entire family had jointly worked hard for a few weekends in order to have everything turned on and cleaned in our home prior to our arrival, even my computer was working! Last year I had problems with my ageing computer and my banker sent a staff person out, who quickly put the wires in the right place, which was another small town perk.

We have already celebrated some family birthdays. Our daughter Lily who may not want me to share her age, and our two year old great-grandson, Jasper shared the same cake.

On Saturday, we helped to celebrate great-granddaughter Molli's birthday at a cookout. At three, she is already a "take charge young lady." As I reminisced a bit, I recalled the important role that family had played in my own life; through the passing years. I hope Harold and I can provide that same support for the younger generations, as they are growing up in a different world than we did.

Coming home to spring flowers, friends and family in Illinois is an unbeatable combination!

Hometown Happenings--*January 25, 2013*

I've had a busy and eventful day. Early this morning I had to decide whether to venture outside or if it was safer to remain inside because the local news was reporting various incidents occurring on slick roads. I decided that I would drive to the Post Office and if I felt at risk; I could return home. Finding no threatening slick spots: I then drove to the Life Center where I enjoyed playing Skip-Bo and visiting with friends.

I returned home and was writing the above when my phone rang. I took time from writing after seeing the caller was; Maggie, a former classmate. Before long, I was hysterical from laughing and finally got around to asking my friend if I could use her unusual experience to complete my column with a bit of mid-winter humor for my readers. She consented to my request. I think if you have some maturity under your belt like my friend and I, you might laugh with us as we related her story to Halloween ventures that occurred when we were students at Toledo high School (THS)! I'm referring to "Outdoor Toilets" appearing on the Court House lawn the morning after Halloween. That happening would often bring the Sheriff to THS to identify the naughty students, so they could participate in returning them to their original sites and probably receive some lecturing, along the way. Halloween mischievousness had also been prevalent in earlier generations, as my friend told me her Mom had related the story that one year her classmates had tied some farmer's milk cow onto the entry porch of the Court House.

Here's my friend's story:

She reported being puzzled this morning to see a large truck pull into her driveway, as she had not scheduled any deliveries. Thus, she waited for someone to come to her door. Some time elapsed and the truck left without her speaking to anyone. However when the truck left, to her dismay, she could see they had unloaded a Portable-potty in her front yard! She called her son as she had no idea what was going on and at that time it was no laughing matter. Her son came and found some identifying information on the structure to contact. However, before they contacted the owner some pieces of the puzzle had began to fall into place, as they knew a major auction (which could require a portable toilet) was scheduled to be held tomorrow, south of Toledo's Square. When they called the owner, he informed them that the auction site was indeed where it should have been delivered. There were some similarities in the addresses that brought the "potty" to my friends front yard. Their house numbers were the same and both homes were the same distances from the Toledo Square: only in different directions! The misplaced "potty" was soon picked up and redelivered to the correct site.

Thus, when my friend shared her story of her "Unordered front yard delivery" with me; we were able to laugh as we saw its similarity: to earlier Halloween pranks!

When one ventures out in our little Village one never knows what the new day holds. Think what I would have missed if I hadn't had the courage to venture out.

How Do We Become Us?--*June 15, 2002*

Value, worth, magnitude, enormity, substance are all pricey words which come to mind when considering the influence one person can have on another. Have you ever tried to weigh or measure another person's influence on your life? Or, more scary, the influence you have on others? Your children? Your spouse? It would be neat if we could measure influence in some familiar unit like pounds or ounces. Life would be simple if we could say each day we need to dole out six ounces of good influence, ability to complete tasks or sensitivity training to each child. However, with people, interactions are not like weighing produce in the grocery store; never that simple. Our interrelations are so much more complex.

Father's Day and its significance is what has brought me to such deep thoughts as I try to comprehend my father's impact on my life. First I need to issue a disclaimer. I am not so naïve as to think I can truly measure anyone's influence on another person's life, only discuss some outcomes, feelings, thoughts and impressions. You can do the same. Each of us has only one birth father, thus, that role is very important in one's life.

Some of my earliest feelings of accomplishment came from having my father's approval. When I would see him approaching our farm home in the car, my sisters and I would race to open the swinging gate for him to drive through into our farmyard. We always got a smile of approval and the firsthand chance to see what goodies he might have purchased in town. With any luck, there might be a few pieces of Mary Jane penny candy in the grocery sack. Walking with him about the farm was a treat. This feat didn't come easy because of his stride. He had one rate; fast forward, but the association was worth the effort.

Dad had built a Ham radio station in the corner of our living room (W4AOJ). The borders and experiences of our rural Carolina farm community were stretched with excitement and wonder during our early years in the 1930's when Dad invited us to converse with a ham operator in California or one on a ship, in the Pacific Ocean. We also communicated on the code bands. This early technology was a bit like our contacts on our computers today. Keep in mind this was pre-TV. We also had access to a regular radio; if there was money for a battery. Batteries were luxuries that came after groceries and other essentials, like medicine and school supplies.

Another family activity was foot races after work. Because I was poorly coordinated and younger than my sisters, Dad gave me a handicap which amounted to being moved up from the starting line. These fun activities did not have monetary cost, rather time, which had to be taken from our intense work schedules. We lived on a labor-intensive farm and during planting and harvesting times all the family had tasks in the fields which left little time for relaxation. Nevertheless, while hoeing cotton or working in other field crops we participated in intellectual activities such as learning the states and capitals.

Years later, on the night my Father lay dying his mind was very clear, and my two older sisters and I gathered and reminisced with him late into the night about some of our earlier childhood activities. We still adored him even as we had during our exciting and stimulating upbringing. Throughout our childhood, he had taught us our lives had purpose, value and worth. Today, the enormity, substance and magnitude of his influence lives on, in my heart and life.

Hopes and Dreams Flower Like Surprise Lilies—

August 8, 2002

Our horizon is never quite at our elbows. ~~~Thoreau

Earlier this week, as Harold and I headed out for our morning walk, he pointed to a short stem at the edge of the sidewalk. I exclaimed it can't be time for surprise lilies, already! It is. The next morning the stem was twice as tall and the following morning there was six buds on the top of the stem. I am reminded how much the surprise lily's metamorphosis is like the continuance of events occurring in our lives.

The surprise lily sends up leaves like other spring bulbs but the leaves die down without flowering. If you did not know the plant's life cycle, you might dig it up and toss it out, thinking it is a dud. I wondered if this is where the term "late bloomer" comes from when they mean a person is slower than others in developing certain skills or succeeding in some endeavors.

Don't take your hoe to the lily plant when it fails to bloom in the spring. Late in summer, as mine did this week, the flowering stem appears, all by itself with six buds. Each day, one or two of the buds turn into beautiful pink flowers, until all the buds are opened.

Let's explore similar timed sequences which occur in the goals we work towards in our daily life. On different occasions, I have put a lot of time and effort into planning an event and then the whole thing seemed to flop. When that occurred, I had felt that I had literally wasted my time and energy. However, as time passed and sometimes when I had least expected it, my original goal materialized.

Perhaps that is how my parents felt about me at one time. They had the goal of sending all seven of their children to college at EIU. During my senior year in high school, I married and dropped out of school. Many years later, when my youngest son started to kindergarten, I enrolled at EIU, along with my sister; Pat. At that time, my parents provided encouragement and help, as did my husband and my older children; who were in high school at the time.

My children thought, it was good to have mom in college, the same time they were in high school. They said, I better understood the times you could give your best effort in class and still bring home a B on your report card. Twenty-two years after I dropped out of high school, I graduated from EIU.

Don't give up on goals you want to achieve. When you see surprise lilies in full bloom this week, let them be a reminder to you that some of your hopes and dreams can and will be realized when you least expect them if you have not given up.

Eventually my parents' most cherished dream was fulfilled, as all seven of their children were enrolled in EIU at various times during a thirty-year span. They also lived to see several of their grandchildren graduate from EIU.

Sometimes a person's hopes and dreams are contagious and live on in the lives of others. Amber, my parents' great-granddaughter has hopes of graduating from EIU in 03'.

Looking Onward and Upward—
December 31, 2010

There are many ways of stating it: "Turning the Page", "Wiping the Slate Clean," "A New Beginning". Whatever one might choose to say, I'm past ready for the new year to arrive! I know I should not be wishing my life away and I'm not completely ready to leave 2010 behind.

I'm going through normal procedures in setting goals for 2011 although I nor anyone else can predict what it holds, I choose to face it with a positive attitude. I want to do my best to live in a way to maintain good health. I know that means eating and exercising appropriately while avoiding things that could endanger my health. I am gifted with loving and supportive neighbors that are like a security blanket, now that I'm living alone, without family nearby.

I am no longer a caregiver and, I plan to return to volunteering as I had enjoyed doing in earlier years. As then, I had tutored both adults and children who were learning to speak English and had also, assisted an elementary teacher in her classroom. I suspect those needs still exist and will check them out when school resumes.

Another goal I want to look into is to publish my columns in a book as many of my readers has encouraged me to do from time to time. I'm sure this is a project that would consume a lot of time and energy while being one that I would enjoy, although my friend Kathy Swearingen Wolf shared that it is very time consuming. But that's a given for any worthwhile undertaking.

Now as I look back a bit, perhaps I have been too hard on 2010. Although it contained Harold's final illness and death, at the same time loving friends and family stepped forth to help in so many caring ways that I will never forget. Also, God above gave me energy, plus the rest and love that I needed to care for Harold through each passing day. So on this the last day of 2010, I want to use this last opportunity to thank God above and all of my loving friends and family for their sustaining help during 2010!

Now I can draw the curtain with peace in my heart and be prepared at the crack of dawn tomorrow to begin working on my 2011 goals.

I wish each of you a Happy New Year and hope that each of you achieve: your fondest goals during 2011.

Life, Friends & Death : Plus Faith

Death and friends are topics that have engulfed me during this Christmas season, forever impacting my life. The reason for this is my first born child, Roger, died unexpectedly of a massive heart attack on the 23rd of December.

No doubt, many of you have had similar experiences as my three sisters each had lost a child to premature death during their lifetime, with my sister Pat losing two sons. The rest of you knew as I did, at least intellectually, that death is a normal part of living as some of us have been separated by death from our grandparents, parents, and friends even some of our sibs but do not expect our children to precede us in death.

Thus, Roger's death came as a devastating blow. My first instinct possibly was denial combined with anger as normal comprehension and logic seemed to temporarily vanish. It is still difficult for me to address my son's death with logic and/or insight. However, there are some things that I am aware of that I not only want to address and feel a strong need to share in order to cope with the consuming anguish for the lack of a better word to express the sense of unreality that surrounds me at times.

I am keenly aware that I have not been singled out for some different occurrence than any normal person can and does experience during their lifetime.

However, the death of a child is not something that we normally expect nor think about or have had prior experiences, in how to cope.

We live in a high tech society that prepares us for many potential unexpected crises. For instance, every since I started to school I have participated in fire drills. Since becoming a mother we have discussed in our home how we would exit in case a fire. During my career days when ever I traveled, I always counted the number of doors between my room and an outside exit or stairway before retiring for the night.

Still, I never had any preparations for the death of a child~~~~

Another After School Episode-
-September 29, 2003

One event often causes us to recall another one. When I had e-mailed last week's column to my sister, she suggested I share the story about another time I had been accidentally kept after school.

That event had occurred a year or so earlier than the hurricane, at the same elementary school in Ocean View, Virginia. During that long ago school day, I had developed a headache and my teacher had sent me to the nurse's station to rest for a while. I went to sleep on the cot in the nurse's station. I was awakened very sick when the janitor had found me in the nurse's station when he had arrived to clean after school.

There had been a series of events which had caused that to happen; it had not been neglect on any one person's part.

First, the nurse had not been in attendance on that day when I had gone to sleep.

Secondly, my classes were departmentalized, thus what had happened in one class, the next teacher had no direct way of knowing.

Finally, after school, no one lined up to get on the school buses because there were none. Those living near the school walked home. Many students, like myself, who lived by the Naval base purchased weekly passes and walked to the public bus stop in order to catch the bus that went closest to their home and then walked the remainder of the way home.

Then, my mother did not expect me home at an exact time because public buses did not stay on schedules and if one bus was full, you waited for the next one.

Often after school, I had gone directly to a baby-sitting job. There were many opportunities to baby-sit in the Naval housing project where I had lived during the war as there were many Navy wives with young children living there who had husbands at sea. They would go by bus to the Naval commissary on the base to buy groceries and other supplies after school when sitters were available, as few people owned cars.

The janitor who had found me sleeping in the nurse's room called the police to take me home as all the staff had already left the school.

My parents secured medical attention for me the next day, as my fever had spiked through the night. To make a traumatic long story short, I ended up in a contagious hospital located in Portsmouth, which then was a ferry ride across the river from Norfolk, Virginia. I was critically ill, as I had been diagnosed with spinal meningitis.

I have vague memories of that experience, as I was comatose part of the time with a fever of 107 degrees. My parents could only stand outside the door of my hospital room and look in, with love and little hope.

Because my father was in the U. S. Navy, a wonderful thing happened that saved my life. A brand new miracle drug; Penicillin was flown in from the Walter Reed Hospital in Washington, D. C. for my use.

In a short time, my condition dramatically improved. Later I swam at the pool located on the Naval base each day after school for about a year, which proved to be restorative therapy for me.

That experience profoundly impacted my life in many ways. I am, yet today, an optimist who believes it is possible that good things can come out of bad situations and that life and love are God given gifts to cherish and share even as Dr. Fleming through research gave the world the healing gift of Penicillin.

One's Childhood Culture Contains Indelible Ink

Even though I was transplanted from a Southern culture to the Midwest more than sixty years ago when I was in high school, my Southern upbringing continues to reveal my heritage to others in four distinct areas: food, mannerisms, speech, and writing.

Sometimes, when I have ordered my favorite breakfast: two eggs over easy on rice or grits my server will ask "What part of the south did you grow up in"?

Prior to Harold (a native Midwesterner) and I being married, we had not shared breakfast. Thus the first time I prepared rice for breakfast he assumed I would serve it as a hot cereal with milk and/or cream sprinkled with sugar and cinnamon. It about made him sick to his stomach when I served the hot rice with salt and pepper topped with two half raw eggs.

However, in time he learned to love grits or rice served with eggs over easy. Maybe it was due to the fact I often served them with homemade southern- style brown and crunchy dropped-biscuits made from scratch, As a child, I had felt my legs being switched by my Dad with a hedge branch a couple of times for failing to address an adult with his or her appropriate title: Miss, Mrs., or Mr.,(as most people continue to address their teachers) Aunt, Uncle or etc, if a person was of legal age. In that respect I was not a slow learner because Dad thought it was a gross breach of manners not to address any adult with respect.

When I moved to Illinois this established habit seemed to be offensive to many younger adults as well as some mature ones. For example, if I addressed a person, as Mr. Jim Smith, he would reply, "You must mean my dad, I'm Jim."

When I had transferred from a large urban high school in Norfolk, Virginia to my rural high school in Illinois that had less than a hundred students in the school, few had known anyone with a southern accent. My classmates would sometimes laugh or giggle when I attempted to answer a question. It took me awhile to understand they were not making fun, rather they found my accent to be unique and different.

However, I really was self-conscious when I entered my area college, Eastern Illinois University(EIU)in my late thirties when my youngest son had entered kindergarten. This was before it was common place for adults to attend college.

I had struggled with registration and standing in the long book lines. I also had feared that the recent high school graduates might not be accepting, which turned out not to be true. They had welcomed me into their study groups and when tests were returned shared their grades.

Thus, I was both angry and embarrassed when my professor in my Introductory Speech Class had singled me out in class because of my accent saying, "Mrs. Dobbs, you must go to a speech therapist and get permission to remain in this class."

I quickly picked up my books and left the class, trying to maintain my composure. When I timidly consulted the speech therapist he sent me back to my class to tell my professor there was nothing wrong with my speech pattern as I correctly spoke a regional dialect.

When it comes to writing, various readers have commented on my use of regional colloquialisms.

My writing also identified my heritage my first day of college class. My sister Pat had also entered EIU at the same time. After registration we were thrilled to learn that the university's computer had been enrolled us in the same beginning literature class. We had decided not to reveal the fact that we were sisters as we figured it would be tough enough being the only adult students, and besides, we had different names and no one had ever thought we looked alike.

Our common heritage revealed our identify to our professor, Mrs. Robertson, the first day. Our first assignment was to write a one page essay about a familiar body of water.

We completed our essay and left the class together. Before we spoke, we instantly knew that Cowhorn was the subject, we both had written about revealing our identity on day one.

Cowhorn is a small stream the color of ice tea that flows out of a swamp onto white sandy soil at a bridge crossing a country road, near our childhood farm home in Eastern North Carolina. It is where Pat and I had both learned to swim.

Thus, it was no surprise the next day when Mrs. Robertson requested that Pat and I remain after class and then shared how amazed she had been reading both our essays about Cowhorn. Even though they had been quickly written, unedited from our childhood memories, she clearly knew we were describing the same body of water and must be sisters.

The Gift of Restored Sight--*June 2008*

Are you an organ donor? I have been one for several years. I never had dreamed that I would be a recipient one day. Last month I had a successful corneal transplant that has wonderfully restored my sight in my left eye!!! There seemed to be no words to fully express my appreciation.

Below is the letter I asked to be sent to my donor's family that was my attempt to say THANK YOU.

I hope that you will consider becoming an organ donor if you are not currently one. You can become one by expressing your wishes on your Drivers License and informing your family. Mary

Sunday, May 25, 2008

A thank you to the family of the person who donated my new cornea:

From the depths of my heart I want to say thanks but I am struggling to find the words that express my appreciation. It seems that the normal words that I used to express my thanks seem insufficient or inadequate in this situation.

Sight is a gift that one may mistakenly take for granted until it is threatened.

I have been an organ donor since the 80's, but I never dreamed that one day I would be a recipient.

I have a rare heredity disease named Fuchs' Dystrophy that eventually destroys the cells that a person uses to see in both eyes. Transplanting a healthy cornea that has been given by a donor can restore a person's sight.

I had the corneal transplant earlier this month, which has restored the sight in my left eye. It was a miracle to see after my surgery and my vision continues to improve daily.

A few nights after my surgery, I was riding in a car with friends and I could clearly read the street signs, which earlier had been indistinguishable. My sight in my left eye was so clear that I could have seen to drive, something I have not done at night for a long time.

I cite this example to express my appreciation to you, the family of the person who gave me this wonderful gift. I will be forever thankful and want you to know how much this gift means to me.

I am a great-grandmother and I can say this is the most valuable gift that I have received during my lifetime.

Due to the rules I can't thank you in person so I'm writing this letter so my doctor or the Eye Bank can forward it to you.

I have faith in God above and give thanks to Him and my surgeon; who is an expert and has played an important role in improving my sight by helping to create the DSAEK surgical process that he used. Nevertheless it could not have been done without the gift of the donor's cornea.

A Grateful Recipient

Whose Side of the Bed?--*September 30, 2002*

There are happenings and activities that we deal with routinely but seldom discuss with anyone other than our spouse or argue with ourselves in private, to determine the best solution.

Last night my home seemed a bit too cool, so Harold turned the thermostat up and before long my feet and hands felt warmer. However, when I went to bed, I was cold. I started twisting my bedcovers. I tried to tuck the covers under my feet to shut out the cold air, without getting out of bed, but met with little success.

Whenever I think about getting my bed covers arranged just right, many past episodes surface; some that are humorous as I look back and other happenings that make tears surface.

As a young child, I often shared the same double bed with my older sisters. That was fine in the winter; when we had a soft and fluffy feather tick on our bed.

For the younger generation, a feather tick is a large pillow filled with feathers that covered the mattress. My body could sink into the featherbed, as in a cocoon and be immune to cold drafts. On very cold nights, Mother would heat bricks and wrap them in towels, to warm our feet. That was how we kept warm before we had electricity in our farm home.

Occasionally my thoughts return to the time when my Dad had experienced a damaging stroke. Those days were difficult for all of us. My Mother and my youngest brother Frank; were Dad's primary caregivers until his death. As often as I could, I came by after work and visited with him in his bedroom. Before I left, he always asked me to tuck the covers around him, particularly under his feet. I recalled wondering why that was so important when the room seemed to be a perfect temperature. Now I experience the cold feet syndrome on summer nights and understand perfectly why Dad wanted his covers snuggly tucked around his feet.

I am blessed with a loving husband, who frequently, if he hasn't already gone to sleep, gets up and tucks me in when he senses I'm struggling with the bedcovers. On second thought, it may be in self-defense that he tucks in my covers to keep me from edging my cold feet onto his side of the bed.

Who knows for sure, cold feet may be worse than sand in your bed, as Harold never has cold feet.

Sisters--*April 5, 2001*

For there is no friend like a sister
In calm or stormy weather; ....

To lift one if one totters down,
To strengthen whilst one stands. Christina Rossetti

What wonderful truths! And to think I was gifted with three and yet have two. Recently, Harold and I were house guests of my next oldest sister. Memories were everywhere! We could scarcely enter into a conversation without reminiscing. Does that mean we are over the hill? No pun meant. If we are, I claim ownership as I happily celebrated my seventieth birthday during my visit with her and other extended family and friends. I was gifted with two older sisters and one younger. My oldest sister Carolyn no longer resides on earth. However, she will always reside in my heart. She was a extraordinary role model. Maybe you also had an older sibling, one who experiences life's stepping stones first and leaves a trail of" bread crumbs" for the younger members of the family to follow. We younger sisters didn't make it easy for her. We sneaked and read her diary, giggled in the next room and peeped behind the curtain to see her date arrive. We meddled in her room and tried her make-up and did all the troublesome things that younger sibs do to aggravate an older sister who was trying to retain some dignity while treading the untried territory called maturing.

My sister Pat, who I recently visited is closest to me in age. Growing up we shared a bed which had a feather tick on it in the winter. If you are too young to know what a feather tick is, ask your grandmother or search on the web I bet some innovative person has defined it there.

Anyway, our yard in North Carolina was full of sand, not grass. Instead of mowing we swept the yard with a broom made of closely woven tree branches. No matter how we tried to avoid it, sweeping and all, sand ended up in our beds. My favorite way to aggravate my sister was to get out of bed and shake the sand from the bottom sheet on my side of the bed onto her side when she was trying to sleep.

Needless to say my actions would bring her out of bed as soon as I had crawled back in bed to return the sand to my side of the bed. If I was feeling conciliatory, or more important, if I didn't want Mother to hear and enter the fray with a switch, we both got out of bed, shook out the sand together and then went to sleep. My youngest sister is much younger. I only knew her as an occasional baby sitter or when she was being a pest as I had been to my oldest sister.

Everything that goes around comes around. Later, I developed a meaningful relationship with her as an adult.

And by the way, during my recent visit with my sister, she did not put sand in my bed. She was gracious. Memories and love sufficed.

Mother's Continuous Gift

A Mother is not a person to lean on:
but a person to make leaning unnecessary. --Dorothy Fisher

What a struggle when parents are in the midst of transporting, cleaning, cooking, and earning a living to grasp the fact that they are shaping their child's values and outlook for life.

When in the midst of parenting there is little time for parents to plan, evaluate and grade their performance in the most important job of their lives. Then how does it happen that some children reach maturity as responsible contributing members of society, while others do not.

I am not so naive to think that there are simple answers to complex problems facing parents today. Some children fall through the cracks no matter what their parents do. Yes, before I speak and you ask, I have raised three grown children, none perfect, who like you are working to earn a living with like concerns and needs. Yes, my husband and I struggled in our parenting role and my children now enjoy pointing out some of our methods, with tongue in cheek.

Two of my children are several years older than their younger sib. The older two have claimed that I gave their younger brother some privileges much earlier than they received them and they thought it was unfair. I told them that they may be right. Furthermore, I was practicing on them as I had no prior experience in the parenting business when they came along.

I am thrilled as to the number of parents today who fully share all of the parenting role, even at times with the father being the primary caregiver and/or house parent. They are doing exactly what I have observed is best for child rearing during my 25 years of professional involvement with children and their parents and or caregivers. Which is:

Stay involved hands on at every level! If you are cleaning, transporting, or whatever talk, listen, sing, keep the channels open. If you haven't been involved, begin. Your children and you will love it once your child realizes it is for real; not merely a sporadic trap to lecture them.

I wanted to write something today to honor my Mother for Mother's Day.

Many of the above ideas were first used by my parents when I was a child. I was born on a labor intense farm. Each member of the family began doing chores at an early age to help the family survive during the Great Depression. More lasting than the work, I remember the exciting intellectual contests my parents organized and participated in with us as we worked, such as learning to spell the states and their capitals, as well as other skills. We discussed the places my parents might visit on a trip around the world some day. We did these mental exercises while our hands were busy hoeing in the fields, sorting tobacco in the sheds, feeding the chickens and mules and/or picking cotton in the fields. When my children were young, I did not have my Mother's parenting wisdom. I had retained the good memories and interacted with my children, to a lesser degree. Every time I see children operating hand held games, I think how much better, if they were building memories interacting with their parents and sibs.

In my heart, today, I say," Thank you Mom and Dad."

TOMORROW IS A NEW DAY: FOR LEARNING--
July 11, 2011

If I had my Life to Live Over
I would have talked less and listened more. ... I would have shared more of the responsibility carried by my husband. ... but mostly given another shot at life, I would ...look at it and really see it... . Erma Bombeck

This season it has been very difficult: getting things ready and closing my condo in order to return to Illinois. I've become keenly aware that doing it by myself, without Harold's help; is what has made the big difference even though my health issues has had some slowing effects. Harold always was a person of action, instead of words. When he saw something that needed to be done: he simply did it, instead of talking about it or waiting for me to volunteer to help. Occasionally, when I did offer to help, he would assure me that he could handle whatever he was working on by himself, while adding that I could make the lists of what we needed to do so we wouldn't overlook some of the necessary tasks.

I now know exactly how Erma Bombeck must have felt when she penned her words above as doing the jobs by myself, even though my cleaning lady and friends helped with the physical part, I was made keenly aware of the responsibilities Harold had always undertaken without a murmur.

Even though, I know he thought doing things was part of being protective and loving, I now know, I could have insisted upon being more helpful in sharing responsibilities.

I can't change the past, nor would I want to change most of it as Harold and I had a loving relationship that grew with the passing 62 plus years that God had permitted us to share. But as the saying goes: "Tomorrow is the first day of the rest of my life," and there are changes I can make.

My children and grandchildren practice many of the same loving and caring things that they learned from their Dad and Granddad and no doubt feel that they want to try to fill the gap and do some of the same caring things for me, that Harold had done.

An example is when I returned to Illinois , my Florida cell phone did not receive services in Toledo and there was a delay in retrieving and connecting my land phone number; so my kids discussed the problem via their phones because they did not want me to be without phone services. They both have Verizon mobile phones, which permit them to communicate without tolls with each other, and Lily has found, receives services anywhere in the U S as she travels a lot in her work. They decided to get one for me. David and Shirley added me on their family plan, and Shirley stopped on her way home from work and picked up a phone for me. The next day David and Keaton, who were en route to Indy, where Keaton was racing, delivered the phone to me. They took the time to program in our family's numbers, plus other numbers I most likely would be calling, and then demonstrated how to use my new cell phone. Thus, with time, thought and action: my children quickly solved the dilemma of my being without phone services! Nevertheless, my children are in the midst of their careers and have loving spouses, children and grandchildren of their own, that are important priorities. Thus, I need to steer them from thinking that they need to be caring for me.

Hopefully, the next time they volunteer to help me with a project, I need to speak up and say that I can take care of it myself; unless it is something like the phone issue that I could not easily do by myself. So time will tell if I'm too old to learn new tricks. However, in trying to do more things for myself, I do not want to ever lessen the time I can be with my family to visit and/or share the joy of seeing my children, grand children and great-grandchildren(all my in- laws count the same as my children and grandchildren, as I love them all the same) that God had gifted Harold and me with; during our shared journey.

Coping with the Reality of Death—
October 24, 2010

Accepting reality was easier for me to do; during the happier stages of my life. In reverting back to my longtime habit of checking definitions in the dictionary my Scrabble Dictionary, which is always brief, states: "something that is real" as its meaning for reality. The passage of seven weeks, since Harold's death has taught me that the reality of death, is, indeed, something that is real and sometimes overwhelming; yet something that I think I can survive with God's help, plus continuing to apply some of the values that I learned as a child from my parents .

Since Harold's death, I have been unable to sit at my computer and express my inner feelings in writing. Instead, I have published letters that I had received and saved from a happier time, our 50th Anniversary celebration. I have gone through various stages of grieving and now have arrived at these conclusions: I now know and accept the fact, that I will not see Harold again on planet earth, other than in my heart, dreams and memories.

In essence, I am no different from the millions of other women who have lost a loving husband. Meaning, I have not been singled out to somehow be treated differently from all the other widows that I read about in the obituaries. However, I now have more empathy in my heart for others whenever I read about their loss.

I have experienced the loss of many important members of my family: my parents, three sibs; of which two(Carolyn & Pat) like my brother Jim and myself were inspired by our parents to pursue careers in education, my first born Roger who was a loving son for 59 years, and now my loving husband. The death of my husband seems to be the most difficult, because 63 years of my daily life thus far had been shared with Harold in a loving relationship. That equals 80 % or 4/5th of my total life to date! However, I now know all of these other family members, as well as Harold were gifts from God, and now their memories of love and what they taught me about life and living are gifts that will continue to enrich my remaining years.

Through the passage of these past seven weeks, the love, friendship, kind deeds as well as the words and prayers of many have made my road easier to navigate. I extend my heartfelt thanks.

Also, I know that none of my aforementioned deceased loved ones would want me to spend time being depressed and out of reality because of their passing. Instead, they would have wanted me to utilize what I have learned from their lives. I need to use each new day to pursue the unfinished goals that we had worked on together to make our world a better place for all who follow.

For me this includes promoting the values that I first learned from our parents, such as doing all I can to help others to obtain an education. My parent had the goal of helping their children to obtain all the education they could acquire. Harold had been willing to go the second mile for me to continue my education in college after we were married as I had dropped out of high school. I began college after all our children entered school, which enabled me to obtain the training and opportunity to teach others and to take an active role in the early stages of governance and the development of programs at LLC. During my tenure on LLC's governing board, Burnham Neal, whom I had known, since he had dated my oldest sister Carolyn when she was in college, invited me to serve on the Neal Foundation. One of my first assignments on the Neal Foundation was to help write a Scholarship Program which has enabled seniors at CHS, for several years, to apply for and receive scholarship funding from the Neal Foundation in order to attend LLC or EIU. Through Burnham's ongoing generosity, students from CHS and other schools now have access to scholarships provided by him and the Neal Family.

After I had retired from work, I had loved spending time volunteering in classrooms and tutoring both children and adults in Florida. Now that I again have some available time, I realize I can once again volunteer to do the same, as the need for volunteer help had increased because of the state of our overall economy.

I've shared my family's interests in education that has profoundly impacted my life to point out to all who find themselves, like me, in retirement, trying to move from the pain of losing someone dear and near that you can honor the memory of your love ones by volunteering. You could be like me: choose whatever field your loved ones inspired you to develop skills and/or interests in during your working years. There are many other choice, the arts, education, sports, childcare, cooking, and healthcare to name a few.

My cousin and dear friend, Marilyn Diel Gabel recently shared this bit of wisdom: "A loss creates a void in our heart~~ like a piece of missing puzzle." However, I'm slowly discovering that reality doesn't mean you must toss out the whole puzzle;, rather continue to put your life in place as you would fit in the pieces of the puzzle. Keep the remaining viable parts and values in your life that have served you well thus far.

CHAPTER 7
Historical Happenings
9/12/01--The Morning After--*September 12, 2001*

This morning I woke up at 3:30 A M. I tried to tell myself that
yesterday was a nightmare that could not be real. Not so. I tried,
without success, to ease my mind into returning to sleep for a few hours
as my mind kept replaying the horrible scenes of our planes being used
as flaming human bombs.

My mind raced back in time to a Sunday afternoon in December of 1941
when my parents were entertaining a marine from a nearby military base
(Camp LeJuene). He had been invited into our home to share Sunday
dinner. My father had built his Ham radio station in the corner of our
farm living room and had been demonstrating how he made contacts on
the 160 meter band (W4AOJ were his call letters) with other amateur
radio operators. When all of a sudden the message was broadcast that
Pearl Harbor had been attacked and all military personnel should return
immediately to their bases and that all amateur operators should shut
down their stations.

Then, I was a young child. Nevertheless, I sensed the enormity of the
situation by observing how my parents responded to the curt message.
Our visiting marine guest left our home in the middle of our meal to
return to his base. My father sent my sister and me across the field to our
uncle's home to share the stark news that Dad had heard on his amateur
radio receiver. In time, the invasion and war became a reality in my
family's daily life, as my father enlisted in the Navy.

Last night I was able to contact my niece Katie who works in Manhattan.
She shared that she had watched the attacks on T V in her high-rise
office located near the United Nations Building. When she and her
associates saw the U N Building being evacuated, they went down to the
street level and saw hundreds of people walking from the devastation of
what had been the Trade Center Buildings. She said most of the people
were moving along the street quietly and orderly. Later in the day she
walked to Grand Central Station and fortunately was able to board one of

the first trains out, for her commute home.

Tears bathed my face and I felt relief to know Katie was safe in her home as my mind and heart felt nauseating pain for all of the hundreds of families who had not, and will not received the reassuring message which I had just heard.

As I stare into my computer screen while listening to the early morning news reports, I search for words and/or ways to comprehend the hideous tragedy that had been inflicted on our country and our people. No words of reason come forth that I can understand.

However, the words and methods which I had used when I had taught American History, in the classroom, to young students flashed across my memory. I had wanted each student to know that our history was more than learning dates; rather, it was about people and how they lived and helped each other. I had tried to teach what a privilege it was to be an American, how our forefathers had worked, planned and had shed blood to create our form of democratic government.

When I had taught, the main message I had wanted to implant was that it would be up to them, as young students, to work together with others everywhere, towards keeping our democratic form of government strong and safe throughout their lifetime through voting and remaining involved. Every year my students participated in mock elections in our classroom, visited government offices and attended a session of court. Today is a day for all Americans, including them, you, and me, to continue to labor together as our forefathers did to keep our democracy strong and safe for us and for all those who will surely follow in the generations to come. Together, with God's love we will succeed.

What Now?--*September 21, 2001*

We are now into the second week of one of the greatest crises our country has experienced for a very long time. We have witnessed horrible and unbelievable scenes on our T V's that have been implanted in our hearts and minds.

Listed below are four steps, which was a consensus opinion of a group of financial leaders whose firms had been stricken in the World Trade Center:

1. Be calm,
2.Tell the truth,

3.Put people before business,

4.Then get back to business as soon as possible.

As I read through this list, I thought New Yorkers who had just lived through the trauma of their lifetime had their priorities in order. Items one and two seem to be essential. You can't panic or deny what has happened if you are going to be able to accomplish number three: help people meet their needs. Work is therapeutic. We all have witness on a lesser scale what relief there is in returning to our daily routine following some crises.

Especially troubling to me has been the reports of a few of our citizens verbally and physically abusing other Americans who are of Arabic or foreign descent. We sometimes forget that all of us were once immigrants except Native Americans. I have seen news reports of families, particularly Muslim women and children, being afraid to go shopping or to their churches to worship. To harass or intimidate people of different faiths is acting like the terrorists.

A couple of years ago I took a class on understanding the religions of the world. The class compared the likenesses and differences of the Christian, Jewish and Islamic (or Muslim) Faiths. Clerics from all three faiths presented the fundamentals and beliefs of their people and then answered questions from the students. Until then I had known very little about the Islamic religion. The terrorist behaviors of killing and taking their own lives are contrary to the mainline Islamic faith. Unfortunately, in the past we have experienced the impact of religious cults that have had origins in our own country. Do you remember the man who led over 900 people to their deaths by drinking poison a few years ago?

Many people of the Islamic faith living in The United States (about seven million) and in other countries are as upset about the terrorist attacks as we are. Many of these countries abroad are working with our government in order to rid our world of the terrorists and prevent future attacks.

I share the fears and anxiety which all of us have experienced as we have come to terms with this horrendous enemy called terrorists, who are bent on destruction of people and their property. Terrorists are different from any enemy that our country has confronted before. They move across borders and live and co-mingle in many countries of the world, including our own. They attack innocent victims without warning. The barbaric attack on us has made caring people and nations of the world realize none of us is free from the threat of an attack. I was moved to tears when

I watched 100,000 of our Canadian neighbors gathered in a memorial service in Ottawa singing our national anthem. There is strength in freedom-loving people coming together and seeking wisdom. The outpouring of support, compassion, prayers and love from around the world tells me that together this cowardly enemy can be identified and conquered.

Measuring Our Use of Time--*December 28, 2009*

"Imagine a world in which every single person on the planet has free access to the sum of all human knowledge." (Jimmy Wales, Founder of Wilkipedia).

How do we measure and use our time? With the New Year fast approaching, bringing 2010 calendars and blank new record books, it doesn't seem like a year has past since we tried to balance and close out 2008.

Another way to look at time is the fact that 2010 will complete the first decade of the 21st Century, which causes me to realize that the birth and death of love ones is a way I often measure the passage of time.

The first week of 2000 gave Harold and me, Logan, the first of our five great-grandchildren born in this decade, followed by: Jackson, Molli, Jasper and Caleb. Logan was born, on my mother's birthday, almost 100 years later. Her life spanned a large part of the 20th Century. My life, thus far, has spanned both centuries making my life a generational bridge.

Along with the joy of my great-grandchildren born in this decade has come the death of two loved ones close to my heart, my sister Pat and Roger; my first-born son. My caring journey with them, which spanned most of their lives, has made the passage of that time seem more precious and fleeting.

New life is like a blank page to be written upon with wonder and love. My descendants will live in a world that has more access to the human knowledge to fulfill their hopes and dreams; than Mother or I. Nevertheless, reality and past experiences tell me that the younger generations will be confronted with some of the same bumpy and unforeseen roads to travel that we have encountered, when it comes to making choices. They will arrive at crossroads, as we did, that have no clear directions like those described so pointedly in Robert Frost's poem, *The Road not Taken.*

As we anticipate the joys and, yes, possible disappointments now hidden in 2010, let's ask for guidance from the One who knows the future as we face each new day. Thus, when and if we complete this first decade of the 21st Century we can say with Frost:

"Two roads diverged in a woods, and I,
I took the road less traveled by,
And that has made all the difference,"

Justice O'Connor has Removed Barriers--*July 4, 2005*

Justice Sandra Day O'Connor's twenty-four years of service on the Supreme Court has raised the benchmarks for all women while promoting equal rights for all Americans.

Webster's definition of the word barrier includes the following words: "obstruction, sticking point, wall and barricade," among others. Many women know what some of these words feel like.

Tradition, public opinion and lack of precedence have been hindering factors for women. Although our Constitution guarantees equal rights for all, it remains a work in progress.

As I approach this subject, I cannot write as an observer, because I have been an active participant in the ongoing journey of seeking equality for all women. In 1975, I had been the first woman elected to serve on my local Community College Board of Trustees in my fifteen-county district in Illinois.

Thank progress. Today; I do not think one's sex is an issue for candidates who seek to serve in that or any other district. Several women have since been elected to serve.

As I look back to 1975 when I first had been elected to serve, some of the happenings now seem humorous, but I assure you, they were not then.

Our U.S. Constitution reinforced women's rights to serve in elective and/or governmental appointive positions after the Nineteenth Amendment passed in 1920; giving them the right to vote.

President Franklin Roosevelt removed some barriers when he appointed Miss Frances Perkins in 1932 as his Secretary of Labor, becoming the first woman to serve in a president's cabinet.

President Ronald Reagan made history in 1981 when he appointed Justice O'Connor as the first woman to serve on the Supreme Court.

Charles Lane, writing in the Washington Post (7/02/05) said, "The first woman on the court thus became the most powerful woman in the United

States-a fact that was acknowledged even by her conservative rival on the court, Antonin Scalia, who said in a statement that 'She has become a star.'

The statistics show that during her tenure she shaped the jurisprudence of this Court more than any other Associate Justice."

This is the same woman whom law firms had refused to hire after her graduation from Stanford University in the early 1950's. She had grown up on an Arizona ranch and immediately began working to remove barriers.

All of our lives have been touched by her steadfast interpretation of our Constitution. She has been a positive role model and has removed many barriers for all citizens who seek equality in many phases of their lives. Currently about one-half of students entering law schools are women.

Recently, I spoke with a young attorney, Sarah B. Holsapple-Miller, who graduated from law school about fifty years after Justice Sandra Day O'Connor. She reported considerable progress has been made for women attorneys since Justice O'Connor graduated from law school. She said, "I had no problem finding employment as an attorney," She added, "I am employed by a firm that has fourteen attorneys and three of them are women."

Let's all honor and thank Justice Sandra Day O'Connor for her 24 years of outstanding service. The next woman President Bush appoints to the Supreme Court will have fewer barriers because Justice O'Connor has left guideposts and an outstanding heritage for all who follow.

Memories: Pearl Harbor Day--*December 7, 2012*

I was reminded when watching an older gentleman being interviewed on the news that Pearl Harbor Day occurred 71 years ago, today. The news reporter said most people know it only as a date in history. I began listening closely as I clearly remembered Pearl Harbor Day. The man being interviewed, had been on one of the ships that Japan bombed long before Hawaii was a state.

I think it's an important date to recall. Most of you will remember it as a historical date, but for me it was engraved on my memory as a child. Here are some significant historical facts because this date could have changed our history if our young men had not stepped forward on short notice, with many giving their lives during the five years of the "BIG"

War! Pearl Harbor was our major Naval Base, located in Hawaii in 1941. Japan had staged a surprise bombing attack: killing more than 2400 men plus wounding several servicemen and civilians. Japan's surprise attack destroyed eight US battleships; sinking four of them plus destroying 188 airplanes. Other U S Naval vessels were, also damaged..

On December the 8th, 1941 President Franklin Roosevelt declared war on Japan. But this was only part of the trauma of WWII, as that same week we entered war with Italy and Germany in Europe!

The above are actual facts that I learned from history. Following are my childhood memories that I recall.

December the 7th of 1941 was a Sunday that my parents had invited a U S Marine stationed at a nearby base home with us after church, to share dinner with our family. We had finished our meal, and my Dad was showing off his Amateur Radio "Ham" station that he had built in the corner of our living room. They were chatting on a broadcast band, probably the 160 meter band when an emergency message came on telling of the horrific attack on Pearl Harbor! Following the initial report, it ordered all "Ham" operators to shut down their amateur stations and for any service-men to return immediately to their bases.

Our Marine guest quickly collected his belongings and my Dad took him back to our little village, where he caught a bus back to his base. I, as a child, didn't fully comprehend the significance of what had happened, but knew it wasn't good by my parents' response of concern. My Grandma Hill and another of her sons lived across a field from us. Dad sent my sister Pat and me across the field, to share the information about Japan's surprise attack on our Pearl Harbor Naval Base with them as we did not have phones. My Uncle and Grandma who were upset by our news; returned home with us to learn more details. We had an old fashion battery-powered radio to listen for more news; it's battery was almost used up; making it very hard to hear!

Even though my Dad had served in the Army Air Force after WWI and was too old to be drafted, with several children, he immediately began talking about enlisting. He felt it was his duty to do so. He enlisted in the U S Navy in a few weeks!

Eventually, his actions forever changed my life from a North Carolinian farm girl, to a Navy brat, to one who would spend most of the remainder of her life, after the successful conclusion of WWII, in Cumberland

County, Illinois.

A Bit of History and Reminiscing About: Lake Land College's Creation and the Illinois Community College Act of 1965--*September 24, 2011*

Today, I was sorting through old books and stuff in an attempt to get rid of some. To begin with, I am a "Saver of Stuff" and have difficultly tossing anything. Thus, most anything relating to Lake Land Community College (LLCC) and the other community colleges that I had once been closely associated with as a member and the State President of the Illinois Community College Trustee's Association (ICCTA), was simply moved into other stacks.

I placed one book on top to pursue as this week's column material *History of Lake Land College: The First Ten Years 1967- 1977.* This book holds special memories for me, as I had been involved in its publication. As an undergraduate I had been a history major and then was teaching history to elementary students. Allan Keith who was serving as; LLC's Director of Public Information, had a lot to do with the actual assembling of the book.

I first had been elected to LLC Board of Trustees in 1975 and had the privilege of serving with two men from LLC's original Board: Floyd Curl of Neoga and Robert "Bob" Johnson of Shelbyville as well as knowing another original member, Dr. L. E McNeill, as he was my Dad's close friend. When we were compiling LLC's 10th Anniversary History; a wonderful advantage was that many who had been involved in its creation and/or formative years were still actively involved and available to contribute or be interviewed.

I put my stack of books aside, as I had business and a luncheon scheduled in Mattoon today, which took me past LLC's beautiful campus. It's almost impossible to comprehend its growth and outreach since its official beginning 45 years ago with the purchase of 304 acres of ground by LL's first Board of Trustees.

I think I can safely say today: that no other institution or investment using tax money can compare with the immeasurable benefits that LLC has and continues to provide in the field of education, for its residents, as well as their communities. Upon returning home from Mattoon, I have been rereading and remembering happenings involved with the writing of LLC first history to commemorate its 10th birthday. Thus the remainder of this column will be a combination of these facts and memories.

This first History of LLC and its formation contains valuable information about the residents of six downstate rural Illinois Counties working together in order to successfully create affordable post high school education for its citizens. There's probably not a family currently residing in our LLC district, (which contains, the largest CC geographical area within Illinois,) who cannot say, that their family has benefited, in some fashion from: LLC!

Through the years of my trusteeship at LLC, I participated in numerous graduation ceremonies, where I had parents share that their child was the first member of their family to attend and graduate from college and that some of them had also taken beneficial classes at LLC's Extension Centers.

Below are some direct quotes, plus information that I've added, which I think you will find of interest taken from LLC first history book. Thus, I will not credit each entry, separately:

"On September the 24th 1966, nearly 12,000 people went to the polls to cast their ballots (with 9960 voting yes; including me). ... . LLC District No. 517, originally consisting of the Counties of Coles, Clark, Cumberland, Edgar, Moultrie and Shelby, was now a reality."

"'Annexations will provide a stable and economically sound future for the college in the years ahead, as well as provide a sufficient population to maintain a well balanced offering of programs. We feel this is extremely important to all communities of the district.' Robert Webb-- President's Eight Annual Report, June 1975' "

"LLC first opened its doors in September of 1967 when 627 students enrolled at the National Guard Armory in Mattoon."

"A low tuition rate of $3.25 per quarter hour was attractive to many students."

"But the story of CC's in Illinois does not begin with the September meeting....in Mattoon. Joliet Junior College, founded in 1901 under the sponsorship of the University of Chicago, is considered to be the first public junior college in the United States."

"The LLC master plan projected that 312,500 gross square feet of permanent buildings would be required to house the programs and services to be offered by the college."

233

"On (Saturday) December the 12th of 1967, the voters overwhelmingly approved the bond referendum of $3,910,000 to be paid off in 17 years at a local tax rate, no higher than .07 cents per $100. of assessed valuation."
"Richard Nichols, a graduate of the Cumberland high School, was the first student to apply for admission to LLC in the spring of 1967. In the fall of 1976, Miss Julia Barton, a graduate of the Effingham High School, became the 25,000th to enroll for credit courses in the College. What better testimony could be offered to demonstrate the validity of the feasibility studies... some 10 years ago which showed there was a need for a comprehensive CC to meet the educational needs of citizens in the area."
"In the years ahead, with proper care and management, the LLC campus will be a scenic and educational attraction for students and community groups from the area." This was a prophesy that has been fulfilled!
I think the last paragraph in this book summarizes it well:
"A listing of the personal efforts of countless individuals who have contributed to the success and achievement of LLC during the past ten years would be endless. Few would disagree, however, that the single most important factor in the success of LLC has been the determination of the Board of Trustees and College staff to fulfill the objectives and principles established by the citizens who founded the college, to value the worth and integrity of the individual students, to place equal importance on students pursuing career and college transfer programs, and to provide an opportunity for all individuals irrespective of their economic or academic background to have an opportunity to pursue their education."

ABOUT THE AUTHOR

Mary Hill Dobbs was born on a bright leaf tobacco farm in Eastern North Carolina during the Great Depression and grew up experiencing the pain of a segregated society, although fortunately her parents were not segregationists. Her mother was a native of Illinois, and her dad though a native North Carolinian had been out of the South, when he had served in the Army Air Force (AAF) after WWI. He had met and married her mother when he had been stationed at Chanute Air Force Base in Illinois and took her to his N C home to live, after he was discharged.

Mary was first introduced to column writing as a child, when her parents had jointly written a human interest column entitled, DOWN ONSLOW WAY for the "Raleigh News and Observer" in the 1930's .

Mary's father had enlisted in the U S Navy during WWII and after its end her family had reestablished their home on the Illinois farm where her mother had been born. Her mother had continued her column writing during the 1940's in Illinois, which was published in the Mattoon Journal Gazette under her by-line: "Down Cumberland Way".

At the age of 16 Mary. fell in love with and married her husband Harold. They shared 63 happy years. After dropping out of school at 16 she secured a GED diploma when she reached the age of 21.

Mary first entered EIU at the time her youngest son entered Kindergarten. She graduated with a degree in Education and a major in History. Afterwards, she began teaching in elementary school.

As education had played such an important role in her life, that she decided to seek a seat on the relatively new: Lake Land Community College's Board of Trustees. No woman had previously ran or had been appointed to serve. She was successful and this gave her a role in the future planning and directions for LLC.

She returned to EIU and received her master's degree in Counseling. After that, she switched her career to social work and worked in child welfare.

Thus when she retired and became a Snowbird in Naples, Florida with free time , she began writing a column .During 20 years as a Snowbird, Mary has written about her diverse background that included her growing up in a Southern segregated society. Her career and life experiences were chronicled in her hometown newspaper, "The Toledo

Democrat" and later in two Naples newspapers; "The Golden Gate Gazette" which discontinued and then in "The Collier Citizen." Now that Mary is no longer a Snowbird, she continues to write her weekly in "The Toledo Democrat."

Made in the USA
Charleston, SC
11 May 2014